THE
ULTIMATE
SPA
BOOK

THE ULTIMATE SPA BOOK

Pam Martin Sarnoff

WARNER BOOKS

A Warner Communications Company

TRAVELLER'S
BOOKSHELF

PHOTO CREDITS: Charles Abbott, page 19; Robert M. Bruno, page 41; Luis Castañeda/The Image Bank, page 194; Michael Clark, page 142 (bottom); Robert Ames Cook, page 51 (top); John Durant, pages 56, 206; Kenneth Johansson, pages 12, 15; Littlejohn, page 148 (bottom); Herral Long, page 78; Philippe Morel, page 216; Rob Muir, pages 115, 116, 218 (bottom); Guido A. Rossi/The Image Bank, page 141; Hubert Schreibel, page 96 (bottom). All other photographs courtesy of the respective spas.

Warner Books, Inc., 666 Fifth Avenue, New York, NY 10103

A Warner Communications Company

Packaged by Rapid Transcript, a division of March Tenth, Inc.
Designed by Stanley S. Drate/Folio Graphics Company, Inc.

Exercise drawings in Part III by Wendy Frost

Printed in the United States of America
First printing: November 1989
10 9 8 7 6 5 4 3 2 1

Library of Congress Cataloging-in-Publication Data

Sarnoff, Pam Martin.
    The ultimate spa book / Pam Martin Sarnoff.
    ISBN 0-446-51520-5
    1. Health resorts, watering-places, etc. — United States —
Directories. 2. Health resorts, watering-places, etc. — Caribbean
Area — Directories. 3. Health resorts, watering-places, etc. —
Europe — Directories. I. Title.
RA805.S27   1989   89-40041
613'.122'0296 — dc20   CIP

IN MEMORY OF
my dear father . . .
who, when he was dying of heart trouble,
placed his hands gently on my shoulders,
looked me in the eye with the greatest love,
and said simply,
"Pam, I wish you health."

Contents

I

SPAS IN THE UNITED STATES

II

SPAS OUTSIDE OF THE UNITED STATES

III

LIVING THE SPA LIFE AT HOME

THE ULTIMATE SPA BOOK

A Personal Comment

WHEN I BEGAN THIS PROJECT, LITTLE DID I KNOW THAT I WOULD BE spending the better part of two years traveling from spa to spa testing the waters—to say nothing of the classes, treatments, services, and accommodations offered at nearly one hundred of the world's finest health resorts. Me, Pam Martin Sarnoff, about whom a friend once commented, "She won't even go in an elevator without her husband!"

I also did not know that other people would be tackling the same sort of project—but primarily through the mail, without leaving the portals of home and thus entirely dependent on the words of press agents and the advertising department of each spa. That's an easier course, certainly, but not as trustworthy when it comes to a client's-eye perspective on facilities and programs to choose among.

It is my hope that presenting candidly the facts and feelings of life as actually experienced at each of the spas will give you an accurate picture of what to expect and help you choose the spa that best suits you.

The benefits of a satisfying spa experience extend far beyond the enjoyment of the time you are there. As a result of my continuing spa experiences, I have, little by little, stretched not only my body, but that other muscle—the mind. Spa life is structured to put you in touch with yourself, to help you eliminate stress and realize more of your inner potential. As Sigmund Freud said, "Being entirely honest with oneself is a good exercise." I know that my thinking has become more honest in regard to what is causing stress in my life; I now see more clearly what *I* must do to keep healthy and happy and to enhance the lives of those I love by so doing. If introducing you to the world of spas leads to that same result for you, the work on this book will prove more than worthwhile.

So many people have been helpful to me in getting this book together. I am very grateful to them all.

Special thanks go to:

My wonderful, supportive children—Nancy, Richard, Jeffrey (and his Maria).

The friends who shared valuable insights—Gregg Abbott, Harriet and Robert Cohen, Lou Davidson, Arthur Emil, Shirl Grayson, Anne Johnson, Jenette Kahn, Susan Kaskel, Martha Knight, Jerome Markus, Joanne Matthews, Nancy Mayer, Ann Miziaszek, Inger O'Brien, Blanca Palomeque, Sharon Kay Ritchie, Mary Ann Stubbs, Luanne Wells, and especially Karen Collins-Eiland.

Nancy Luce, an inspiration—now, as always, "far from the madding crowd."

The grand group at Warner Books—Larry Kirshbaum, Nansey Neiman, Jackie Meyer, Ling Lucas, and Ellen Herrick.

Ellen Mikulka, who transcribed all my yellow pages of scribble into readable type and was unbelievably helpful with myriads of travel arrangements.

Jamie Raab, my bright and shining editor, without whom I would have been lost.

Deborah and Michael Viner, whose sage advice and interest in the project made a real difference.

My husband, Bill, the most important helper in my life as well as my book. He tried out the men's facilities in dozens of spas. He read and reread my words, always encouraging me to "keep up the good work" or (more often) to do a little better. To him, my thanks and my love forever.

Well, dearest Mom, I did it!

4

The Spa Experience

ARE YOU ONE OF THE WOMEN WHO WORRIES THAT A SPA MIGHT BE intimidating?

Are you a man who feels he would be entering a women's world by going to a spa?

Are you concerned that taking a spa vacation might be sinfully self-indulgent—and way beyond your budget?

Are you convinced that you're too out of shape even to attempt to get back into shape?

The reassuring fact is that these concerns needn't keep you from enjoying the reinvigorating benefits of a spa experience. There has been a veritable explosion on the spa front in the last decade. Spa retreats and resorts are no longer places where only the idle rich take "the cure." In the United States alone, there are spas to fit every need, personality, and budget.

Why go to a spa, you might ask? Perhaps you've gotten a little flabby, a little potty, a little stiff, a little frantic, a little bored. You are drinking, smoking, eating, and worrying too much. You appear washed out; you feel washed up. You know you're looking too old, too fat, too wan . . . *and, finally, you are ready to do something about it!*

What you need is a place to relax, lose some weight, tone up, get pampered, and drop those bad habits. A new look! A new outlook! A new lifestyle!

Never fear—there is a spa just right for your torso (and mind-set). Visiting a spa is the glorious getaway of the 90s.

Two years ago, I set out on the Ultimate Spa quest to discover, describe, and rate the best spas in the United States, the Caribbean, and Europe (with primary focus on American spas). To do so, I visited each spa, worked out, talked to clients. I checked out everything from decor, location, ambience, and surroundings to beauty services, treatments, classes and facilities, available sports, food and diet, staff, and programs for improving one's mental outlook. In addition, questions of cost, the guest mix, clothing needed, unique offerings, and ongoing programs interested me, as I knew they would interest you. Each spa had its own personality and point of view, I found. Some gave luxury a new name; others offered just the basics (many with a special down-home graciousness). I worked out and sat down to supper with celebrities and millionaires, with mothers and working women who'd decided it was finally time to splurge on themselves, and with couples who were seeking a better lifestyle, individually and together. It turned out to be a wonderful personal voyage of discovery. The pampering was delicious; often the food was, too.

I had never been all that concerned about health and fitness. Now I know we must be dead serious about it . . . our lives might very well depend on it. I know the spa experience has brought healthful, joyful changes into my life.

This book will let you know what you can hope to get out of your own spa visit—your personal quest for fitness, fun, health, and beauty.

At the end of each spa description you'll find a quick sketch of what to expect. Details in the text will fill out the picture. Spas are arranged alphabetically in the text. There are geographical listings in the appendix for convenient reference. There you will also find the "Top Spas" lists, which have been carefully compiled. (It wasn't easy—there are so many good ones).

I've included my personal plan for living the spa life at home in a special section, so that when you return home you can prolong the wonderful effects of your visit.

I hope that you will enjoy it all.

Twenty-five Reasons to Go to a Spa

To live up to your potential both physically and mentally
To minimize the effects of aging
To establish new eating habits
To feel healthier
To feel happier
To tone up
To reduce weight
To quit smoking
To quit drinking
To look more attractive
To increase athletic skills
To prevent diseases
To help cure common ailments
To treat specific male or female problems
To stretch your body
To stretch your mind
To eliminate or reduce stress
To have fun
To meet people ("plug in" socially)
To achieve a better body and more balanced personality
To be pampered
For family togetherness
For individual activity
For solitude
For relaxation

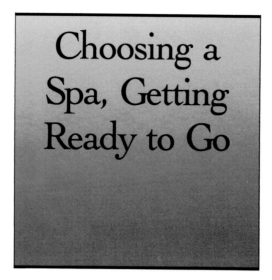

Choosing a Spa, Getting Ready to Go

THE FIRST STEP IN SELECTING A SPA IS TO NARROW THE CHOICES. Decide what you want: Do you want a rigorous workout program, or would you prefer one that stresses the pampering aspects? Can you survive a spartan diet plan or would you rather have gourmet meals? Do you want a structured program or free time to use as you wish? Are you looking for a family atmosphere or a super-sophisticated ambience? Does a retreat appeal to you more than a bustling hotel resort? Would you be unhappy without a tennis court, golf course, or other athletic facilities?

What is the *most important* aspect of a spa vacation to you? Come to terms with your desires; pick two or three possibilities. Then pick up the phone (or write) and ask the spa director or reservations manager a few crucial questions.

- If you're not locked into a time frame, ask about special deals throughout the year.
- If you want certain services at specific times (such as a massage at 5:00 P.M.), see if you can book them in advance.
- Should you require their assigning you a roommate to defray cost, inquire about who that might be.
- Find out if they will meet you at the airport.
- Ask about the rooms available at that time, including details on color scheme, furnishings, and view—whatever is of interest to you and will affect the quality of your stay.

PACKING CHECKLIST

Pack as light as possible for the spa of your choice. The list here includes virtually all your necessities. If an item is followed by an asterisk (*), it means that some spas provide it. Read the text for that information.

- ☐ toothbrush, toothpaste
- ☐ (inexpensive) watch (most spas have alarm clocks, but not all)
- ☐ hairbrush, comb, blow-drier*, shampoo*, conditioner*, shower caps*, other hair needs
- ☐ camera, film, flash units
- ☐ cosmetics, moisturizer*, tweezer, razor*, shaving cream, Band-aids, cotton swabs, sun cream, other grooming needs
- ☐ credit card, money, checks, airline tickets, visa, passport, keys to your home and car (pack in carry-on luggage)
- ☐ any medications needed (pack in carry-on luggage)
- ☐ glasses, sunglasses, contact lenses (take an extra pair; pack in carry-on luggage)
- ☐ Walkman or similar portable cassette player
- ☐ rain gear, hat with sun visor, cold weather gear
- ☐ swimwear, wet area footwear*
- ☐ bathrobe*, sleepwear
- ☐ aerobic shoes, hiking shoes, other shoes
- ☐ exercise socks (several pair), other stockings
- ☐ underwear (several bras, underpants, etc.)
- ☐ leotards*, tights, headbands
- ☐ shorts*, t-shirts
- ☐ sweatsuit*
- ☐ sports gear
- ☐ casual or other evening wear
- ☐ books*, notepad and pen (stationery is generally provided), diary
- ☐ flashlight*

- [ ] safety pin to pin daily schedule to robe
- [ ] plastic totebag to use all day*
- [ ] detergent
- [ ] business cards (but leave your work at home!)

Don't forget to allow empty space in your suitcase for your spa purchases.

THINGS TO KNOW BEFORE YOU GO

- Consult your doctor to find out if you have any food or other allergies, and if you should avoid heat treatments or any specific exercises.
- Plan to spend extra money on a la carte services, cosmetics, and side trips.
- Tell the folks at home *not* to call you with any problems that can wait until your return.
- Don't overpack. Do take a camera.

. . . AND AFTER YOU ARRIVE

- Take advantage of the opportunity to relax your defenses, let down your hair, and just be you.
- Keep notes on any information important to you.
- Be absolutely honest with the staff about age, allergies, addictions, dietary habits, physical failings, etc. You'll find them discreet and helpful.
- Go with the flow, squelching feelings of skepticism, impatience, superiority, or inferiority. Enter the program with an open mind and willing body, but have fun with it, too.
- Ask questions. Don't be reticent about asking the experts for advice and information.
- Don't feel guilty about the time and money you're spending on yourself. You deserve it.

THE COST

In order to give you an idea of how much each spa might cost, I've divided them into five categories.

One week — high season — single occupancy

Inexpensive	under $1,000
Moderate	$1,000 to $1,500
Moderately Expensive	$1,600 to $2,100
Expensive	$2,200 to $3,000
Very Expensive	$3,100 up

The estimated cost is calculated on what your per person bill will probably total if you stay for *one week* at normal high season spa program rates without optional services (single occupancy). *Please keep in mind that many spas give you a break in price if you double-up with a roommate. In some, high and low season rates vary substantially, and almost all spas run special promotions during the year.*

I
SPAS
IN
THE UNITED STATES

The Ashram

CALABASAS
CALIFORNIA

FEWER THAN A DOZEN ADULT spa-goers arrive at the Ashram each Sunday for a week of denial and trial—no unhealthy or fattening foods, no coffee, no smoking, no liquor, no drugs, no luxury. They come to face reality and to change their bodies and/or mind-sets accordingly. They do this fortified by the constant support of their fellow participants and the staff. Because of the smallness of the group, the close quarters, and the overall emphasis on togetherness in the program, a family-type atmosphere quickly evolves.

It's important to think twice before you make your reservation at "The A." You may hate it, you may love it. It's hard work, but the results are rewarding. Once you're there, you've made a commitment to live life on the Ashram's terms. You stay with the program until the bittersweet end. And why not? That is what you came for; that is what you paid for; and that is the only way

you're going to feel it was all worthwhile when you leave.

Although spa guests may feel that they are somewhere on a remote part of the planet, in actuality, the Ashram is situated just off elegant Mulholland Drive. Surrounded by wild terrain and mountains, it enjoys a setting designed by nature. You are transported there by van from Los Angeles International Airport or other designated transfer point, and must leave your own car behind. (There is no easy, quick escape route!)

The two-story main house—old, cozy, and nondescript—sleeps the whole gang, two to a room, with a total of three bathrooms. Comfortable slumber is assured by excellent mattresses, down pillows, and physical exhaustion. The staff changes the linens every other day and keeps everything tidy. Meeting and eating goes on in the living-dining room. Don't even think about room service. Everyone sits at a common table for each meal.

Off the kitchen, a laundry room buzzes with active folks depositing personal dirty laundry in one bin (to be retrieved twenty-four hours later) and sweaty Ashram spa clothing in another. A constant supply of red "A" sweats, t-shirts, robes, and caftans is kept piled up for use while there. Also housed in the laundry room are the scale and tape measure, the necessary evils of any self-respecting weight-loss program. In the gym upstairs, modest exercise equipment (not state-of-the-art, but sufficient and user-friendly) welcomes the weak and the muscular.

In addition to the main building, Ashram facilities include a hot tub, a

ADDRESS
P.O. Box 8009
Calabasas, California
   91302
TELEPHONE
818-888-0232
CREDIT CARDS
None

pool, sundeck, solarium (for all-over tanning), a geodesic dome (for yoga classes and massages), and three small structures used for massages and exercise.

Sunday, the day of your arrival, is showtime. The curtain goes up with you stripping down to your skivvies. Anne-Marie Bennstrom, the head honcha, takes your blood pressure, weight, and body measurements. She looks you over, sizes you up, and *tells you* about your personality and needs, using your physique and her intuition as a guide. Before long, you realize how sincere she is and how devoted to the integrity of The Ashram. You feel you'd bend over backwards for her—if only you could bend over backwards. The next stop is "the Shed" for five minutes or so on an exercise bicycle to determine your body age.

Hiking activity begins that very first day. The many beautiful trails offer varying lengths and inclines. None of them are treacherous, but some are strenuous and seem to go straight up. Judging group ability, the staff assigns walks and hikes that become more rigorous, as the week progresses. (By Thursday, if you're on a roll, the ten-mile hike proves to be a euphoric experience.) Guides with walkie-talkies keep the flock from straying. Sometimes you walk alone, sometimes with others, and occasionally accompanied by deer. The hikes are mandatory, but there are shortcuts and pacing is geared to individual ability.

The daily schedule remains fairly constant. By 6:30 A.M. you are in "The Dome" for a session of yoga—breathing and stretching—a gentle way of waking up. You see the sun rise, feel the cool air, and settle in for a little breakfast—very little! Then, with canteens slung on, the troop marches off for a serious two-and-a-half-hour hike. Upon return, revitalizing but not too tasty "green juice" is served.

After a rest period—short but sweet—a voice bellows, "Okay, ladies and gentlemen, let's go!" That means you're off for calisthenics, using free weights under the tutelage of a man built like a cannon. This period is neither short nor sweet, but it is effective.

Pool aerobics, which generally follow, are enjoyable, and the water volleyball games are honest-to-goodness fun.

After lunch and some free time, come more calisthenics and aerobics classes, given by women who are in magnificent shape. The good news is that some time between the first hike and the second (ah, yes, there is a second), everyone gets a good, strong massage. These are given daily.

The second hike is taken in the late afternoon around sunset. Supper follows, then you listen to a lecture or watch a movie.

Staff members glow when they talk about The Ashram, describing it as a sensual and religious experience. The interrelationship of the physical, emotional, and spiritual self is stressed. The aim is to treat all three simultaneously. To supplement that, part of the focus is on recognizing the external forces that affect you and learning how to respond to them in a productive way. Lectures and discussions cover such topics as self-acceptance, nutrition, emotional balance, the New Age philosophy of

brotherhood and peace, and how to maintain the gains made at The Ashram.

The program tests your physical limits. Not only do you exercise continually, but your food intake is strictly monitored, and many experience a certain amount of light-headedness, nausea, annoyance, and pain—existing on 600 to 700 calories a day while keeping abnormally active tends to put a crimp in one's style. Cry-babies and those who cop out are not treated with much tender loving care. Guests are expected to do the whole program. The idea is to surrender to it, to entrust yourself to it. If at some point, you feel, "Okay, enough is enough," it's probably not. And there's no use praying for a "snow day." Whatever the weather, the program prevails. Even in a tropical heat wave, the mountain is there and up you go! The best thing to do while there is not think at all—just do the program.

The food is very fresh and good. Somehow most people find it ample—hard to believe when you know that breakfast consists of fruit juice and a potassium pill (for nondieters, add toast with almond butter); lunch consists of a couple of pieces of fruit and a salad; and a typical dinner means steamed vegetables, a baked potato, *or* lentil soup. Rarely is a dessert served, but there are snacks such as cantaloupe popsicles, and for those who feel faint or listless, tuna provides the remedy. Certain individual fasts are approved and supervised.

The theory that prevails here is that weight reduction is not as important as the loss of inches. It is possible during one's stay to lose several pounds and many inches. When it's time to leave, getting into those loose travel togs is the proof that patience and fortitude pay off.

A mixed bag of people choose The Ashram. There are a few strange types, but most are regular guys and gals (substantially more of the latter.) The down-to-earth philosophy with its twist of mysticism attracts some; the inner and outer body benefits appeal to many. The crowd tends to be younger than the usual spa population, but there are guests of all adult ages—even seventy plus—all of whom leave feeling and looking younger and healthier.

Clothes are unimportant at "The A." Part of the deal is that everyone dresses alike in the spa clothing. However, you should pack hiking and aerobic shoes, swimwear, sleepwear, socks, shorts, toiletries, and underwear.

The Ashram is a grand spa for the right person. Before you go, establish in your mind that you can cut the mustard—physically and emotionally. It's like camp. They actually discourage the kid in you from calling home on the hall pay phone.

Fortunately, many guests manage to toe the new line when they get back to their usual routines. The gift of The Ashram cookbook with suggestions that are not hard to follow is a help.

As the days at The Ashram pass, a countdown is typical—five days to go . . . four . . . three . . . Even for those who love the routine, a week is enough. Gregg Abbott, a friend who gave me the male point of view on this unique retreat, raised his herbal tea on the final night and toasted, "Here's to never having to come back." Now he says he *would* go back, and, in retrospect, found the experience intriguing and highly rewarding.

Appropriately, a t-shirt proclaiming, "I SURVIVED THE ASHRAM," is lovingly given to each guest before departure.

GETTING THERE

Fly to Los Angeles and prearrange your pickup point by van with The Ashram. For L.A. residents, it's easy—just call the spa.

RATING

Overall: Boot camp for sophisticated dieters, de-toxers, and body toners

⊕ Results; staff

⊖ Rudimentary facilities; lack of privacy; no pampering or coddling

Main thrust: Cleansing out of calories and cobwebs

Cost: Moderately expensive

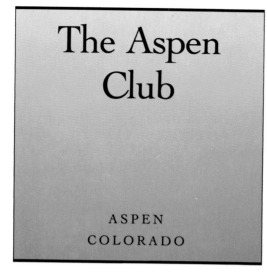

The Aspen Club

ASPEN
COLORADO

ADDRESS
1450 Crystal Lake
    Road
Aspen, Colorado 81611
TELEPHONE
303-925-8900
CREDIT CARDS
AE, V, MC

WHETHER YOU WANT TO socialize with the Holly-wood–Texas–New York set or just hit the slopes, the spa, and then the sack, Aspen can provide the background, the pizzazz, and the bill. It's not an inexpensive little mountain resort but it's got the laid-back chic that keeps 'em coming.

A good aerobic walk from the middle of town lies The Aspen Club. Though it has existed for years as a private club, it now broadens its appeal with spa facilities and guest accommodations at the charming Victorian-style Hotel Jerome right in the middle of town (and the action), The Aspen Club Lodge, or one of the Aspen Club Realty properties. Transportation to and from the facilities comes gratis.

An able director, Dr. Julie Anthony, the attractive one-time tennis great, confides, "I always stayed clear of the word *spa*—we want to be medically correct and really scientific." Realizing that many spas are now geared toward serious goals, she continues, "We still don't want to attract the person who wants eyelash tints and herbal wraps. We teach people about their bodies. *There are ways to live not denying yourself but still not destroying yourself.*"

You'll like the setup: a classy alpine-style building framed by nature's top-of-the-line offerings. The condos all around blend into the scenery. Inside the club you'll find a reception gallery flanked by a pro shop and a boutique. Beyond that are well-equipped, clean, compact locker and wet areas for men and women—amenities offered include shampoo, conditioner, shaving lotion, body lotion, hair blow-driers, cotton swabs—with a speedy swimsuit drier, great showers, sauna, steam room, and Jacuzzi. Massage rooms are nearby.

Divided into three separate zones, the workout space is awesome, with up-to-the-minute weight-training and body-toning machines plus cardiovascular equipment and stretching pads par excellence. Plug your earphones into your aerobics machine and switch to the television viewing of your choice. (NOTE: There are no towels out in the workout area, so bring one from the locker area.)

The facilities for basketball, volley-ball, squash, and racquetball are as impressive as any I've seen anywhere. Players on the ultra-pro indoor tennis courts can be viewed by guests sitting in the informal fast food restaurant area. I was so distracted as I watched Jane Fonda on the StairMaster, Ryan O'Neal on the squash court, and Martina Navratilova on the tennis court that I hardly had time for my workout.

I attended exercise classes given in a rather unassuming gym with a resilient floor. Best for those who know what they're doing or can readily follow the leader—but good for all—the classes supplement a range of aerobic, stretching, and toning activities.

A special expansive room exists for the Pilates Method. If you haven't heard of this procedure for toning *every* millimeter of your body, this is the place to learn and do it under the tutelage of a practiced master of the method.

Housed at The Aspen Club as well is the Fitness and Sports Medicine Institute. If you need to get physically rehabilitated, renewed, or simply ready for action, you've come to the right spot. Superb equipment is available, and an advanced medical staff stands ready to expertly examine and advise you to help remedy knee injuries and other sports-related maladies.

Outside facilities include six lighted tennis courts (used by many tennis luminaries as well as beginners and people at all skill levels in between), Jacuzzi, ungroomed cross-country skiing and walking paths, and a volleyball court.

With merely a nod in the direction of true pampering, The Aspen Club fits into no known spa mold. Its emphasis is on fitness and real sports. Also, you can get very good nutritional guidance and lose weight. In fact, that's why most women sign on.

Personalized is the key word here. Each spa-goer is interviewed by phone and by mail prior to arrival and a customized program is devised. It will include whatever sophisticated testing

(e.g., stress test, electrocardiogram, body fat measurements, lung function evaluation, nutritional analysis) is deemed necessary. Whatever the activity you're interested in, be it exercising, hiking, skiing, even shopping, one-on-one attention is an integral part of the overall plan. A personal fitness guidebook is professionally prepared specifically for you while you are there and will prove invaluable after you depart.

Since The Aspen Club provides nothing in the way of clothing except bathrobes for massages, bring your own spa and sportswear, as well as shoes, necessary personal items, sunglasses, and seasonal casual (but chic) après-spa wear.

Getting there probably won't be half the fun, but once you arrive and see the mountains and the picture-perfect Western town with its combined turn-of-the-century and modern panache, you'll be glad you made the trip.

GETTING THERE

From many cities you can fly directly into Aspen. From others you can fly to Denver or Grand Junction and then drive to Aspen or take a commuter plane to the local airport. Call the spa for complimentary transportation from there.

RATING

Overall: A serious, personalized action spa and club with an exceptionally impressive fitness and sports medicine area

⊕ Fitness equipment; nutrition and exercise counseling; interesting upscale guests; sports medicine; skiing and hiking; court sports

⊖ Have to share the facilities with club members and guests of Aspen Realty properties; no beauty parlor on the premises; necessary to travel to the spa each day

Main thrust: Helping you to achieve and maintain your personal best

Cost: Expensive to very expensive

Aurora House Spa

AURORA
OHIO

IMAGINE A PICTURE-PERFECT white clapboard house dating back to great-great granddaddy's time sitting on a suburban road, with a complex of buildings, gardens, and pool situated discreetly in back. Inside, spa guests spend their time being pampered and beautified with world-class facials, massages, and nail and hair care, with a dash of aerobic activity. If this image appeals to you, you'll feel right at home at the Aurora House Spa near Cleveland, Ohio.

Victoriana fills each room, evoking memories of a less complicated past. The manicure tables are actually old Singer sewing machines. But a little kitsch is a happy diversion from the usual sterile premises for beauty and body work.

The living quarters consist of fourteen pseudo-Victorian junior suites and one executive suite, all with whirlpool tubs somehow fitted into the small bathrooms. A complimentary bottle of champagne and a handy wall hair drier—plus all the usual furniture and amenities—greet each arriving guest. Soothing colors such as dusty rose, maroon, beige, and white decorate the interiors.

Aware that the emphasis here is on relaxation and beauty, I was amazed at the number of *couples* who arrived on the weekend. However, before long I realized that the men were having as much fun as the women. They may have been dragged there kicking and complaining all the way, but they left with beer bellies a little less bulgy, rough-and-ready psyches all calmed down, scraggly hair trimmed in the latest style, and skin creamed and gleaming. Even members of the Cleveland Browns have left their bench in order to return from the Aurora sittin' pretty! Most of the folks are from Ohio and neighboring states. All ages are welcome, and there is no minimum stay. Business groups have found it to be a pleasurable-profitable meeting environment.

Spa programs range from one to six days. On Saturdays and Sundays, forty or more may arrive for a la carte services and lunch. Those who opt for the six-day plan receive room and meals, fitness sessions (gym and water), walks (brisk or "it's up to you"), "environmental habitat," dulse or salt-glo treatments with loofah sponge, deep cleaning facials, further facial and throat treatment, thalassotherapy, aromatherapy, body wrap cellulite treatment, pedicure and manicure with paraffin, reflexology, European hair conditioning, haircut and styling, and makeup application (for women). In addition, guests can use the Jacuzzi,

ADDRESS
35 East Garfield Road
Aurora, Ohio 44202
TELEPHONE
216-562-9171
CREDIT CARDS
MC, V, AE

steam cabinets, and sauna. Request single or double occupancy rooms, as you wish.

If your reaction to the mention of "environmental habitat" was a big question mark, the answer will surprise and delight you. The "habitat" is a fascinating contraption: You lie on a wooden bed in a glass enclosure for a timed sequence of environmental changes. First, the lamps shine, as relaxing as the tropical sun. Then come clouds of steam, followed by hot "winds" to blow away any remaining tension. Finally, simulated raindrops begin to fall. When you emerge, you have been subdued, simmered, and showered.

A heavy-duty beauty treatment to consider is the *repechage* facial, which involves applying four layers of nourishment: (1) seaweed filtrate, (2) hydrating cream, (3) seaweed mask, (4) mineral mask. The result is deep pore cleansing and a mask that comes off in one piece.

Other facial specialties include the tight-and-tone nonsurgical face-lift and derma peels given in a series under the supervision of highly trained technicians.

Delicious and well presented, both the low-cal "spa cuisine" and multi-cal "gourmet" menus seem to please every-one. There are many selections and, as far as I could tell, all are winners. Eating lunch in the Victorian Parlor is delightfully relaxing. (As I looked around at everyone dressed in the maroon robes and matching turbans provided by the spa, it occurred to me that we appeared to be members of some sort of cult!)

Bring exercise and swim clothes, casual dinner clothes, and proper shoes. Even if you decide to take a side trip to the nearby Sea World or the Football Hall of Fame, you will spend your days in sweats or slacks. You should pack boots, sweaters, and jackets for the colder months.

GETTING THERE

Fly to Cleveland's Hopkins Airport. Take a taxi for the short trip to Aurora, or prearrange pickup by the spa. Drivers will spot the spa easily where Rte 13 meets Rte 82.

RATING

Overall: a best bet for beauty

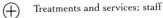 Treatments and services; staff

No athletic facilities; close to road

Main thrust: Rejuvenation while being worked over from head to toe

Cost: Moderately expensive

P.S.: The owners, Mario and Joanne Liuzzo, also own the Manan Island Inn and Spa on Manan Island, New Brunswick, Canada. This is a secluded retreat for spa-goers who want summer solitude. (Call 1-506-662-8624.)

The Spa at Bally's Park Place Casino Hotel

ATLANTIC CITY
NEW JERSEY

ADDRESS
Park Place and the
   Boardwalk
Atlantic City, New
   Jersey 08401-6709
TELEPHONE
609-340-4600
1-800-772-7777
CREDIT CARDS
All major

THE SPA AT BALLY'S IS A BIT of a surprise. It is an island of subtlety in that ocean city of excess!

Everyone's heard about Atlantic City, the home of the Boardwalk and mecca of slots and other casino thrills and spills. Bally's, one of the huge, glitzy hotels separated from the Atlantic Ocean by the five-mile-long Boardwalk, is best known as a gambling haven, but it also houses an impressive spa.

Downstairs at Bally's, your senses are stunned with bright lights, swarms of people, and lots and lots of slots and other casino action. Upstairs and in the new tower guest building, you'll relax in a quiet, clean, comfortable room with all the usual upscale hotel amenities.

The Spa at Bally's cost over $20 million to build, and management has every right to be proud of the results. It is a very appealing area, geared toward pampering those who think the odds are better on the massage table than at the gaming table. It is located on the eighth floor, just past the attractive full-service beauty salon. Etched glass doors lead into the spa cafe, check-in, and boutique area, at one end of which are four major glassed-in racquetball/handball courts. The floor in these courts is spring-loaded.

Guests of the spa appear to be men and women of middle income from the East Coast, whereas the lobby and casino are populated by people from all walks of life.

The 40,000-square-foot, two-level spa area is manned by a small, caring staff who will help you through your exercise schedule.

Past the sports courts on Level I is an aerobics/toning/stretching/yoga classroom (classes are good). Then comes the superb multilevel indoor pool area with its gorgeous tropical plants, seven beautiful whirlpool baths (one for the handicapped), an outdoor fireplace surrounded by a circular bench (cozy in winter), lounging beds and chairs, a sun deck overlooking the ocean, four massage cabins, a coed Finnish sauna and inhalation room, plus the Olympic-size swimming pool (with underwater sound system), where aqua classes are held.

Overlooking this section of the spa and the ocean is Level II, consisting of an exercise equipment room with treadmills and exercise bicycles (electronic read-outs on all), a StairMaster, rowing machine, Nautilus machines, and free weights.

The men's and women's wet areas, done in teakwood, are separate but almost equal: showers, lockers, sauna, steam room (the men's is a Turkish

steam bath with a vaulted ceiling and intricate tile work), and massage and treatment rooms. The women's area offers (at a good deal extra) the use of the "MVP (Most Valued Player) Suite"—a marbled marvel with private massage table, whirlpool/steam tub room, and sitting area.

All hotel guests and health club members are allowed to use the spa on a pay-as-you-go basis. For spa program guests, classes, treatments, and services are woven into the half-day to three-day schedules. These include massages, private whirlpool, herbal wraps, loofah scrub, and—in some plans—beauty parlor services, discounts in the spa boutique, and coins for the one-armed bandits.

Calorie-counted, balanced meals served in the spa cafe and other Bally's restaurants for people in the spa program generally provide 1100 calories per day. Room service is an option. There is no extra fee for food.

Bally's provides hair blow-driers, curling irons, shampoo and conditioner, bathrobe and slippers. Pack swimwear, a sweatsuit, aerobics gear, and casual seasonal clothing, plus one dressier outfit in case you want to see a night-club show. Be aware that only sneakers with light-colored soles are allowed in the fitness center.

Atlantic City may not appeal to everyone, but the Spa at Bally's is definitely a best bet!

GETTING THERE

Most folks arrive at Bally's by private car, bus, or cab. The drive from New York takes 2½ hours; from Philadelphia, 1 hour. Buses travel between Atlantic City and the Port Authority Terminal in New York City many times a day.

RATING

Overall: I'll bet you a quarter you'll like this spa.

⊕ Ocean; Boardwalk; lovely spa facility; caring spa staff

⊖ Unattractive city; hotel denizens more oriented toward a night at the tables than a day at the weights

Main thrust: A place to be pampered

Cost: Moderate

Bonaventure Resort and Spa

FORT LAUDERDALE FLORIDA

ADDRESS
250 Racquet Club
   Road
Fort Lauderdale,
   Florida 33326
TELEPHONE
305-389-3300 (direct)
1-800-327-8090
CREDIT CARDS
MC, V, AE, CB

WE HEARD FROM THE competition that Bonaventure uses the spa as a jewel to romance conference groups. Perhaps this is true. In any case, a rousing business is done in the spa and it is a first-class facility.

In 1982, when it was built, Bonaventure chose a relatively unknown actress named Linda Evans to be its spokeswoman. Her rise to stardom proved to be a great boon to the resort and spa. Without a doubt, the intensive ad campaign paid off. However, guests continue to flock to the spa for more personal and practical reasons: Bonaventure offers an excellent variety of services and activities for both gearing up and winding down in a comfortable low-key spa setting.

This combination hotel, convention facility, and health fitness spa consists of several buildings separated in some instances by concrete parking lots. Fortunately, the truly beautiful par 70 and par 72 championship golf courses are right there to add glamour and greenery to the vistas.

Attractive also is the main swimming pool/lounging area and the Renaissance Grill with its tropical rain forest motif. Subdued in tone, but often buzzing with activity, the lobby, boutiques, bar, and informal cafe are the hub of the main building. Here, too, is the Bonaventure's "World Conference Center"— 83,000 square feet of space, equipment, and services to cater to the needs of the most demanding of the Fortune 500 companies.

Decorated in pastel and earth tones that are soothing (but a little too somber for my taste), the guest accommodations satisfy the requirements of any traveler, although occasionally a call to housekeeping might be needed to speed up the bed turn-down. Although there are four buildings of guest rooms and suites (totaling 493 units), spa guests are placed in those nearest the health and fitness center. To compensate for the fact that it is a spread-out resort, jitneys are provided at all times to take you wherever you wish to go at Bonaventure.

Due to the variety of conference groups visiting here and the size of Bonaventure, this resort does not have a definable year-round personality. By and large, the conference group of the moment sets the tone (and that can be anything from rowdy to dignified). This phenomenon also has its effect on how people dress. Often those who come for high-powered meetings are more formal than the average spa guest might be. Certainly, men should bring a jacket. Spa program people tend to

25

dress *very* casually even for their three meals a day in the spa cafe located in the hotel.

Offering everything from a short-term spa experience to an in-depth program, the two- to ten-day plans are popular with all types of women and men. The Princess Yasmin Khan-Jeffries comes for seven days several times a year, as do many housewives from throughout the United States. Conventioneers may opt for a la carte entrance to the spa or sampler plans entitled "The Perfect Day" or "The Beautiful Day." Children under sixteen *must* find a different place to play.

Men and women have separate spa areas, including outdoor swimming pools and sun decks. The two spas are practically mirror images of one another, though the pink of the ladies' area darkens to a more macho maroon in the mens'.

State-of-the-art Keiser and Precor equipment makes the exercise gyms outstanding. Notable, too, are aerobics rooms with cushion-on-cushion flooring covered with special carpeting. (Only *low*-impact aerobics classes are given.) After massages, Swiss needle showers, hot and cold plunges, saunas, steam, whirlpools (drained and refilled for each guest), loofah rubs, herbal wraps, facials, and aroma therapy, one can further relax in the siesta room or sunbathe nude behind the ficus trees (it's so nice to have a wall made by Mother Nature).

The number of hand, foot, nail, and hair services offered by the men's barber shop and especially the women's beauty salon are mind-boggling.

Top products are available for guests'

use in the locker areas, and Evian water is everywhere. Spa clothing provided for the length of your stay includes leotards, warm-ups, bathrobe. (Slippers, exercise shoes, and swimwear must be your own.) Come equipped for the tropical sun and for unexpected changes in the weather.

The calorie-counted diet menu consists of several choices for each meal, with a suggested total daily calorie intake of 900: 200 for breakfast, 300 for

The Princess Yasmin Khan-Jeffries comes for seven days several times a year, as do many housewives from throughout the United States.

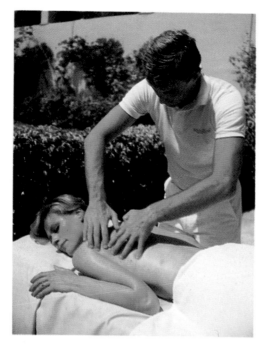

Because Bonaventure is so near the thriving community of Fort Lauderdale, one can always take a short side trip for jai alai, greyhound racing, the Flamingo Gardens, or superior shopping. The front desk will arrange these excursions.

lunch, and 400 for dinner. The honor system is used here. How effective it is depends on your willpower. Bonaventure helps those best who help themselves.

Shortly after arriving, a spa guest receives a complete medical exam and diet recommendations. Individual day-by-day programs are suggested, often starting with a brisk walk at 7:30 A.M. or a brisker walk at 7:00 A.M.

For the sports-minded, there are excellent golf facilities, twenty-four tennis courts (many with lights), biking, volleyball, racquetball courts, paddle boats, and the Bonaventure Saddle Club for beginner and advanced equestrians.

At night the Players Lounge is open for dancing, entertainment, and video games.

GETTING THERE

Getting to this mecca of sports, fitness, and beauty (combined perhaps with a healthy helping of business) is simple. Fly to Fort Lauderdale International Airport (25 minutes by cab) or Miami International Airport (40 minutes).

RATING

Overall: Join the crowd, tune in and tune up.

⊕ Help-yourself diet program; exercise equipment; golf and tennis; beauty "makeovers"

⊖ Hard to find solitude on the premises; too many cement parking lots

Main thrust: Beauty and relaxation for women; sports for men; fitness for all

Cost: Expensive (moderately expensive in off-season)

Cal-a-Vie

VISTA
CALIFORNIA

CAL-A-VIE CALLS ITSELF "THE Ultimate Spa." In many ways it is.

Certainly, Cal-a-Vie offers a superb climate for spa activities. The overall building and landscape design has been executed delightfully. *Cuisine fraîche* by a true master spa-chef pleases the palate and sustains the energy. Each spa-goer is treated as a cherished guest and receives individual attention every step of the way.

However, if seclusion is not your style, this probably will not be the best of all worlds for you. It's true that San Diego is nearby, but Cal-a-Vie itself is secluded and most guests tend to stay put. If you're looking to escape the demands of everyday life, this is the place to come.

Delicately salmon-hued, tile-roofed buildings cluster around a large swimming pool to form the nucleus of the 125 acres owned by Cal-a-Vie. Surrounded by rolling hills, this microcos-

mic Mediterranean village casts a stress-reducing spell even before the T'ai Chi, yoga, lectures, treatments, and classes begin. Esthetically, it's lovely. Guest rooms, villa-like in appearance, are decorated with quiet flair. Only twenty-four people are accepted at a time, and each person is assigned one of the twenty-four accommodations. No sharing. Each room with its terrace, European carved armoire and desk, comfy chintz-covered bed, separate bath and shower, gift toiletries, daily bottle of mineral water, telephone, radio, and splendid view is yours and yours alone in which to luxuriate and unwind.

Doors are left unlocked all day. Valuables may be stored in safety deposit boxes in the office. Ground floor rooms have a security alarm system. All rooms have a panic button, but no need has ever arisen for panic, alarm, or keys!

A few steps from the guest quarters and pool area are the reception building, the spa, gyms, the boutique, and tennis court. If you're into brisk morning walks or hikes, you'll find the surrounding grounds captivating.

The Morning Room, a special nook where the group gathers informally, is where you'll find your very own newspaper. The dining room is enhanced by a glowing fireplace that makes the evening meal an intimate social pleasure.

Within this tranquil enclave, a serious spa program flourishes. The seven-day plan is individualized for each client (anyone over sixteen)—room, board, classes, treatments and beauty services, a personal adviser, use of spa

ADDRESS
2249 Somerset Road
Vista, California 92084
TELEPHONE
619-945-2055
CREDIT CARDS
AE, MC

clothing (turquoise warm-ups, t-shirts and shorts, bathrobes, jackets, and slippers), and personal laundry service. A complete fitness evaluation is part of the basic package. As is true in many spas, the aim is to give you a happy start on a healthy lifestyle that you can continue long after you depart.

The big fitness five at Cal-a-Vie are:

1. Cardiovascular endurance
2. Proper body composition
3. Muscle stamina
4. Flexibility
5. Body awareness

Most guests join in a bracing walk before breakfast, at which time each finds a beautiful little logo-shaped card inscribed with a personal schedule for the day. The philosophy never varies: exert after breakfast, inert (or almost) after lunch! In effect, all the physically demanding classes are in the morning: low-impact aerobics, water aerobics, posture, weight training, stretching. (Equipment consists of Keiser and Universal stations, free weights, tramps, treadmills). You can cut class at any time to enjoy a game of tennis, take a swim, golf (for a fee) nearby, or just play your own brand of hooky. Afternoons are devoted to more relaxed activities: yoga, T'ai Chi, massages, facials, "body glo," reflexology, hair and scalp treatments, hand and foot treatments (the paraffin dip makes your feet feel fabulous), thalassotherapy (seaweed wrap), aromatherapy (massage with various oils), hydrotherapy (with underwater jets), and beauty services. Rousing games of water volleyball never fail to attract the morning or afternoon frolic-loving group, especially during the coed weeks or men's weeks, which are scheduled several times a year. Otherwise, it's a woman's world.

How nice it is not to have to decide where you want to eat the next meal or to deal with marketing, cooking, and cleaning up the mess! Breakfasts and dinners are served in the dining room; lunch is generally poolside. Delicious and beautifully presented, the food arrives on informal white china or charming glass plates shaped like fish. Weekends bring out the Villeroy and Boche vitro-porcelain, made in Luxembourg and decorated with sweet violets. Crystal goblets add a slight touch of formality. For arrival and departure dinners, wine or champagne is served.

The chef's well-tended garden provides most of the produce used in the menus (which feature primarily fruits, whole grains, legumes, and vegetables) and for the snacks and hors d'oeuvres. Don't expect a steak and french fries. Sometimes the food is unrecognizable, but it is always top quality.

Suggested caloric daily intake for women is: reducing diet, 900 to 1000; maintenance diet, 1200; gaining diet, 1500 to 1800. For men: reducing diet, 1000 to 1200; maintenance diet, 1200 to 1500; gaining diet, 1500 and up. An optional weekly cleansing day of liquids is offered. The culinary highlight is the chef's famous pizza! A sample dinner menu I had consisted of:

Garden greens and sprouts salad
   with lemon thyme dressing
Boiled Mahi Mahi with curried corn
   sauce
Artichoke and mushrooms sauté
Baby red potato
Tarte aux Pommes

Surrounded by rolling hills, this microcosmic Mediterranean village casts a stress-reducing spell even before the T'ai Chi, yoga, lectures, treatments, and classes begin.

an emphasis on eating slowly and eating proteins first.

Attending the chef's "show and tell" lecture makes for an evening of informative fun. You sit in his kitchen watching him nonchalantly prepare a culinary dream and listening to his pearls of wisdom. At the end, you feast on the innovative dishes concocted before your eyes.

Pack lightly and wear the spa clothes they give you for your stay. Of course, you'll need socks, gym and walking shoes, leotards and tights, swimwear, and personal items. During coed weeks, women generally wear their own casual attire for dinners.

Cal-a-Vie makes the transition to real life a bit easier by including a delicious meal in your departure package. This is not the usual brown-bag variety, but one tastefully arranged in a charming floral container. Can't you just imagine two ladies waiting for the plane at San Diego Airport, one savoring lunch from Cal-a-Vie, the other from The Golden Door and comparing contents and calories. The simple delights of spa vacations!

A balanced diet of 50 to 65 percent carbohydrates, 15 to 20 percent low-fat proteins, 10 to 20 percent fresh fats and oils is followed. Cal-a-Vie suggests that you continue this throughout life, choosing foods high in fiber and low in salt, fat, and/or refined sugar, using natural herbs and spices for seasoning, and eating a variety of foods without combining too many at one meal. Part of Cal-a-Vie's philosophy of nutrition is

Canyon Ranch

TUCSON
ARIZONA

ADDRESS
8600 Rock Cliff Road
Tucson, Arizona 85715
TELEPHONE
602-749-9000
1-800-742-9000
    (U.S.A.)
1-800-327-9090
    (Canada)
CREDIT CARDS
V, MC, Discover

CANYON RANCH IS A WINNER. Whether you are a jellyfish or a jock, you'll be happy here — and feel healthier when you leave. There is something for everyone, and that's true almost every hour of the day. America's star fitness spa combines nutrition, fitness, and stress management with an A-1 facility. The Ranch sends you home satisfied that you've enjoyed a life-enhancing vacation.

The grounds of Canyon Ranch are appealing in an unusual sort of way. The lushness of a tropical resort is not found here; but the mixture of cacti, flowers, shrubs, trees, tiny bridges, and rocks is soothing in its naturalness. The Catalina Mountains in the background add scenic grandeur.

In the clubhouse, simple and comfortable decor prevails. Decaffeinated coffee is always piping hot and waiting for takers, and this is a pleasant place to sit and say "hi" to the faces that will soon become familiar. A boutique close at hand draws in the shoppers. The dining room, located in the rear of the clubhouse, is simple but attractive, populated by guests in athletic gear, leotards, and casual wear. Lone diners should ask to be seated at the captain's table, where they meet new people at every meal. Clustered around the clubhouse are the rest of the buildings.

The regular guest rooms are clean and have all the necessities, but not much charm. On the other hand, the casitas are terrific, each with its own living room, dining room, bedroom, bath, patio, and laundry. (It's a great convenience to be able to dump your dirty laundry in the washing machine each day.) Some casitas have second bedrooms that can be locked off and have their own entrances. These are available as regular rooms and are very nice. Casita living requires a short uphill walk from the spa, clubhouse, and evening programs (lectures, movies, games). Smoking is taboo in all public areas and guest rooms. However, it is allowed on the guests' private patios.

Once settled in, you'll walk over to the clubhouse for orientation. At that time, portfolios chock full of information—including lists of activities and treatments available—plus personal daily logs are distributed. You meet the other new arrivals, tour the spa facilities, get your locker key and bathrobe chit, and hear about all the activities and programs. Then you'll be pointed in the direction of the nurse's office for your checkup and advice. Immediately after that (or maybe even before), if you're smart you'll make a beeline to the computer center to try to get the time slots you want for the lessons and treatments that require an appointment. (Obviously, *everyone* wants that massage at the end of the day.) Each of the four-, seven-, and ten-day packages allows for some free services. However, wise spa-goers spend a little (or a lot) extra to take advantage of more of the unique and excellent opportunities.

In addition to the regular spa packages, an "Ultimate Challenge" program is offered for those who really want to push themselves to the limit. Programs geared to those who want to stop smoking, need help for arthritis, or seek long-term lifestyle changes incorporate medical and psychological counseling with exercise and services. Summer rates are attractive for the budget-minded who don't mind the heat.

Male and female spa areas in the huge spa building offer complete beauty care, herbal wraps, aromatherapy, massages, pearl body polish (using crushed pearls), facials, steam, sauna, Jacuzzi, and inhalation rooms.

You must sign up for hiking, tennis, squash, basketball, volleyball, and other games. Classes (there are thirty-five or so a day) include aerobics, yoga, stretch, dance, meditation, and back strengthening. The use of exercise equipment and machines requires only your desire to participate.

Canyon Ranch consistently comes through with well-trained, appealing instructors and a wide range of state-of-the-art weight and exercise machines. Cushioned floors, mirrors, and good lighting grace every gym and sports court.

Along with swimming, a popular sport at the Ranch is tennis. The six courts are lighted and in use well into the evening. Those who win the tourneys seem proud to strut around in their prize Canyon Ranch t-shirts! The Ranch van transports golfers to a nearby course.

Being a hiker from way back, I was especially impressed by the caliber of the walking and hiking program. There are one-, two-, and four-mile brisk walks at the crack of dawn each morning. That is an easy, delightful way to segue into the day's activities. For those who enjoy a lengthier time on scenic mountain trails, there are hikes for novices, intermediates, and gung-ho types. *Be aware that even the intermediate hikes are tough.* Small backpacks with breakfast or lunch are provided, as is transportation. These hikes all have guides who make sure you're okay every step of the way.

Medical fitness, nutrition, and wellness experts are available for private consultations. There are also evening lectures on these subjects. Canyon Ranch offers a much more advanced psychological program than any other spa. Private sessions, though costly, are worthwhile.

Now, about the food: It's hard to figure out how food could be so consistently delicious and filling and still be super-healthy and very low in calories. You can stick with the suggested diet menu or order whatever you want . . . and in multiples! (Each serving is calorie-counted.) A New York mogul who tends toward tubby was so impressed with the food at the Ranch that he sent his chef there to learn the culinary secrets. If you are your own chef, you'll probably want to take the *Canyon Ranch Cookbook* home with you.

As you've probably gathered, casual

Mel Zuckerman, Canyon Ranch's owner, says, "Self-esteem and being in control is what it's all about."

34

is the dress of the day—and the night. Be sure to bring a very warm sweater or jacket. Nights get chilly in the Southwest. Comfortable, proper footwear at all times is a must. Bring your jeans. You'll also need gear for aerobics classes, swimming, and sports.

The newest innovation at the Ranch is the Life Enhancement Center, which accepts up to forty people at a time who eat their meals, take their classes, enjoy their therapies, swim, and relax in a Jacuzzi or steam room in a brand-new (mini) spa building. Here one has the opportunity to participate in a group experience geared to those who are very overweight, have a health risk condition, or simply want a more disci-

plined spa week. (Of course, the rest of the spa keeps the welcome mat out for them.) Mel Zuckerman, Canyon Ranch's owner, says, "Self-esteem and being in control is what it's all about."

Life at the Life Enhancement Center is more nurturing and insular than at the regular spa, and guests need not make choices about their food schedule. At the Center, they avoid the slightly competitive atmosphere and fervor of activity elsewhere at the Ranch that comes with a highly motivated, savvy "do it" spa population—and from the sheer number of bodies keeping busy. In high season (middle of September until the middle of June) 250 or so guests at a time call this retreat home. Don't let that dissuade you from a visit. There's no place like it in the world.

Who are all these people? Anyone who can afford it, it seems. You'll see singles, couples, and groups from all over and of all ages, sizes, and shapes. The client list includes business tigers and social lions and nice ordinary folks. Basically, it's an attractive group of active people.

GETTING THERE

Transportation to and from the Tucson airport is provided by the spa. The Canyon Ranch van driver greets you with cold Perrier water and a warm all-American smile. Driving from the Phoenix airport takes 2½ hours.

RATING

Overall: A spa for all reasons; a spa for all seasons

⊕ Fitness program; instructors; hiking; food; wellness programs—particularly stress reduction; good male–female ratio

⊖ Ordinary rooms are ordinary; an air of competitiveness

Main thrust: Total fitness

Cost: Very expensive (bargain packages in summer)

Canyon Ranch in the Berkshires

LENOX
MASSACHUSETTS

WHEN MICHAEL DUKAKIS heard about Canyon Ranch breaking ground in Lenox, Massachusetts, for a new health and fitness spa, he remarked, "One more gem in the crown of the Berkshires." I feel very comfortable in suggesting that it will be not a mere gem, but a major jewel! Turn to the description of Canyon Ranch in Tucson, Arizona, for a broad view of what to expect. The new spa will be the Northeastern version, with state-of-the-art exercise and other equipment, an exciting menu of classes and diet food, plus stress management opportunities.

The chosen site is superb—a grand Versailles-inspired turn-of-the-century mansion called Bellefontaine. It is a remarkable historic estate. Mel Zuckerman, the founder of Canyon Ranch, undertook a complete restoration of the building's brick and marble exterior and gardens.

The blueprints reveal a 100,000-square-foot spa and a 120-room inn of modern New England style, connected to each other and the mansion by glass-enclosed walkways. The program will feature fitness classes, body building and muscle toning, treatments, and therapies. In addition, sports enthusiasts can swim in the indoor or outdoor pools, run around the track, or play basketball, volleyball, squash, racquetball, and tennis. Post-activity relaxation is made easy with steam, sauna, Jacuzzis, and inhalation rooms.

We're not through yet. There are miles of trails for hiking, biking, walking, and cross-country skiing in exquisite natural surroundings. Autumn, when the leaves turn, is a wonderful time to be in the Berkshires.

The Tanglewood Music Festival and the Lenox Art Center, both well known to culture buffs, are merely minutes away.

Each season brings its own charms to the Berkshires and its own weather-dictated dress necessities. You will need seasonal sportswear (it's cold in the winter, hot in the summer), very casual lounge wear, spa and swim gear, appropriate shoes, and all personal items. No one dresses up at the Ranch.

Mr. Zuckerman promises that this Canyon Ranch, like its big brother in Arizona, will continue the family tradition—"a vacation experience focused on exercise, nutrition, stress reduction, and permanent lifestyle improvement." That's a lot to deliver, but the driver knows his way.

ADDRESS
P.O. Box 2170
Kemble Street
Lenox, Massachusetts
   02140
TELEPHONE
413-637-4100
CREDIT CARDS
V, MC, Discover

36

Carmel Country Spa

CARMEL VALLEY
CALIFORNIA

"WE LEAVE BEHIND A bit of ourselves wherever we have been" is not merely a philosophical thought to the women who go to the Carmel Country Spa—it's a prayer! The agony of dieting is turned into fun at this small, laid-back hostel.

Unassuming and unintimidating, the premises consist of the exercise treatment area, beauty salon, boutique, pool, Jacuzzi, volleyball/badminton court, low gray guest buildings, and an all-purpose room. In that room you buy your cosmetics, eat your dinner, watch television, and pay your bills. Furnishings are best forgotten, but the friendships made there seem to stick. I talked to several repeat guests who were very enthusiastic about spa relationships.

Visible from the central room is the flower-filled pool area and lovely valley below, a vista guaranteed to soothe the stressed and delight the relaxed.

Guest quarters (twenty-five in total) are minimal. Most rooms have chenille-covered twin beds, a desk, television, telephone, bureau, and small bathroom with shower stall. (When the owners decided to do a little upgrading, the guests who were consulted said they preferred a bigger gym to better rooms.)

On arrival at most spas, one is asked to fill out a comprehensive health and fitness questionnaire. Here the form simply asks your sex, height, weight, occupation, smoking habits, and if your interests include tennis, golf, badminton, volleyball, table tennis, bridge, backgammon, crochet, knitting, and macrame.

Spa guests are predominantly middle-aged women, although weight-conscious young adults are welcome.

Massages, facials, body wraps, salt and oil rubs, and all beauty services are available. Assorted low-key exercise equipment shares part of the aerobics room. Badminton/volleyball courts and a swimming pool are on the grounds, and there are more golf courses per square mile than you can shake a club at in surrounding areas. The John Gardener Tennis School is a mere half-mile away. You can easily arrange bicycling by the sea to strengthen your legs and ease your mind.

The typical daily schedule begins with breakfast, followed by a morning walk, stretch class, a cup of broth, low-impact aerobics, pool class, lunch, pool class, aerobics, yoga, a nonalcoholic "happy hour," dinner, and then perhaps a lecture on a subject such as how to eliminate phobias and/or bad habits,

ADDRESS
10 Country Club Way
Carmel Valley,
   California 93924
TELEPHONE
408-659-3486
408-659-3798
CREDIT CARDS
V, MC

38

You can do everything in your bathing suit—even eat dinner. This is a place to be totally comfortable.

how to lead a more healthful life or how to eat for better nutrition.

The program is specifically geared toward weight control, and the majority of guests tend to be overweight. The strict diet program here consists of 700 to 800 calories a day, with the main meal at lunchtime. The ingredients of each meal combine to maximize weight loss. You must drink eight glasses of water each day. You will be given multivitamin pills to supplement the meals and keep body functions regular.

For the lucky few who arrive with the singular purpose of relaxing, the spa promises to provide all the food they desire. Fruits and vegetables are home grown or from the neighborhood. When in action, the barbecue pit is the center of attention. Guests can't wait for the two evenings when the chicken parts go from pit to pit.

You *can* follow a strict vegetarian diet here if you prefer.

Clothes and makeup are incidental at Carmel Country Spa. You can do everything in your bathing suit—even eat dinner. This is a place to be totally comfortable.

Attempting to be nothing more than a friendly, low-key refuge with a diet program, Carmel Country Spa is a nice place to rest, relax, and reduce.

Dr. Wilkinson's Hot Springs

CALISTOGA
CALIFORNIA

D R. WILKINSON'S HOT Springs looks antiseptic and has a group of clean-cut young attendants to make things run smoothly. Still, it is definitely an offbeat spa experience; to some, it is also off-putting. It is open all year and dispenses services for the stalwart that induce laughter, healing, and sweating—along with trepidation and relaxation.

Calistoga sits at the foot of Mt. St. Helena where the hot springs bubble up. This small town is considered quaint by some, honky-tonk by others. The trees are old; so is a large portion of Dr. W's clientele. However, inquisitive yuppies are appearing in fast growing numbers.

Men's and women's bathhouses, three mineral pools (one indoors), and motel make up the whole of Dr. W's establishment. Don't expect *anything* fancy, but the motel rooms are efficient—some have full kitchens, all have television and telephone. White tile is about the most luxurious material in the bathhouse.

The main event here is mud. Is there something a bit degrading and a little weird about immersing yourself in mud? you might ask. Perhaps, but if you can get past that, you'll probably have a good time—certainly you'll have something to talk about at cocktail parties. In truth, I can't say it's for the uptight. This is "down-home cure and fun time."

Going for the whole routine means about two hours of this peculiar kind of pampering. A staff member will greet you and show you to a simple dressing room where you'll hang your clothes on a hook and don a towel. You are escorted to a mud-bath room. One of the two tubs filled with warm mud will be yours for about twenty minutes. After covering your hair with a shower cap, you'll lower your body into the rather gritty mud and, with the help of the attendant, cover everything below the neck. At this point, the thought may occur to you, as it did to me, "What if someone else sank deep into the mud and is lying under there lost and forgotten!" There is no need to worry. The mud stays in place and so does the body. The feeling of being suspended finally overtakes the fear and, with a cold cloth on your head, you give in to a strangely total relaxation.

After sweating out all those nasty impurities, you arise, rub the stuff off, and shower.

Now it's time for a natural thermal mineral whirlpool bath—another twenty minutes of rejuvenation and, this time, rejoicing. Following that is shared

ADDRESS
1507 Lincoln Avenue
Calistoga, California
94515
TELEPHONE
707-942-4102
707-942-6257
CREDIT CARDS
V, MC

women, diabetics, and skin disease patients should pass the mud and waters by. Those with muscular aches, rheumatism, or a stressed-out feeling may notice a healing effect. The theory is that the heat and sheer weight of the mud and water relax your mind, joints, and muscles and encourage blood circulation and detoxification. Who am I to question an age-old nature remedy?

The mud is flushed with boiling water after each use. We are told that any bacteria are killed by the over 100° temperatures in combination with the composite minerals and volcanic ash.

Obviously, dress is extremely casual at the spa. Sulphur fumes and satin duds don't mix too well.

And there *is* a funny smell from the minerals. Still, it's hard to turn your nose up at it. An amazing number of people come to "take the cure" or just for a few giggles—white-collar executives, blue-collar workers, no-collar drifters with a few bucks, and a sprinkling of silk-collar celebrities.

The main event here is mud. . . . if you can get past that, you'll probably have a good time—certainly you'll have something to talk about at cocktail parties.

time in the steam room (each person sitting on his or her teeny-tiny towel). Then you are wrapped and bedded in the "cool room" to sleep—perchance to dream.

The final step in what Dr. Wilkinson's calls "the works" is an old-fashioned massage. The motel room will look pretty good to you now. Even driving a car looms as far too strenuous an activity to contemplate. However, a couple of hours later, you'll be ready to hit a new restaurant, a jazz concert, a couple of craft shops, or maybe just hit the road.

Near the famous mud and water happenings, you can enjoy golf, glider and balloon rides, hiking, Sunday jazz and ragtime concerts, plus visits to numerous top-notch vineyards. Dr. Wilkinson's spa could be a short stop on a wine-sampling vacation.

People with heat problems, pregnant

GETTING THERE

Dr. Wilkinson's Hot Springs is located in Napa Valley. To get there, fly to San Francisco. Then drive the 80 miles or take a bus to Calistoga.

RATING

Overall: A real experience—perhaps comical, maybe clinical, possibly metaphysical

⊕   Mud; natural thermal mineral water

⊖   No frills; a bit bizarre

Main thrust: Renewal through mud and waters of the hot springs

Cost: Inexpensive

Doral Saturnia International Spa Resort

MIAMI
FLORIDA

ADDRESS
8755 N.W. 36th Street
Miami, Florida 33178
TELEPHONE
1-800-331-7768 (out of
state)
1-800-247-8901
(Florida)
305-593-6030
CREDIT CARDS
AE, V, MC, DC, CB

"HOW YA GONNA KEEP 'em down on the fat farm after they've seen Doral?"

Thirty-three million dollars after the idea to fashion an American spa after the famous Terme di Saturnia of Tuscany, Italy, struck Susan and Howard Kaskel, a superstar was born, and they named it the Doral Saturnia International Spa Resort. Supremely serene and exquisitely elegant, every inch of the grounds, hotel, and spa facilities commands your respect (and respects your commands!). The atmosphere exudes Italian grandeur. This, my friends, is Oz *a la moda!*

Visualize ballustraded stairways leading to European gardens of flowers, trees, and formal topiaries; perfect expanses of lawn; lots of Italian marble and terra cotta; tiled Tuscany roofs over earth-toned buildings; pineapple palms in stately guard; walls of fossilized keystone from the Florida Keys; a hundred-foot cupola topping the Spa Center—and topping *that* a real gold ball . . . Are you beginning to get the picture? Add several fountains with lovely small bridges, an outdoor juice bar par excellence, a statue of a toga-clad man pouring an urn of water over a seated woman (the spa's logo), a natural hydra-cascade beneath which you can sit and luxuriate under the rush of invigorating (maybe even curative) mineral water, and a beautiful outdoor pool area with the best-designed outdoor furniture I've ever seen. In daylight, it is awesome. At night, with the lights under the trees, it is magnificent. The Doral Saturnia International Spa Resort is a twenty-four-hour treat of a retreat.

The visual delights continue indoors. Exceptional are the four life-sized murals echoing Botticelli's "Primavera" and "Birth of Venus" in the reception area, the stunning Art Nouveau spiral staircase of glass and brass transported from a chic Parisian boutique, the Giacometti-inspired lamps, the drop-dead crystal chandelier in the restaurant, and on and on.

Throughout the spa and hotel, the furniture and furnishings have great style and panache. The Doral Saturnia's brand of understatement makes a big statement. Marble, terra cotta tiles, and plush carpets in muted hues are elegantly accented by giant urns, imposing statuary and columns, trompe l'oeil painting, and etched glass "walls."

The well-trained, energetic staff, dressed in the attractive spa uniform, greets guests in the lovely reception areas and lounges, making sure every courtesy is extended. Guests mingle in

43

the two restaurants, eating gourmet diet food within view of the glass-roofed grand cupola and the large indoor pool, separated from them by pristine etched glass panels. A favorite meeting place is the cozy library, where reading the international newspapers, magazines, and books and playing billiards or "Trivial Pursuit" provide diversion from physical pursuits.

The forty-eight guest accommodations start with "Luxe Suites," graduate up to "Grand Suites," and culminate in "Supreme Suites." Each boasts a view of greens, fairways, or gardens. Not one is without the absolute necessities—a gracious foyer, a living room with full entertainment console, a seductive bedroom, a sybaritic bathroom, and a terrace. So even the bottom-of-the-line suites ensure top-of-the-line living. For instance, #39 has a lovely foyer with wet bar, golf club closet, chic white tile floor, appealing black and white furniture in the living room, a VCR and cable TV with remote control. Breakfast is served on a flowered private terrace. The sumptuous bedroom with its king-sized bed is connected to four (yes, four) separate bathroom spaces, all marbled, of course—*two* vanity rooms, a toilet-bidet-sink section, and a private Jacuzzi tub and shower.

The thirty-six "Grand Suites" have even more glorious foyers and living quarters, plus not one but two marble Jacuzzi baths and dressing rooms.

Then there are the five "Heaven can wait" accommodations dubbed "Supreme Suites," each named after a place in Italy. My personal favorite is #28/Rome—navy and beige, fabulous foyer with everything, including a wet bar; spacious living room decorated with elegant classical furniture; two divinely inviting bedrooms and two full bath and dressing areas; great statuary, murals, frescoes, and carved moldings. It makes you feel a bit self-indulgent. But, listen, "When in Rome . . ."

If you prefer the sleek, modern look, try #12/Sardinia, with its assorted baskets, fish nets, and other nautical niceties. And #20/Venice is so, so romantic with its glassed-in living room and Venetian murals, glass, and fabrics. The best of contemporary Italian design can be found in #48/Milan. Finishing off the list of super-suites for the super-rich is cheerful #52/Capri.

Two separate safes provide a secure home for valuables in each accommodation. Gold fixtures adorn all toilets and sinks. Privacy is honored—just flip the switch inside your door and a brass plate outside will light up with those (other) three little words, *Do not disturb.*

In the spa reception lobby, an enormous clock on the wall (Roman numerals, of course) reminds you that it's time to get down to the business of the day: fitness, nutrition, stress management, and total personal image.

Starting with an examination and evaluation, the experts will develop a personal workout plan, diet scheme, and relaxation program, leaving the selection of classes, lectures, and demonstrations up to you. The options are numerous. When you leave, a re-evaluation will send you on your way with a home plan and a hot-line number.

In operation from September through May, all spa programs offer use of facilities, classes, lectures, airport

equipment, and services. So many products are out for use in the dressing areas that it is hard to break away from the mirror and step into one of the big showers with its own individual dressing area. The colored "barroom doors" for each stall provide privacy.

In the wet areas, you'll find saunas, steam rooms, whirlpool, cold plunges, loofah rooms, herbal wrap rooms, fango rooms (where the volcanic mud from Tuscany is used), Swiss showers, hydrotherapy tubs (with—can you believe it—seventy jets), and innumerable massage rooms soothingly done in a number of subtle shades. (If you're a Pisces, ask for room #22—it's sea foam green.)

Called the Institute di Saturnia, the beauty salon and its many facial rooms are exquisitely marbled in quiet, complex patterns. Shell motif glass fixtures light the walls with a warm glow. All esthetic services for face, hair, skin, hands and feet are done at carefully appointed stations by well-qualified beauticians. Terme di Saturnia products may be purchased for "do it yourself" use.

In the two coed workout rooms, state-of-the-art exercise equipment stretches, tones, and strengthens every conceivable muscle. Besides the eleven David machines, Precor treadmills, Life rowers, Lifecycles, Schwinn cycles, and StairMasters, you can try snazzy free weights encapsuled in rubber. All the equipment is very, very quiet—the better to hear your own heartbeat!

Also coed, the aerobic, yoga, dance exercise, body toning, and stretching classes in the gyms keep the action going all day every day. Spring-loaded

Supremely serene and exquisitely elegant. . . . The atmosphere exudes Italian grandeur.

transfers, accommodations, and meals. If you've got seven days or more to spare, your choices are personalized schedules with emphasis on (1) health and fitness, (2) beauty and image, and (3) sports. Four-day and day-by-day programs are options for time-budgeters. (Money-budgeters, beware of all programs.)

Guests tend to love the peachy peach robes with the Saturnia logo and the gray and white sweatsuits, shorts and t-shirts, leotards, and slippers provided. A wide range of exercise gear is also available in the resort's well-stocked boutique.

Spa facilities and spaces for both sexes are spectacular in terms of decor,

There are serious programs at the Doral Saturnia for those who wish to stop smoking, reduce stress, and/or improve their image.

Diet is of paramount importance for everyone. Here fat points count as well as calories — 60 percent carbohydrates, 20 percent protein, and 20 percent fat seem to make up the winning parlay. You'll enjoy the truly delicious calorie-counted menus as well as the cooking lessons and lectures on nutrition — for these, an outstanding demonstration kitchen was built in the Spa Theater. A screen lowers in front of it for movies, slides, and other entertainment.

Plan to use Saturnia's spa clothes. Bring your own athletic shoes, socks, swimwear, and a couple of resort outfits.

For a plush renewal vacation Italian style, right here in America, this is the place.

floors, walls of ombré gray "silk," expansive windows, and mirrors inspire teacher and student alike. Along the barres, sumptuous gray towels hang at two-foot intervals.

Both indoor and outdoor pool areas beckon with their aqua-exercise and lolling possibilities. The five championship golf courses of the adjacent Doral Country Club and numerous lighted tennis courts get heavy use. Additional sports options are croquet, volleyball, horseback-riding (care for an Arabian?), an exercise course, and that old Italian favorite, bocce. High in the spa, you can jog around the banked oval $1/22$ of a mile track (that means forty-four times around for a good aerobic workout), which is climate-controlled, has its own sound system, and boasts a great view of the trompe l'oeil painting inside the famed cupola.

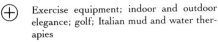

GETTING THERE

Fly into Miami International Airport. Complimentary transfers to and from there will be arranged by the spa.

RATING

Overall: Even if you don't look like a god or goddess, you'll live like a king or queen.

(+)   Exercise equipment; indoor and outdoor elegance; golf; Italian mud and water therapies

(−)   Ocean so near, yet so far

Main thrust: Luxurious living combined with serious spa-ing

Cost: Very expensive

The Equinox Hotel, Resort and Spa

MANCHESTER VILLAGE
VERMONT

ADDRESS
Manchester Village
Vermont 05254
TELEPHONE
802-362-4700
1-800-362-4747
CREDIT CARDS
All major

THE ROLLING HILLS OF VERmont could capture anyone's heart. Add to those, real ski-able, hike-able mountains and pure, fresh air you can breathe and you've got a great place for a New England spa-resort. The owners of The Equinox Hotel realized this and turned the charming, sprawling, white-shingled building into just that. If only they had made the spa part twice as big. As it is, it will suffice for several spa programmers (they'll take up to fifteen) plus inn and conference guests who participate on an a la carte basis.

The town of Manchester Village is a happy combination of early colonial and late Ralph Lauren—colonial because of municipal laws that keep the buildings in that style—with historic statues and sites and a liveried horse-drawn carriage that clippity-clops its way through the streets; Ralph Lauren because this is the buzz word for visiting shoppers. (Well, that famous mer-

chandise outlet is affectionately referred to as "Ralph's" by the local gentry. It is one of many discount operations here—not at all tacky and manned by helpful sales people.) For lovers of American country antiques, the whole town is a treasure chest. So, I guess The Equinox is sort of a spa-shop-sightseeing-ski stop.

Situated at the base of Equinox Mountain, the resort has a lovely view. The 154 rooms and suites are decorated simply with pine furniture and bland colors, all with television, telephone, and private bath. Also available for rental are three-bedroom condominiums a few steps away.

Weather permitting, guests can enjoy the clay tennis courts, swimming pool, and nearby eighteen-hole golf course.

Located behind the hotel in a separate building (with the same architecture), the spa compresses a lot into a little space. There is a workout room with Nautilus equipment, NordicTrack, free weights, and exercise bicycles; separate men's and women's sauna and steam rooms, an exercise class room, and a heated swimming pool. Somehow they managed to squeeze in tiny massage, loofah scrub, herbal wrap, and hand or foot paraffin treatment rooms here and there. If you don't want a male therapist for the massage or wrap, let them know. Otherwise he might find you blushing all over. (Actually they try to keep one's modesty intact with towels—but with ridiculously small towels.)

Walking or hiking in the area invigorates and tones the body while lifting the spirits. Ask a member of the spa staff to guide you to hidden ponds and

Families are welcome at the inn, but only those members who are over fifteen are allowed in the spa. Spa programs offered run from one day to one week and are fashioned for each individual. All include room and meals.

Things have changed at The Equinox since Mary Todd Lincoln, Ulysses S. Grant, and Teddy Roosevelt summered there. The guest list is less impressive, but the place has dignity and charm — and a low-key, pleasant spa.

up mountain trails. Enjoyable, too, are the all-level exercise and weight training classes, treatments, and informal health and fitness chats.

Your locker comes outfitted with robe and slippers. Bring spa clothes, sports gear, seasonal clothes (winters are cold), personal items, and, for men, either tie or jacket for dinner. Incidentally, the spa menus are tasty. You have the option of eating from the regular hotel menu, too.

GETTING THERE

From New York City by car, 4½ hours: Take the N.Y. Thruway to Rte 87N; continue to 787N to N.Y. Rte 7 (in Troy) to U.S. Rte 7 in Bennington, Vt., to Exit 3 in Arlington. Go north on 7A for 10 miles to the Equinox. Boston is 4 hours away; Albany, New York, 1 hour.

RATING

Overall: A small, but serious spa in a grand old inn, surrounded by rolling hills, mountains, history, and super shopping

$\oplus$ Individual attention; outlet and antique shops and skiing nearby

$\ominus$ Cramped quarters in spa; outdoor activity restricted by weather conditions

Main thrust: General wellness and fitness

Cost: Moderately expensive

The Four Seasons Hotel and Resort at Las Colinas

IRVING

TEXAS

ADDRESS
4150 North MacArthur
   Blvd.
Irving, Texas 75038
TELEPHONE
214-717-0700
1-800-332-3442
CREDIT CARDS
All major

THE FOUR SEASONS AT LAS Colinas near Dallas is the best-kept secret in Spadom. For the price it can't be beat. With a personalized fitness and beauty program in a cheerful facility, plus a reassuring, well-trained staff, plus tasty meals that teach "moderation without deprivation," the sum is as impressive as its parts.

Las Colinas is a newly developed section of the Dallas metropolitan area, 400 acres of which belongs to The Four Seasons. The Resort's main building, an attractive brick structure, encompasses a 315-room hotel and conference center, a full-service spa and beauty salon, an awesome sports club, a boutique, and the Las Colinas Preventative Medical Center. Outside the main building, but still inside the yellow brick wall, which is banked with myriads of flowering plants, the property goes on and on. There is an outdoor pool for swimmers, sunners, and water-resistance

exercisers from the spa; eight lighted tennis courts; a quarter-mile jogging track; and two eighteen-hole championship golf courses, one of which is the home of the PGA Byron Nelson Golf Classic. It is around and through this beautiful golf course that the early bird spa-goers take their morning walk.

For *indoor* action, the Sports Club-Spa section features a pool for swimming laps, more lighted tennis courts, six glassed-in racquetball courts, a center court that seats 500, a couple of squash courts, a cushioned one-eighth-mile jogging track, and anything you might think of in the way of exercise and weight training equipment. To wind down, perhaps a game of billiards, shuffleboard, or darts in the game room would be just the right tempo.

"Wait a minute," you may be thinking. "This sounds overwhelming, huge, and impersonal." Well, it is—for the first day. Then, as your waistline begins to decrease, so does the place. By the third day, it becomes home—you know your way around; everyone is your friend; you feel comfortable, even cozy. At the end of your spa program, you'll feel like giving the entire gang a big goodbye hug, especially the spa personnel.

Spa programs range from a la carte to eight days/seven nights. The "long week" includes (1) complimentary transportation between Dallas/Ft. Worth International Airport (fifteen minutes) or Love Field (ten minutes) and Las Colinas on request; (2) deluxe room and delicious board, low-cal or otherwise, in the hotel restaurant, the spa, or your room (gratuities included); (3) a comprehensive health and lifestyle profile (body composition, nutritional analysis, etc.); (4) fitness consultation; (5) unlimited access to educational programs, classes, and sports and fitness facilities. There is a wide range of choice in classes, which are also open to the many Club members—weight training, aerobics, stretching, body toning, yoga, dance, and self-defense. The separate men's and women's spa facilities include saunas, cold plunges, steam rooms, whirlpools, tanning beds, and tanning deck. In addition: a variety of one-hour massages, herbal wraps, loofah treatment, herbal baths, facials, one-hour private lessons in the sport of your choice, and personal fitness coaching opportunities are offered.

My first "sports massage" was given to me at this spa, and it was incredible. The (great!) Dane who was the therapist explained that a series of such massages can actually cure problems that some people have operations to alleviate. I can believe it. He also told me that in Russia everyone on the Olympic teams gets 300 sports massages a year!

The Four Seasons wouldn't think of sending you on your way without a shampoo, haircut, styling, manicure, and pedicure. You might even be able to work in a worthwhile makeup session. I've been to every free make-over demonstration at beauty counters from coast to coast, but I learned more at this spa than anywhere else. How nice it was to have someone actually look at my face rather than paint by numbers.

You can spend your free time rooting for the Dallas Cowboys if you come during football season—the stadium is only minutes away. Also within easy distance are the Arts District and The Galleria shopping mall.

What few hours you have left will be spent in your room. Nothing wrong with that—each accommodation is sound-proofed, temperature controlled, and has a balcony (try for a golf course or pool view).

Bathrobe, slippers, shampoo, conditioner, and lotion are provided by the spa. Bring your own workout clothes (though you can borrow some from the spa), personal items, seasonal clothing, and any sports gear needed. The "formal" restaurant requires jackets for men, but one can dine casually at the attractive Cafe on the Green, which is also in the hotel building.

As you leave The Four Seasons Spa, you'll receive a complete, very informative notebook outlining your personal health and fitness profile and lots of helpful advice.

GETTING THERE

Pickup at Dallas area airports by hotel car or van is complimentary for those on spa programs.

RATING

Overall: A staff and spa program bound to please—especially for the price

⊕ Friendly staff; trained spa personnel; great sports options; sophisticated medical facility on premises; good value

⊖ No mountains, sea, or other natural wonders; facilities shared with Health Club (although members have their own locker rooms)

Main thrust: Self-knowledge and renewal

Cost: Moderately expensive

The Golden Door

ESCONDIDO
CALIFORNIA

ADDRESS
P.O. Box 1567
Escondido, California
92025
TELEPHONE
619-744-5777
CREDIT CARDS
None

WHEN YOU WALK INTO The Golden Door, you'll enter the inner sanctum of perhaps the most highly reputed spa in America. When you cross the charming wooden footbridge and see the serene, low buildings, Japanese rock gardens, sand rakings, Kai (carp) pool, and discreet waterfall, you'll quietly murmur, "Wow," being careful not to disturb the silence which is also golden. And when you leave after your week's stay, you'll say, "Sayonara," knowing that, like almost every other guest, you will want to return before too many suns set on your busy life.

Strangely enough, there's nothing truly glamorous about The Golden Door. The simplicity of the place is what is so striking and so stylish. Japanese in structure and furnishings, this copy of an old *honjin* inn is a delightful setting for rejuvenation and quiet rejoicing. The Szekely family hit on the right spa formula here and have stuck with it.

Having been around for about thirty years, "The Door" is a sage old spa and has touched a lot of lives, even though only forty guests a week are accepted. Each enjoys a private accommodation with bath and shower, radio, telephone, and a tiny Japanese garden—again, more hush than lush. Samples of beauty products, personalized stationery, and Golden Door clothing (in the right size) await you at check-in. You'll be provided with gray sweatsuits, purple shirts and shorts, bathrobes, slippers, and a blue and white Japanese robe to wear to dinner. Before you even leave home, an exercise videotape will arrive to help loosen up any squeaky joints in preparation for the spa program.

While I was there I heard women say again and again, "It's so special." No one can succinctly define this special quality that The Golden Door most certainly has, but everyone has felt it. Perhaps it is the delicate balance maintained between keeping you on track and letting you be your own boss. Also, the tranquility of the setting allows you to relax with yourself. There's no pretense and no makeup necessary . . . well, maybe a little during "Couples Weeks." After the first lunch, when you are interviewed by the spa director and nutritionist, your decisions are over for the balance of the week. You spell out the program you want and all the arrangements are taken care of. Each morning a paper fan will appear with your breakfast, and on it will be your schedule for the day—hour by hour, reflecting exactly what you want to get out of the week. Your meals will be

served to you without menu or options, containing the proper number of calories and omitting any food you find even mildly unpalatable.

Available for relaxation at any time are the saunas, steam room, and Jacuzzi (Japanese family tub), next to which is a herbal wrap room with several beds. Not large or commodious, the wet area also houses the Swiss showers, regular shower stalls, and a couple of toilets. There are only hooks for clothes. Guests use their own rooms for changing and wear robes to and from this area. For extracurricular exercise, there are two heated pools and two tennis courts. However, the staff plays down the tennis, since that doesn't qualify as part of the regular program (to which they strongly encourage guests to stick).

A typical day at The Golden Door would go something like this:

After the *early* morning wake-up call, it's stretch and walk time. (This can be anything from a short stroll to an invigoratingly brisk five-mile hike up and down "the mountain," stopping for water and orange slices.) Then comes your reward for that effort—breakfast in bed! After that, the choices are warm-up exercises (in the garden or one of the gyms); a class in aerobics, back exercises, dance, stretch, or T'ai Chi; weight training with Camstar machines or free weights; or a workout on the exercise bikes or treadmill. Then it's treat time with an hour of beauty services, perhaps a facial or body wrap. Before lunch by the pool, there is time for more classes, a lecture, or pampering (manicure, pedicure, hair care, and makeup). The pool aerobics class after lunch is popular. In mid-afternoon,

opportunities for a hike, special class (such as jazz dance), or water volleyball are offered, followed by yoga, meditation, or a quiet twilight stroll. Five P.M. brings a masseuse to your room for a full massage. At the sound of the Japanese gong, hors d'oeuvres and "cocktails" are served, then it's dinner in the dining room. For those who are not yet ready for their nightly Japanese hot tub and sleep massage, there is a choice of evening lecture, flower arranging lesson, cooking class, parlor games, and other activities.

For "Men Only" weeks (three two-week periods a year) and "Couples Weeks" (generally following the men's weeks), the schedule is slightly changed and embellished with low-key competition.

Any problems you have with knees, back, neck, or other parts of your body are identified by color-coded dots and squares on your nametag. This negates the need to explain your weakness to each class instructor. Without fail, he or she will say your name before commencing a stretch or exercise that might be wrong for you and suggest you do it in an alternative, nonharmful way.

In addition to the regular program for unwinding, "Inner Door" and "Inner Journey" programs are available to a limited number of return clients. (There is no extra charge and you may register for them on arrival.) These strive to integrate body and mind to enhance creativity, increase awareness, and become familiar with right brain/left brain functions. Lectures, yoga, meditation, biofeedback, and stress reduction techniques provide the tools for plowing through your mental garden and zapping the weeds.

Apart from that, we all know that shopping can be soothing. The boutique displays enough high-class bounty to satisfy almost anyone's acquisitive itch.

"Food, glorious food?" Well, maybe not exactly glorious—remember, this is a spa—but it is beautiful, with each fruit and vegetable carved, sliced, and shredded to perfection. Eighty percent of all the food served so artfully at The Door is grown right there. Using legumes, yogurt, cheese, milk and eggs, plus some seafood and poultry for protein, together with fruits and vegetables, a balanced daily menu of about 1000 calories finds its way into the eager tummies of most visitors. Special diets from 750 to 2500 calories can be suggested or requested. Help for eager reducers comes in the form of a well-devised liquid diet once a week. A word to the hungry wise: when the fruit plate in your room is empty, you can ask for a refill (and be sure to leave a note for the maid not to remove that last apple in her zeal to keep your room pristine).

The philosophy concerning food can be reduced to one word: moderation. Eat enough, but not too much, staying away from fats, salts, refined sugar, and red meat. To keep you on the straight and narrow, when you leave, you'll take your next meal with you.

The guests, mostly in their forties, tend to be people who "get things done." They are lawyers, doctors, politicians, celebrities, business leaders, and spouses of all the above. Sometimes moms and daughters and husbands and wives share the spa vacation, shedding pounds together and building stronger

family ties. Couples weeks are playful as well as beneficial. Because there is no room sharing even for married couples, it's fun to slip off for a romantic assignation in your partner's assigned room.

Dress is casual. If you choose, bring your own attire for evening—like the Hermès butterfly-covered sweatsuit worn to dinner by the stylish Lucy Jewett. Suggested articles to pack include toiletries and underwear, tights and leotards, gym socks, jogging shoes, aerobic shoes, tennis shoes, swimwear, a jacket or sweater, and sleepwear. You can actually get by bringing nothing but your ticket home. Incidentally, personal laundry is done by the staff every day.

If you've spent most of your adult life picking up after others, pampering your family and business associates, answering calls for a little help here and a lot of time there, get thee to The Golden Door. Now it's your turn to be coddled, aided, and soothed. Of course, much of the time you will be far from idle, going on hikes and attending classes. But it's all for you—*your* body, *your* psyche, *your* future.

GETTING THERE

Complimentary transportation from the San Diego airport is provided by the spa.

RATING

Overall: Society's spa ground

⊕   Ask for anything—the only thing they'll turn down is your bed! Japanese serenity and ambience in gardens and buildings

⊖   Some say it was better when it was smaller

Main thrust: Relaxation, revitalization, and reducing

Cost: Very expensive

The Greenbrier

WHITE SULPHUR SPRINGS WEST VIRGINIA

ADDRESS
Station A, West Main
    Street
White Sulphur Springs,
West Virginia 24986
TELEPHONE
304-536-1110
800-624-6070
CREDIT CARDS
All major

I F YOU, LIKE ALICE IN WONDER-land, feel that you have to run as fast as you can just to stay in place, it might be time for you to slow down at the Greenbrier in White Sulphur Springs, West Virginia. With its own in-house spa, this ante-bellum establishment is definitely anti-stress!

Even with 650 guest rooms, 51 suites, and 52 cottages in its 6500-acre setting, The Greenbrier somehow manages to purvey a serene atmosphere. The decor has an old-fashioned, colorful, and warm appeal. It maintains a charming, refined quality even when bustling with conventioneers. The staff at this mansion-like resort and spa has been well instructed in the resort's philosophy—"ladies and gentlemen serving ladies and gentlemen."

The guest rooms, equipped with all the conveniences, are located in the hotel. Cottages lie a short walk away. Most likely, your spacious room will be decorated with cheery flowered or striped wallpaper and cozy furniture. Views vary, so look out the window before you settle in to be sure you like what you see.

The impressive expanse of property includes a picturesque row of craftsmen's shops where handmade goods are sold. There are fifteen outdoor tennis courts (Har/Tru) five indoor tennis courts, two platform tennis courts, an Olympic-sized pool, a par course for joggers, and the Greenbrier's famous golf courses (one designed by Jack Nicklaus). A panorama of the Allegheny Mountains and pine forest forms an impressive backdrop for all the facilities.

Other activities on the seasonal dockets: jogging, hiking, trap and skeet shooting, fishing, horseback riding, cross-country skiing, ice-skating, shuffleboard, horseshoes, Ping-Pong, bridge, backgammon, and movies, to name a few.

The healing, rejuvenating, or at least *soothing* powers of the White Sulphur Springs water lend a special cachet to the spa. The mineral baths, with completely up-to-the-minute facilities, are the most popular of the wet works.

In the separate men's and women's spa areas, bare bodies abound. Don't hesitate to ask for cover-up towels if that is not your most comfortable (non)attire. Attendants may not supply them automatically.

As is true in most American spas, many more ladies than men go for the three- to five-night spa packages (and a la carte spa use). This quiet world of pampering, with a few aerobic, toning, and stretching classes thrown in, appeals more to the softer sex, who ap-

until dinner. It's not impossible to lose weight at The Greenbrier, but neither is it easy. The abundant and tasty food served requires great self-restraint. Consider room service to avoid temptation.

Casual clothing, swimwear, and spa gear—that's the dress code for day. (Spa programmers receive a Greenbrier exercise suit.) In the evening, women put on a bit of silk and a string of pearls and gentlemen don their sports jackets and ties. Be sure to pack a shawl even in the warm months. Because you probably will not want to negotiate the hallways in your bathrobe here, bring a cover-up.

Spa-goers at the gracious Greenbrier unwind and renew, maybe even get a bit more fit in the process. At the end of each day to insure the guests' peace and quiet, a sign is hung in the hallways which says

"IT'S SLEEPYTIME DOWN SOUTH"
Pleasant dreams at The Greenbrier . . .

preciate the beauty services, facials, body wraps, loofah scrubs, body buffs, and water therapies. Men haven't really caught on to the restorative virtues of that part of spa life, but they do appear for a massage or a session with the fitness exercise equipment—rowing machines, exercise bicycles, treadmill, and free weights. (The gym, indoor pool, and exercise classroom are coed.) Everything is Cadillac quality, even the exercise mats.

For those who haven't quite gotten their home fitness routine together, an individual consultation with the exercise physiologist is a must.

Also on the premises is a well-respected medical facility called The Greenbrier Clinic, providing diagnostic and preventative health care by doctors holding impressive credentials. Many people from all over choose to undergo their annual physical exam at the Clinic.

The spa day is interrupted when tea time begins—a big deal at The Greenbrier. Of course, high tea is anything but low cal, so, dieters, beware of this civilized custom. It's better to hold off

---

GETTING THERE

Fly to the Greenbrier Valley Airport, located 15 minutes from the resort/spa. (You can take an air taxi from Roanoke or Charleston.) Another choice is Amtrak. If driving, follow I-64 to the Greenbrier turnoff.

RATING

Overall: A Southern exposure to a European-style spa and world-class sports facilities

$\oplus$ Lovely ambience; excellent sports; White Sulphur Springs water treatments; fine spa equipment

$\ominus$ Spa programs appeal mostly to women; large conference population; weather unpredictable; difficult for the undisciplined dieter

Main thrust: Mental and physical stress reduction through exercise, the powers of pampering, and natural mineral water therapies

Cost: Moderately expensive to expensive

The Greenhouse

ARLINGTON TEXAS

CONTRARY TO REPUTATION, The Greenhouse is no longer just for Eastern bluebloods or Southwestern matrons spoiled by the profits from those "black gold" wells.

Back in 1965, The Greenhouse served as a drying-out retreat for wealthy women of Texas. Then it became a safe haven where Big Daddys sent wives and daughters for pampering, dieting, and shopping while they took their sons hunting and fishing. Yes, ma'am, those were the days when men were men and women were shippable!

Today, women from all over the world, whether involved in careers or home-making, arrive under their own steam, carrying their own credit cards and pursuing up-to-date ideas like adopting a healthier lifestyle. Some save up all year for this one rewarding week. Others dip into nonstop bank accounts to charge and recharge at The Greenhouse every few months.

So, join the gang! Escape cruel reality for the gracious never-never land of The Greenhouse (a never-*ever* land for men). There you will get prettied-up from head to toe, pampered into divine delirium, fed and exercised out of your old body into a new.

Although the area around The Greenhouse is no longer wide open spaces, there is still a feeling of privacy, security, and even seclusion within its grounds. As you drive up to the portals of the estate, you see manicured lawns, a walk-jog track, tennis courts, and the outdoor pool area (a popular hangout for exercise class cutters who prefer pursuing a high-priced suntan to physical strain.

The Greenhouse lives up to its name in architecture as well as atmosphere. The focal area is the glorious central indoor pool, over which a dome-shaped latticed skylight lets the sun shine through. Interior balconies all around are festooned with lush hanging plants.

The oval area around the pool is a spectacular setting for exercise classes, lounging, and drinking the ever present herbal tea and lemon or mineral water (alcohol and carbonated beverages are taboo). This also becomes the shoot-the-breezeway en route to activities where smiles and warm greetings are exchanged.

Radiating out from the pool area are the lovely dining room, parlor, and drawing room; the massage and treatment area with shower, sauna, steam rooms, and whirlpool; two gyms (one equipped with exercise machines and weights); offices; and guest accommo-

ADDRESS
P.O. Box 1144
Arlington, Texas 76010
TELEPHONE
817-640-4000
CREDIT CARDS
V, MC, AE, Neiman
  Marcus

dations—all singles except for two double suites generally occupied by mother-daughter teams who want to share the quiet hours. On the second floor are more single rooms, the boutique (offering stylish merchandise), facial and beauty areas, and the nurse's office. Soft colors and California-style decor throughout make the ambience soothing, casual, and dignified. (A little updating would push it to perfection.)

Every guest room is stocked with *Town and Country* and other magazines, as well as full-size packages of skin and hair products. Bathrooms are stocked with fine linen and hand towels plus a stack of the terry kind, and also tea rose and glycerine soap. In the desk drawer you will find beautiful pale green stationery adorned with a pink rose—and stamped envelopes! Unpacking at The Greenhouse is a pleasure, with plenty of closet space, drawers, and vanity surface.

On arrival, the doctor gives you a cursory exam in your room and determines what your caloric intake should be while there (850, 1200, or 1500 per day—served in the dining room, by the outdoor pool, or in your room). After a fitness evaluation by your personal instructor, you'll be all set for the action and relaxation.

Gracious living at The Greenhouse is distinguished by numerous thoughtful touches, appropriately beginning with the daily wake-up call—a knock on your door followed by the entrance of an attractively groomed maid carrying your breakfast, which she places on a charming wicker bed tray. After drawing the drapes, she exits, leaving you to luxuriate in bed with your breakfast,

served on fine china (a different pattern each morning). Decorating the tray is a yellow rose of Texas, a cheery note from the spa director, and your personal schedule for the day. In the side slot you will find the morning newspaper.

Every morning, after a brisk walk, there are wake-up exercise sessions and stretching, toning, and water classes on each guest's schedule. Tennis, a relaxation class, low-impact aerobics, yoga, and circuit training are also offered. You go at your own speed, fired by constant guidance and encouragement, which continues when you return home, thanks to The Greenhouse's toll-free 800 advice number. Instructors at this spa (which is under the supervision of one of the spa greats, Toni Beck) use every possible means for keeping classes amusing as well as productive. In fact, the fitness program is every bit as good as the renowned beauty program.

Top-notch estheticians, beauticians, and therapists make each of the forty guests purr with multiple massages, thalassotherapy (seaweed wraps), nail care, personalized makeup demos and practice sessions, hair care, loofah scrub, daily facials, and more. The pampering and petting never stops. Don't turn up your nose. I know it sounds ultra-frivolous, but let me tell you—frivolous is fun!

Every guest receives royal treatment. No one on the staff is ever rude or thoughtless. They really do aim to please. Schedule changes are made cheerfully. By and large, a serene, flexible, do-your-own-thing atmosphere prevails. Taking into account each

Gracious living at The Greenhouse . . . [begins] with the daily wake-up call — a knock on your door followed by the entrance of an attractively groomed maid carrying your breakfast. . . .

person's goals, needs, frailties, and strengths, the crew gives its all to assure everyone an unpressured, productive week.

Exquisite table settings turn low-calorie dinners into a lovely experience. Some meals taste delicious, others less so. Service is formal, with service plates, doilies, finger bowls, and such. For that added touch of class, demitasse is poured in the drawing room after dessert. Wednesday night (or "Quiet Night," as it is called here) sees dinner brought to your room, allowing you the opportunity to keep your hair oiled for the night, watch television, write home, read, or whatever.

Special events include lectures, food demonstrations, bingo, fashion shows, and a shopping expedition to Neiman-Marcus (where you receive the red carpet treatment).

Since The Greenhouse is a woman's

world, leave the sexy little numbers at home and take chic, informal dinner wear, personal items, and very little else. During the day everyone wears the team uniform—spa-provided navy blue leotards, stockings, sweat bands, shorts, and white terry robes. There's no hassle, no competition. Although younger guests tend to dress fairly casually (but no sweats or jeans) even at eventide, most Greenhouse ladies emerge made up and dressed up. At any rate, bring the pearls and consider the diamonds. Whatever you choose to look like at this spa is acceptable. However, since appearances count in the real world, the staff readies your hair and makeup for those two momentous occasions, the trip to Neiman-Marcus and the trip home!

Most of the goings-on go on indoors, so occasionally a guest will experience a tinge of claustrophobia or boredom. In the end, the self-contained ambience of The Greenhouse becomes a plus. It is cozy and comforting, and no one feels lost.

GETTING THERE

For a stay at The Greenhouse, fly to Dallas–Fort Worth Airport or Love Field. On arrival, you'll be met at the baggage pickup area by a spa driver.

RATING

Overall: An indoor Eden where overstressed undertoned women of means lose a little weight and gain a lot of confidence

⊕   Comprehensive program; attentive, caring staff; stunning indoor pool area; elegant living

⊖   In-town site; little outdoor activity

Main thrust: Beauty and fitness with more than a touch of class

Cost: Very expensive

Gurney's Inn Resort and Spa, Ltd.

MONTAUK
NEW YORK

I F YOU CAN MANAGE THE ENERGY to turn over from your back to your stomach, you can do the program at Gurney's. Not that there's a lack of activity for the active, but this spa is basically for people who want to tone up lying down.

Gurney's Inn Resort and Spa, Ltd., spreads out along a beautiful white sand beach edging the Atlantic Ocean at the easternmost tip of Long Island in the fishing village of Montauk, New York. The "Big Apple" is about three hours away by car. Location is a big asset here. The proximity to the sea dominates the mood and activities, especially in regard to the spa, which is variously called The Marino-Therapeutic Contemporary Spa, The Spa at Gurney's, and The International Health and Beauty Spa. Take your pick—they all mean "relaxation and rejuvenation seashore style."

Gurney's is understated, not at all elaborate. The only thing splashy about it is the ocean. In the main building, there is a nautical but nice bar, two large restaurants strategically placed for best views, a nondescript reception area, a small boutique, and conference rooms for business meetings.

Down a ramp, one finds the spa building with its men's and women's pavilions (utilitarian, pleasant, spartan), beauty salon, and the pièce de résistance, a spectacular indoor filtered salt-water pool big enough for classes, laps, and recreational swimming. The glassed-in southern wall welcomes the sun's warm rays and allows for a lovely panoramic view of the beach and ocean.

Several weathered shingle buildings house guests in motel-type accommodations, each with television, refrigerator, bath/shower, telephone, and private deck. Definitely ask for a room right on the beach. It's worth the extra expense to be able to lie in bed and let the sounds and sights of the Atlantic lull you to sleep.

The soothing, leveling, revitalizing effect of the sea atmosphere helps the spa accomplish its goal: to encourage guests to accept themselves as they are and then improve where possible. The program is definitely a gentle one. Elderly and lethargic people who don't want to move around a lot but do want a spa experience come and enjoy the facilities along with the young "salts." Some seek relief through the reputed curative effects of sea water or thalassotherapy, deemed helpful for ailments such as minor skin irritations, insomnia, exhaustion, arthritis, and rheumatism.

Spa programs range from one day to one week, but a la carte participation is an alternative. Plans include tasty,

ADDRESS
Old Montauk Highway
Montauk, New York
  11954
TELEPHONE
516-668-2345
  (information)
516-668-3203
  (reservations)
516-668-2509 (direct to
  spa)
CREDIT CARDS
AE, V, MC, DC,
  Discover

nutritious calorie-counted meals, classes, use of exercise equipment, numerous treatments and services, lectures. Unfortunately, there is only one small gym, and the exercise equipment room could use more exercise bicycles and a couple of treadmills. However, daily beach walks and a well-conceived par course for jogging add to the aerobic options. Accommodations are priced per person, with double occupancy billed separately, and Gurney's will not provide a roommate.

Among the spa offerings are seaweed wrap; thalassotherapy in individual tubs with numerous nozzles and jets using filtered sea water, Roman baths for several Jacuzzi-lovers at a time, Swiss shower, scotch hose, sauna, sun bed, massages, facials, loofah and dry scrubs, aromatherapy, hypnotherapy to stop smoking or overeating, and biofeedback. Beauty services fill in the (in)activity roster.

Water sports are big in the summer season, and the beach beckons the bronzed body set. The spa stocks your locker with a bathrobe, slippers, and a tote bag containing a surprise package of popcorn—25 calories—a bottle of mineral water, tape measure, hair shampoo, and your personal daily schedule. Spa hours are 8:00 A.M. to 10:00 P.M. Bring casual seasonal clothes (winters are very cold) as well as swim and exercise gear, plus all personal items. *Don't* depend on the boutique for necessities. Men are requested to wear jackets at dinner.

GETTING THERE

Call in advance for complimentary transportation from local airports, the Long Island Railroad station, and the Hampton Jitney bus stops. The drive from Manhattan takes you through ever-so-social Southampton and razz-ma-tazzy East Hampton. Upon entering Montauk, you'll sense the laid-back, unadorned difference of the fisherman's deep sea dreamland.

RATING

Overall: A simple European-style seaside spa utilizing the ocean water, air, and atmosphere

⊕   Location; thalassotherapy; large indoor saltwater pool; undemanding regime; good food

⊖   No tennis or golf on premises; generally no special pricing for singles in rooms; spa area is not at all luxurious and needs updating; iffy weather during much of the year and cold in winter

Main thrust: Water therapy and beauty treatments for relaxation and rejuvenation

Cost: Moderately expensive on *double* occupancy basis

The Heartland

GILMAN
ILLINOIS

THE HEARTLAND IS CLOSE TO Chicago, but a world apart. Serenity and peace come with the territory: thirty-one acres of woods, farmland, and lake. Situated on Kam Lake, the estate consists of a white clapboard farmhouse and a three-story barn, which is now the spa. Life in the house turns clients into guests and strangers into friends, thanks to a staff that deserves accolades. Elegant in its own way, The Heartland offers homey, cozy public rooms in which to curl up and listen to fine-tuned Heartland Institute lectures on improving one's lifestyle and general health, eat delicious food at round tables with newfound or old pals, take a yoga class, or just hang loose and browse through the boutique.

Roommates are provided for lone spa-goers who desire double occupancy rates. Fourteen in total, the guest rooms tend to be small but nice—just imagine that you are visiting your country cousin. Older people who don't care to navigate the stairs (there is no elevator) can ask for the room downstairs. That's the one with the tub; all others have shower stalls. Don't look for a freebie package, but you will find a hair blower and an intercom in each room. Part of the stress-free plan is the lack of a telephone, television, or radio in the rooms—all the better to hear the birds singing and the corn growing!

When you arrive and are told to leave your shoes in the cubby in the foyer, your valuables in a manila envelope in the downstairs safe, and your keys *in* your doors (on the outside!), you may experience a brief moment of anxiety. After that you'll glide through your stay without a worry, dressed in Heartland sweats, shorts outfit, slippers, socks, and robes. (You do have to bring athletic and walking shoes, boots in winter, undies, and toiletries.) Spa clothes are replaced almost instantly when you leave the dirties outside your door.

No one prods you to take part in the spa program. You choose your own classes, treatments, and services. A short walk outdoors or a tunnel indoors takes you to the spa for the aerobics classes, exercise equipment, facials, massages, steam, whirlpool, sauna, pool, makeup sessions, manicures, pedicures, hair styling, waxing, and (in the winter, with equipment provided) the cross-country skiing orientation. Safety is stressed in all activities. With caring guidance, you'll learn to use the excellent Keiser Cam II equipment, free weights, exercise bicycles, rowing machine, and Heavy Hands. Fear of failure or fracture need not deter you from partaking of the race walking

ADDRESS
Gilman, Illinois 60938
TELEPHONE
815-683-2182
BUSINESS OFFICE
18 East Chestnut Street
Chicago, Illinois 60611
BUSINESS
TELEPHONE
312-266-2050
CREDIT CARDS
V, MC, AE

10:30—water aerobics
12:30—lunch
1:15—Heartland Institute lecture
2:00—intermediate/advanced aerobics or free weights
3:30—muscle training
4:30—yoga
6:00—supper
7:00—"All the Fun Moves" (see below) or walk
8:00—lecture
8:30—dessert/games/movie, plus tiny snacks

Of course, treatments and services go on all day.

Why does one go to The Heartland? Reasons vary: general fitness, weight loss, proper nutrition, stress reduction, cardiovascular improvement, relaxation, body shaping.

Beyond that (and beyond belief) there's fun and games in the form of "All the Fun Moves." This is a progression of activities designed to bring out the adventurer in you. It takes a few days, but it may be worthwhile to carve the necessary time to participate out of your schedule, instead of opting for a mere weekend. Starting with easy parlor games that instill participants with trust in one another and get them to work together in solving problems, you finally work up to the "big finish." You climb a forty-foot telephone pole, walk on a wire like a circus performer, then slide back to reality (and terra firma). No, I'm not kidding. There is no danger—a harness insures your safety during this mini Outward Bound course. It's not for everyone, but those who get up the courage to do it earn their applause. To realize you can go

To realize you can go beyond your prescribed limits is a joyful experience; to prove yourself a winner . . . that's really something!

(which I thoroughly enjoyed), the low-impact aerobics classes, the par course for joggers, tennis, hiking, or lakeside activities.

NOTE: There is no smoking indoors and no alcohol on the premises. Caffeinated coffee is served only at breakfast.

A typical day's schedule would be:

7:15—stretch and walk
8:00—breakfast
9:00—race walking or aerobics

beyond your prescribed limits is a joyful experience; to prove yourself a winner instead of a wimp—that's really something!

Please don't get the idea that The Heartland is only for those who want to soar like eagles. That's just one small aspect of it. Most of the women and men who arrive are likely to be housewives, business people, and moms and daughters from Chicago who want to relax, lose a few pounds, tone up a little, not be hassled, and indulge in being pampered with a few superb massages and facials.

The underlying philosophy of this spa is that wise nutritional habits form the basis of lifestyle change. The food is gourmet vegetarian plus fish. There is one menu for everyone, but any guest can request a special meal in advance. Women get 1200 calories a day; men 1500. For those who want more, it's there, as are constant snacks: fruit, decaffeinated coffee, and herbal teas. Taking *The Heartland Cookbook* home *and using it* along with a personal plan worked out by the staff will keep you in condition. Aim for no more than 36 percent body fat if you're female, 28 percent for males. The Heartland staff will determine your body fat ratio with use of skinfold calipers, taking into account your height, weight, and age.

Exercise, education, and nutrition are the trio for eliminating the daily irritations that can cause enormous stress buildup. The Heartland shows you how to "cool it" through use of these three magic ingredients to reduce hypertension and cardiovascular disease.

You wear the same (comfortable) clothes as everyone else, with a first-name-only name tag, and it is a leveling and relaxing experience. "Airs" drop off even before the pounds. Unless bright-light excitement is a must, it is hard to imagine anyone leaving The Heartland disappointed. No matter the extent of a woman's or man's sophistication in real life or spa life, the appeal of the place is tremendous.

The minimum age for the twenty-eight guests is eighteen. Most people (predominantly women) come from the Midwest. That's strictly due to the spa's location, not its point of view. More rooms are filled on weekends than during the week. For Chicago residents, a departure portfolio, *The Heartland Connection*, which recommends local professionals in diet, exercise, and wellness, will ease re-entry into the world of everyday noise and pressure.

GETTING THERE

Out-of-staters fly to Chicago. From there, you can taxi downtown, to the Oxford House, 225 North Wabash, where the free Heartland van will pick you up, or you can drive south on the Dan Ryan Expressway to I-57. Go 52 miles to Kankakee exit 308; from there follow U.S. 52/45 for 22 miles (it becomes U.S. 49) to Rte 24; take that for 2 miles. Turn left at The Heartland sign, and it's 2 miles. In all it is an 80-mile drive.

RATING

Overall: A friendly, relaxed, low-key, homey wonder of a spa

⊕   Idyllic atmosphere; staff; race walking; they do the thinking for you; "All the Fun Moves"

⊖   Not much variety in sports; weather can be bad

Main thrust: Lifestyle change through learning and doing

Cost: Moderately expensive

Hilton Head Health Institute

HILTON HEAD ISLAND
SOUTH CAROLINA

ADDRESS
P.O. Box 7138
Hilton Head Island,
   South Carolina
   29938-7138
TELEPHONE
803-785-7292
CREDIT CARDS
None

HILTON HEAD HEALTH Institute is different from most spas. Pampering is not even in the picture, and noses turn up at the idea of merely temporary change. The staff here goes for the long view; after all, there is a life after Hilton Head. They'll show you how to live it.

It all begins in *your* head. You must be prepared to absorb the teachings, and making them a part of your day-to-day existence is imperative. Once those bad habits are exorcised through the three E's—exercise, education, and eating—you're on your way to a life-style change that will endure long after you leave Hilton Head.

The Institute is on Hilton Head Island, a resort community off the coast of South Carolina best known for its outstanding golf and tennis. The hot, humid summer is the least desirable time to be there.

Visitors who come to the island for a stay at the Institute are lodged in lovely cottages in an area called Shipyard Plantation. These have two or three bedrooms, and each has its own private bath, a combined living room–dining room, and kitchen. There is also a washing machine and dryer. The five or ten minutes to and from the main building is a short, pleasant walk, especially after a dip in the heated indoor or outdoor pool.

Taking a good look at yourself is part of the program, but this is not all done with mirrors. A medical screening and exam, "stress-gram," and in-depth interview give the fine medical team here the opportunity to help you see yourself and to draw up a route to a healthier existence. Follow-ups by the physician while you're here keep you on course. Exercise and diet are expertly supervised, and informative lectures on health, nutrition, self-management, habit making and breaking, are an integral part of the regimen.

The Institute offers a "Weight Control Program" and the "Executive Health Program," both of which promote optimum well-being. These programs begin on specific dates throughout the year. "Weight Control" lasts twenty-six days, "Executive Health" twelve days. Both are coed, and many couples enroll. Available, too, are one- and two-week graduate programs, and special instruction is available for bulimics and those who want to stop smoking.

Because the philosophy of this spa is to keep everything very simple so that you can continue the program at home without additional equipment (but with

69

the exercise tape), the gym is minimal. A basic Nautilus, exercise bicycles, and mini-trampolines share the room in which the aerobics classes are given.

Walking is the key activity. Hard-packed, glistening sand beaches make this more pleasant. The addition of a Walkman blocks out possible boredom. Required walks of three miles or more a day (after breakfast, lunch, and dinner) can be taken alone, with a friend, or with a leader. For a change of pace, you can pedal along the many bike paths.

The balanced meal plan—high in carbohydrates and low in fats, sodium, and cholesterol—gets results. Unfortunately, the *food does not get raves,* but you're so hungry you don't care! You just keep focusing on the fact that in dieting the losers are the winners. Daily calorie counts go from the "Low Cal Phase" of 800 to the "Booster Phase" of 1100 to the "Re-entry Phase," which bridges the gap between dieting and long-term maintenance. Meals on the program can easily be duplicated at home. Not only are you instructed in how to prepare the dishes, but also in purchasing appropriate food products.

Behavior modification depends to some extent on an effective mental health program. The Institute comes through with serious professional help, private consultations, and lectures.

The Hilton Head Health Institute is

It all begins in your head. You must be prepared to absorb the teachings, and making them a part of your day-to-day existence is imperative.

70

run by impressive, dedicated people. Fortified by their availability and caring attitudes, everyone wins. The personal atmosphere is congenial and helpful. The straightforward, no-nonsense approach to looking better and living better is refreshing.

Clothing needs vary according to season. Generally, you can wear your sweats morning, noon, and night. Bring swimwear and good shoes (running shoes are suggested). Summers call for shorts and t-shirts. From November through February, warm clothing may be needed. An alarm clock radio, flashlight (in winter months), stamps, books, raincoat, and a Walkman will come in handy.

When the staff at the Hilton Head Health Institute says, "Goodbye—keep in touch," that is not idle chatter. Leave-taking is accompanied by en-couragement to contact the staff during the entire next year for advice, help, and warm understanding. This deters backsliding and buoys up willpower and self-image. You return home a new you, with both increased self-confidence and a support team.

GETTING THERE

To get to the Institute, fly to Savannah, Georgia. Airport limos will take you to Hilton Head Island.

RATING

Overall: Twelve or twenty-six days of behavior modification, and then back to the future

$\oplus$ Lifestyle change instruction and practice; supportive staff; special programs for stress reduction, weight loss, and stopping smoking

$\ominus$ More planned exercise classes and equipment needed; too much free time, especially in evenings

Main thrust: Lifestyle change; weight control

Cost: Moderately expensive

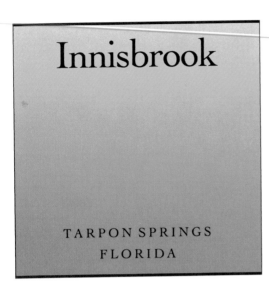

Innisbrook

TARPON SPRINGS

FLORIDA

MORE THAN A RESORT, this is a self-contained community of enormous proportions, with sports galore, superb convention facilities, a health and fitness spa, and entertaining night life. Even with the trams provided for transportation between buildings, you'd be wise to carry your compass and a map of the place at all times while here.

If you're not the kind of person to be overwhelmed by its sheer size, Innisbrook can prove a wise choice for a vacation cocktail with a twist of health. I only wonder how conventioneers can be expected to keep their minds on the bottom line when there's so much going on in the margins. Certainly, if Innisbrook is your destination, bring the kids. There are as many diversions and programs for the tots and teens as there are for grown-ups.

A bird sanctuary with swans, cranes, peacocks, and ducks; a lake filled with bass; manicured lawns; and exotic flowers and trees soften the hard edge of the many buildings. Accommodations consist of well-decorated hotel rooms, suites, and apartments, all containing the essentials for a happy holiday.

Golfers, beware—you may never want to leave. The three eighteen-hole courses are lush and taxing, a golfer's heaven. Several golf packages are available, and talented pros make this the number one sports option. Tennis runs a close second, with riding, fishing, basketball, swimming, bicycling, and scuba diving filling out the roster. Miniature golf, the game room, a nine-station par course for joggers, and a playground appeal to both adults and children.

One need not leave the complex to shop for gifts or clothes. There are minor league boutiques and one pro shop that is major by anyone's standards. You could outfit the entire PGA here!

There are strict rules about dressing. No shirts without collars or sleeves are permissible on the golf courses. Jackets and ties must be worn in some areas. Traveling to Innisbrook with just carry-on luggage would be a true test of one's packing skills since spa and swimwear, sports clothes, and evening outfits for Las Vegas–type entertainment and dancing will be needed.

It would seem almost as if the spa facilities were there just to get your body and mind in condition for the golf and tennis. (Emphasis is certainly on those activities.) There is an extensive line of Universal and Future fitness equipment in the exercise room. Stretch

ADDRESS
P.O. Drawer 1088
Tarpon Springs, Florida
34688-1088
TELEPHONE
1-800-456-2000 (U.S.)
CREDIT CARDS
All major

and aerobics classes are scheduled in and out of water.

Ready and able to help you develop a plan for a healthier lifestyle, the highly qualified staff will do an in-depth evaluation of your physical condition, nutritional needs, and stress tendencies.

Stress reduction and physical examination are accomplished through biofeedback, yoga classes, whirlpool baths, saunas, massages, and facials. "Beautifying the parts" is the job of staff esthetic experts.

And here's the best news yet: A no-tipping policy is in effect.

GETTING THERE

Innisbrook sprawls out over hill and vale not too far from Tampa International Airport. Fly there, prearrange a car to pick you up, and you'll be smelling the azaleas and citrus groves on the property in about 45 minutes.

RATING

Overall: A veritable three-ring circus with business confabs occupying the center ring, golf to one side, a range of sports to the other, and a side show of health and fitness. Step right up, ladies and gentlemen and children of all ages . . .

$\oplus$ Beautifully manicured grounds; innumerable activities available; excellent golf

$\ominus$ Too darn big; not enough emphasis on a spa program

Main thrust: Sports and relaxation

Cost: Expensive

Interlaken Resort and Country Spa

LAKE GENEVA
WISCONSIN

"**G**ET AWAY," "COUNTRY Spa Escape," "Workout Weekend," "Romantic Interlude" . . . these names for the Interlaken packages promise a lot. And they do deliver. You get away from real life, escape into a country spa, and work out. Of course, you must bring your own "romance"— or be very lucky!

The resort itself is an appealing spread of 150 hotel accommodations, 286 villas, and 30 apartments on ninety acres of natural landscape at the edge of the town of Lake Geneva on the shores of Lake Como, Wisconsin. Rooms in the hotel are comfortable and include everything but mini-fridges. Large but cozy, the lovely boutique, indoor and outdoor pools, restaurants, bars, disco, rec room, and tennis courts keep the mood mellow Wisconsin-style.

Summer water sports and winter land sports add to the attraction of Interlaken. For hiking, walking, and jogging, the season never ends. Bicycling is almost always an option.

Not only spa people, but also conventioneers and adult members of family groups can enjoy the mineral baths, tanning machine, facials, massages, saunas, steam rooms, herbal wraps, whirlpool, hydrotherapy, and other services—a la carte or on a spa plan. Spa classes begin after the brisk 8:00 A.M. walk and breakfast. Low-impact aerobics and "aquacize" fill in the weekly schedule, with the addition of one or two all-level aerobics, stretch and tone, and weight-training sessions. The carpeted and mirrored gym is perfectly adequate. In the exercise room, Marcy and Universal machines, plus free weights and exercise bicycles, tone up tired bodies or sculpt active ones with the help of a professional weight trainer. Herbal tea or fruit water is available to rehydrate all takers at all times.

A full-service beauty parlor gets you ready to face the world upon leaving.

Adding a bit of playfulness to eating, the menus are divided into three parts: Act I (breakfast)—Opening, Main Stage, and Sideshow (that's fruit and juices, entree, and cereals and toast); Act II (lunch)—Overture, Green Scene, Main Stage, and Encore (need I describe?); and Act III (dinner)— same as lunch. At each "Act" you check your choices (mindful of the printed calorie counts) for the following meal. Dieters and nondieters eat together in the Lake Bluff Dining Room. That's the way real life is, you know, but if you're low on willpower, I warn you, stay away from the tempting Sunday brunch buffet!

ADDRESS
Route 2, Box 80,
  Highway 50 West
Lake Geneva,
  Wisconsin 53147
TELEPHONE
414-248-9121
1-800-225-5558
CREDIT CARDS
DC, V, MC, AE, CB,
  Discover

Even though the resort's population covers all types and ages, spa program people tend to be mostly upper middle-class Midwestern women seeking pampering, relaxation, fun, and time for themselves. Two or three nights appear to be the usual length of stay.

Spa-goers get bathrobes and slippers but must bring all exercise, sports, swim, and resort wear for the appropriate season. Keep it casual.

While it's true that the spa area is physically not impressive, the attitude of the staff more than compensates, and that goes a long way during a short stay.

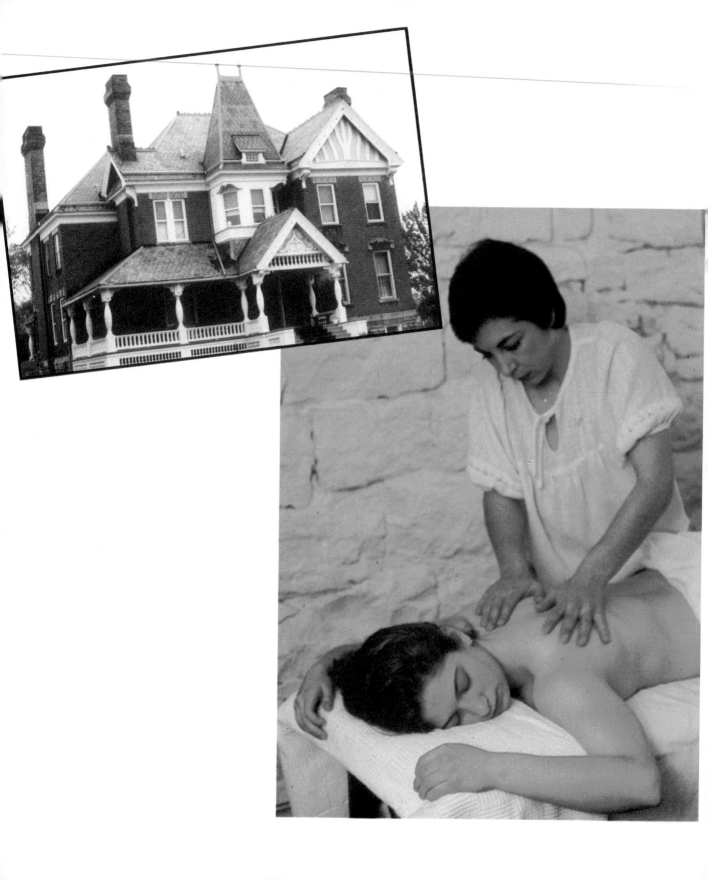

The Kerr House

GRAND RAPIDS
OHIO

"**I** JUST HAD TO COME BACK — *needed* it in order to keep going."

"It's the best thing I've ever done for myself."

"I was here once before, and it changed my life."

These are remarks I overheard from other guests while I was at this little enclave of self-renewal. What a dear, special place! The subtle things that happen here truly can make a substantial positive change in one's outlook, body, and chances for the future. Though the program offered here is serious stuff, it is not heavy going. There are lots of laughs along the way.

Not that it's all perfect. Nothing ever is. No grand and glorious gardens or rolling lawns grace this impressive landmark house, which sits on an ordinary street in the village of Grand Rapids, Ohio, on the banks of the Maumee River. There are no private bathrooms, and even the bedrooms must be shared unless one is willing to pay quite a bit extra. (That is understandable since, fully occupied, only eight guests can be accommodated.)

Because of the smallness of the group, a feeling of camaraderie sets in from Day One. The warm aura of security and sensitivity in this truly beautiful Victorian house, with its elegant authentic furniture and memorabilia of the period, captivates everyone — even those who might find it a trifle musty. Gentleness pervades the atmosphere and the program. As you are coddled, cared for, and eased into a healthier lifestyle, a sense of well-being takes over. The homey, intimate quality of the place adds to the delights of the constant personal attention.

People come here from all over the world not only to improve their bodies, but also their self-image and the way they handle themselves. The director, Laurie Hostetler, shows the way. She is an integral part of the program — and one terrific lady! (If she's not going to be there, rebook.)

The vintage building has recently been renovated.

Lower level: kitchen; informal cheery cafe used for lunches and frequent "tea breaks"; wicker-decorated informal lounge; a petite version of "Ye Olde Gifte Shoppe"; whirlpool; sauna; mineral hot tub; sun bed; treatment areas; a beauty salon of sorts; bathroom.

First floor: two elegant, inviting parlors; offices; lovely oak-paneled dining room; stunning massive staircase leading to the second floor.

Second floor: bedrooms — each different, all decorated with flair; communal bathroom with shower stall, two sinks,

ADDRESS
17777 Beaver Street
Grand Rapids, Ohio
43522
or
P.O. Box 363
Grand Rapids, Ohio
43522
TELEPHONE
419-832-1733
CREDIT CARDS
MC, V, AE

and two toilets and bidets behind separate doors.

Loft: a large carpeted exercise room; a cozy meditation or reading cubby; bathroom.

NOTE: There is no television or room telephone unless specifically requested.

Usually, women fill the guest list. However, the coed and men's weeks have become increasingly popular. Guests' aims tend to be (1) to start a new health regime, (2) to "get centered" and feel in control of one's life, (3) to tone up, and (4) to think through and get a better perspective on a particular situation. The fee determines the fact that most guests enjoy a certain amount of financial success.

Hard-core athletes or frenetic sorts must adopt a new mind-set for the program period. "No pain, no gain"? No! No! Everything is accomplished with as little pain as possible. You take off your makeup, let your hair frizz up or go straight, put on sweats or leotard, and allow The Kerr House to open the gates to the real you, to the fun of being pampered, to a healthier, tighter body and more optimistic outlook.

No one insists that you take part in anything, but maximum accomplishment requires full participation in the program, the core of which is hatha yoga. Don't shrink back. There is nothing weird or mysterious about it. Forget those images of a swami in a turban or a burnt-out flower child mellowing in the lotus position. Hatha yoga, as taught here, consists of exercises for stretching and toning every part of the anatomy, total relaxation, and deep breathing. If you think breathing is one thing you already do well, be assured you'll do it better when you leave. The technique you learn actually enhances your life and may even increase your life-span. Once you get the hang of it, you'll "inhale energy, exhale tension" like the rest of us converts.

During part of the yoga sessions, discussions focus on positive thinking, mental health, stress, and general coping.

Most of the stretching exercises are done on floor mats. My fellow spa-goers, ranging in age from twenty-four to eighty, managed the two-a-day sessions with only mild, good-humored groaning. Daily class time on the individual rebounders (mini-trampolines) add a vigorous aerobic workout.

You've heard of the Big Bang theory of how the world began? Well, The Kerr House teaches the Big Box theory on how to relax in the midst of a world filled with crisis. As you lie on the mat, Laurie has you relax your body from toes to nose. Then, with your eyes closed, you visualize a big box. If something is troubling you, you put it in the box. If someone is bothering or worrying you, you put him or her (or them) in the box. Then you cover the box, set it aside, and let it and its contents leave your mind. It may sound silly and simplistic, but it works for many people. Incidentally, while your eyes are closed, you are covered with a cozy blanket that turns out to be a beautiful antique quilt. If you grow attached to it and feel you can't leave it behind, inquire about buying this treasure.

The rest of the program consists of eating delicious, all-natural meals; massages; manicures and pedicures;

Because of the smallness of the group, a feeling of camaraderie sets in from Day One.

78

reflexology; herbal wraps; use of whirlpool, sauna, and mineral Jacuzzi; nature walks; T'ai Chi; and lectures. Each person's schedule for the day is brought along with *breakfast in bed*.

Unusual activities offered at The Kerr House make time pass almost too quickly. For instance, a professional graphologist brings the group together and reads character strengths and weaknesses from each person's handwriting—masterfully and with great sensitivity and good humor.

When Dr. Bob arrives, it's like a morning at Lourdes! He's an expert in applied kinesiology who performs small miracles—reducing pain and stress, realigning the body, enhancing muscle strength and circulation, and more. Apparently, the trigger points for various muscles are located on the body map somewhere other than you would expect. He knows where to find them and what to do, his diagnostic abilities and chiropractic skills are incredible. (My right leg now exactly matches my left as a result of his manipulating the sixth cervical vertebra in my neck!)

Other diversions are meetings with an astrologist, cooking instructor, personality analyst, or whoever is scheduled at the time you are there.

The 1000-calorie-per-day diet achieves weight loss, though no emphasis is placed upon that aspect of the program. Drinking coffee and smoking are discouraged—the staff is happy to help anyone kick the caffeine or nicotine habit. Alcohol is totally taboo. A harpist or violinist at dinner time perfectly complements the fine food, china, crystal, and candlelight.

Pack according to the season, always including exercise gear, swimsuit; outdoor clothing for walks, caftans, slacks, and dresses for the evenings. Bathrobes, slippers, shampoo and conditioner, lotions, vitamins, and herbal laxatives are supplied, and leotards are sold along with gift items in the petite Kerr House boutique.

In short, *here's what you get:* breakfast in bed; major pampering by a truly caring professional staff; several pairs of listening ears; a feeling of inner tranquility; greater knowledge of yourself plus greater self-esteem; health-improvement techniques to continue at home; a cleaned-out, more supple body.

Here's what you give up: salt, sugar, non-nutritious food, alcohol, smoking and caffeine (probably), sports activity, television, a degree of privacy.

GETTING THERE

Provided by prearrangement, complimentary transportation will await you upon arrival at either the airport at Toledo, Ohio (20 minutes away), or Detroit (1½ hours away).

RATING

Overall: A uniquely intimate, casually elegant spa emphasizing hatha yoga techniques for inner and outer improvement

⊕   Staff; food; ambience; hatha yoga; individual attention; unusual added attractions

⊖   Basically an indoor program; shared bathrooms

Main thrust: Renewal, relaxation, and a plan for a better, healthier life

Cost: Moderately expensive

La Costa Hotel and Spa

CARLSBAD

CALIFORNIA

ADDRESS
Costa del Mar Road
Carlsbad, California
92009
TELEPHONE
1-800-854-5000
619-438-9111
CREDIT CARDS
All major

At La Costa, you can de-bauch or de-tox. The choice is yours.

The resort has the look of a playground for the posh—or at least the rich. The outdoor areas are distinguished by beautiful landscaping and peach-colored buildings. Indoor furnishings are the last word in the California interpretation of European casual elegance. Rooms, restaurants, lounges, and bars furbished with Irish carpets and continental antiques mixed with bamboo and rattan look out onto a walk-through waterfall, one of the two championship golf courses, the twenty-three (grass, clay, or hardcourt) tennis courts, or a swimming pool surrounded by pretty plantings. Cute little La Costa jitneys skittle by with knicker-clad bellmen taking the "swells" to and from their pampering, playing, and body polishing.

The guests are people who know their way around—anywhere. About half of them come from New York (especially in the winter), many live in Los Angeles and Beverly Hills, some drive down from their nearby San Diego abodes, and the rest jet in from all over. And do they bring their clothes! Even ordinary people take on a patina of glamour upon entering this make-believe world. A loyal group, these lovers of the good life return again and again.

Why not? The air alone is revitalizing—the spa is just two minutes from the ocean. Weather is near-perfect. Days can be filled with spa and sports activities or business meetings (there's a 50,000-square-foot conference center). Nights offer peaceful sleep in the lap of luxury or razzle-dazzle in the form of live shows, dancing, first-run movies, and a weekly "theme" pool party.

To enhance guests' enjoyment of the celebrated golf courses, instruction with video is offered for game analysis and improvement. Racquets are kept in play on the tennis courts and practice lanes. There are heated pools for swimming and poolside sunning or scouting the crowd. If walking and jogging make up part of your fitness routine, try the route around the golf course or the special jogging trail (five laps equals one mile). Bicycle riding and water volleyball are popular as well. Less strenuous games can be played in the recreation room (backgammon is still a favorite). And let us not forget the abundant shopping opportunities at La Costa, should that be your sport of choice.

Although La Costa is large, it is not difficult to get oriented to the lay of the land. The main lobby (with its charming mural of La Costa behind the recep-

81

tion desks), clubhouse (with its restaurants, bars, lounges), conference center, and main pool area are all situated together. A short walk takes you to the Lifestyle Center, Nutrition Center, women's spa, men's spa, and the beauty salon. The 482 guest accommodations are scattered throughout.

Spa areas are big and beautiful. Facilities include saunas, rock steam baths, Swiss showers, whirlpools (many private tubs), Roman pools (for more than one person), and solaria. Skin analysis, facials, massages, herbal wraps (in a room with a working fireplace), and loofah scrubs are also available. Exercise classes are given hourly from 9:00 to 4:00 at the pools and gyms (aerobics, stretch, calisthenics, yoga, dance, and a crowd-pleaser called "Rebounder," done on mini-trampolines). Except for water classes, all are coed. The weight room's equipment consists of eight Eagle machines, Lifecycles, computerized treadmills, and rowing machine. You can have a personal trainer for a fee.

All beauty services are performed in the most graceful of beauty salons. The makeup classroom looks like a Fortune 500 business conference room.

Spa programs, offered to anyone over eighteen, vary from one to seven nights. A la carte spa use is an option for non-program guests. The entrance fee includes clothing and use of locker, indoor pools, and steam and weight rooms. Treatments, classes, and services are extra.

The four-night plan includes room (spa rooms are like little apartments); three meals a day (diet or regular); locker; spa clothing (sweatsuit, terry-cloth toga, slippers); a medical and nutritional evaluation; skin analysis; daily massage, facial, and herbal wrap; and exercise classes. Also part of the package are a loofah scrub, manicure, pedicure, spot toning, tanning session, tennis, golf, use of spa facilities, hair care, and (for women) makeup. Lectures on pertinent subjects are given daily.

Serious seekers of a long-term health plan enroll in the seven-night "Life Fitness Program." Its emphasis is on weight control, lowering cholesterol or blood pressure, and managing stress. The week's fee includes a complete series of evaluations: blood and medical, physical endurance, strength, flexibility, pulmonary function, body fat percentage, and nutritional needs, as well as pampering treatments, beauty services, room, board, exercise classes, lectures, and a personalized regimen and dietary plan. Those enrolled in this program have the advantage of individual attention by a doctor, psychologist, and nutritionist. To make the group more cohesive, meals are eaten communally at one long table in the spa dining room. (More information on the "Life Fitness Program" can be obtained by calling 1-800-824-1264 from California or 1-800-426-5438 from other states.)

In one of the spa offices, there is a sign that reads, "He who indulges bulges." Temptation is all around you in life—and, alas, at La Costa as well. As you go to the spa dining room, you get tantalizing whiffs from the other restaurants. In some of the other dining rooms, guests are dressed to the nines; among spa-goers, it's more like to the threes or fours. One hundred seventy-

The resort has the look of a playground for the posh—or at least the rich.

five people can be seated in the spa dining room.

Calorie-counted menus for spa-ers contain no added salt, fat, or refined foods—no oils, mayonnaise, butter, margarine, or whole milk. You are encouraged to accompany meals with vitamin, mineral, and potassium supplements. With each menu, you receive a slip that simply but significantly says:

My calorie prescription is _____
Breakfast calories _____
Lunch calories _____
Dinner calories _____
Total calories per day _____

It disappears into the kitchen with your order.

Each meal has at least three courses, which are amazingly tasty. Totaling no more than 40 calories, dessert choices are custards, fruit parfaits, yogurt, and even cheesecake. That should keep you away from the candy bar in the lobby shop.

The Life Fitness Center at La Costa is serious about its goals and helps those who opt for learning and adopting a new regimen. However, most guests at this buzzing resort go there for golf, tennis, the lighter side of spa life, and a lot of fun.

GETTING THERE

The La Costa service will transport you from the San Diego airport for about one-fourth the price of the resort's limousine service. Driving from San Diego will take about half an hour; from Los Angeles, about 1 hour 45 minutes. The resort is just off I-5.

RATING

Overall: A one-destination stop for innumerable resort and spa activities with a show biz–mogul atmosphere

⊕   So much to do; pretty place; climate; air, golf and tennis; pampering

⊖   Lack of intimacy; impersonal

Main thrust: Beauty and sports

Cost: Very expensive

Le Pli Health Spa at the Charles Hotel

CAMBRIDGE MASSACHUSETTS

CAMBRIDGE, MASSACHUsetts, neighbor of Boston and home of Harvard University, has long been a mecca for eager minds. Now it offers a destination for people who want to combine the pleasures of an urban holiday with the benefits of a spa experience. Le Pli is the place.

The Charles Hotel, which houses Le Pli, lives up to its fine reputation. In the modern, comfortable lobby, an imposing painting of Longfellow's house in Cambridge reminds one that the past counts. The outstanding American quilts hung there reinforce that impression.

Le Pli occupies a tri-level portion of the hotel. Immaculately clean and tastefully decorated in blues, off-whites, and lots of wood, it utilizes its limited space to maximum benefit.

The large indoor, glassed-in pool and sun terrace with its own exercise equipment area, sun bed room, and Jacuzzi combine to make this part of the spa a good place to do laps or simply lie back gazing at the Calder mobile hanging from the ceiling.

In the Cardiovascular Conditioning and Weight Room, Le Pli's Keiser machines are complemented by a Nordic-Track, free weights, exercise bicycles, jogging machines, trampolines, Stair-Master, and rowers. A floor of parquet over plywood over springs in The Studio is gentle on the feet of those taking classes in aerobics, yoga, and dance. Steam rooms, massages, facials, body wraps, mud baths, and hydrotherapy treatments are yours for the asking. The attractive beauty salon offers all esthetic services.

At your initial visit to the spa area, an interview will determine whether you prefer guidelines to follow on your own or a highly supervised regimen.

Working out is the most important activity here, and Le Pli's "Personal Trainer" program benefits all takers. Having one person work with you throughout your stay is an unusual extra—and it's so fitting. The people who come here are an intelligent, demanding group—they undoubtedly have a personal banker, a personal accountant, and a personal maid, so why not a personal trainer?

Anyone over eighteen may use the spa; however, a medical report is required for those over fifty. This ensures that all diets, services, exercises, and treatments are appropriately tailored to your needs.

Because this is an urban spa, traditional sports are de-emphasized. Tennis is available at no cost nearby, but few take advantage of that. Joggers will enjoy a daily run along the beautiful Charles River.

ADDRESS
5 Bennett Street
Charles Square
Cambridge, Massachusetts 02138
TELEPHONE
617-868-8087 (spa)
617-864-1200 (hotel)
CREDIT CARDS
AE, V, MC

84

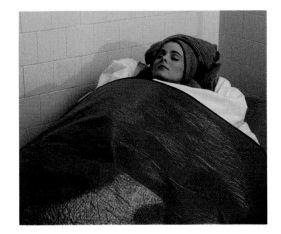

Spa plans of two days or more offer a fitness evaluation, exercise prescription, diet meals, hotel room, massages, body wraps, personal exercise trainer, manicure, pedicure, makeup, shampoo and blow-dry, unlimited exercise classes (there are only a few a day), aquatic exercise, gratuities, service charge, and sales tax. You know up front just how much everything will cost you.

Le Pli Spa plans are available for a day, a weekend, a week, or longer. By far the most favored plan is the "Weekend Program." Upon arrival, you receive a welcome package that includes a Le Pli sweatsuit, the diet book, and your personal spa schedule. There are no "Indian givers" here—these are all yours to keep. Generally, the spa director greets you on your arrival, shows you to your room, and leaves you to unpack.

One of the restaurants in the Charles Hotel offers low-calorie/low-cholesterol food—indicated with an asterisk on the menu. This selection is basically for use of dieting diners not on a spa program. For the program people, a special menu provides the proper intake for each person. Breakfast is served in bed.

Lunch and dinner may be eaten in the spa lounge or the restaurant; most prefer eating dinner in their rooms, happy to be in robe and slippers in front of the TV. The "Fit or Fat" and "Target Diet" menus are well prepared and very tasty.

Weather is tricky in the Northeast. Though hot, sultry air will probably greet you in the summer, and cold winds in the winter, the seasons resist long-term predictability. You'll need only shoes, leotard, and a swimsuit for the spa. They supply bathrobes plus the sweatsuit. Do pack an all-weather coat, an umbrella, and some city clothes. This is a city spa in a city worth seeing.

GETTING THERE

Taxis line up at the Boston's Logan Airport, ready to take you to Le Pli at the Charles Hotel. If it's rush hour, you may have to double up for the half-hour ride.

RATING

Overall: An urbane urban spa

(+) Quality of service; level of cleanliness; personal trainer; Cambridge and Boston sights

(−) Weak on traditional sports; busy city atmosphere; facilities are shared with health club members

Main thrust: Weight loss and unwinding

Cost: Moderately expensive

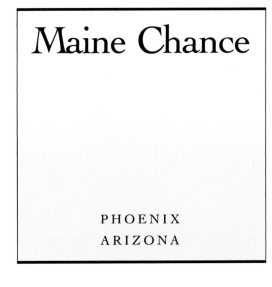

Maine Chance

PHOENIX
ARIZONA

ADDRESS
5830 East Jean Avenue
Phoenix, Arizona
  85018
TELEPHONE
602-947-6365
CREDIT CARDS
V, MC, AE, DC

MAINE CHANCE IS THE grande dame of American beauty spas, opened by that grande dame of the makeup trade, Elizabeth Arden, just as World War II clouds were blowing away and the weary and worn were ready for a cosmetic blitz. It is, and always has been, primarily a beauty spa.

Miss Arden's naive notion that the place would be self-sustaining without any commercial fanfare—that "families" would pass on to other "families" word of her discreet desert flower—turned out to be true. The Fords went there because the DuPonts did, the DuPonts because the Firestones did, and so on. Through the years, from the last Sunday in September until the end of May, society patronesses have left their embroidered white kid gloves at home and headed for Phoenix, Arizona, for a week or so of nutritious low-calorie food, good-but-not-too-taxing exercise, painstakingly attentive hair and skin

care, plus the purest form of top service imaginable.

Surrounded by free-growing desert plants and beautiful inner gardens, Maine Chance sits below Camelback Mountain and seemingly above the rest of the world. It is a precious place—perhaps too precious for some. No one can question the caliber of taste. Simple white buildings house the public spaces, classrooms, treatment areas, and delightful guest accommodations, some of which have private dining rooms and sitting rooms. Each has a unique and elegant look. It's easy to understand why most guests request particular rooms that speak to them in their own esthetic language. There is even a separate four-bedroom house whose occupants have the choice of eating their meals at the private dining table in front of the fireplace there or in the main house.

Twelve *full-sized* packages of Elizabeth Arden products for the body and bath adorn each dressing table.

The spa plan lasts six full days, providing for all meals and potassium, juice, and tea breaks. The program includes optional early-ish morning walks; class fitness exercises (mostly mat work) three times a day; a water workout once a day; the use of steam cabinets, saunas, and pools; and a range of treatments and services—scotch hose, massages, face care, skin care, scalp care, nail care, hair styling, makeup lessons, paraffin wrap. That last treatment, the most popular of all, is given to each guest twice a week.

There is one tennis court, one indoor pool, three outdoor pools, and four bicycles. Optional classes in T'ai Chi, dance, advanced aerobics, back exercises, and face exercise are offered. The equipment room has exercise bicycles and rowing machines.

An important daily activity is a browse through the boutique, where you could easily buy an entire wardrobe. The old Spanish tradition of "a lady never carries packages" is followed here: (1) A guest decides on a possible purchase; (2) a chauffeur carries that item to the guest's room while she follows her spa routine; (3) the guest contemplates the item at her leisure; (4) (now it gets tricky) if the lady opts to buy it, she tears off the price tag and drops it at the boutique; if she decides against it, she leaves it in her room to be fetched by the courier.

The weekly evening routine at Maine Chance starts with a quiet Monday. On Tuesday and Wednesday there are lectures, cooking demonstrations, or fashion shows. Some guests choose to go off into the sunset on Thursday for shopping or a cultural event in town. Friday means bingo, with prizes that make it the biggest night of the week. Guests come to dinner on Saturday with their new hairstyle and makeup, beautifully dressed and bejeweled.

Whether losers, gainers, or weight maintainers, clients enjoy well-balanced meals served in impeccable style. The basic diet for losers totals 950 calories per day. It's breakfast in bed each morning, with the guest's personal schedule for the day next to the vase of fresh flowers on her tray. Dinners in the dining room are graced with sparkling silver and formal china. The main course might be veal medallions with red peppercorns and chervil, barbecued shrimp, baked fish with caper sauce, broiled Australian lobster tails, or roast tenderloin of venison with walnut and brandy sauce. Room service is always available for meals. Lots of fresh honey is used—the spa has its own bees—and all citrus is home-grown.

A pretty pink robe and blue tank suit comprise the daily uniform. (Guests use up to seven tank suits each and, as a group, sometimes as many as 3000 towels a day.) You'll want to bring your own slippers, exercise and walking shoes, personal items, sleepwear, a small tote bag to use during the day, and evening clothes consisting of long skirts and blouses, nice slacks outfits, caftans, and jewelry—*real* jewelry.

The guest books are replete with famous signatures. Adding their Jane Henrys each week in season are about fifty women eager for a few days of rejuvenation with some t.l.c., a personal maid, breakfast in bed served on the china pattern of their choice, surroundings featuring fine art and antiques, and the exquisite light of the desert sun.

GETTING THERE

The spa will send an unmarked station wagon (no sign, just MC on the license plate) to pick up their guests at any Phoenix hotel or at the Phoenix airport. This service is complimentary, as is transportation to all church services.

RATING

Overall: A discreet, unique beauty spa mainly for women with an interest in being pampered and losing weight

$\oplus$ Indulgent service; high-toned; low-key; excellent beauty services

$\ominus$ Up-tight; weak on aerobics

Main thrust: Teaching the Elizabeth Arden beauty tricks in a healthy atmosphere

Cost: Expensive to very expensive

Marriott's Desert Springs Resort and Spa

PALM DESERT
CALIFORNIA

ADDRESS
74855 Country Club
    Drive
Palm Desert, California
    92260
TELEPHONE
619-341-2211 (hotel)
619-341-1864 (Spa)
1-800-255-0848
CREDIT CARDS
All major

THIS IS NOT THE TYPICAL Marriott's. This is not the typical anything. It's spectacular!

Driving up to the Marriott's Desert Springs Resort and Spa makes you feel quite special. Palms line the way, with flowers at their feet. When you walk into the hundred-foot-high lobby, you see beyond the cushy lounge area, beyond the dramatic indoor waterfalls, and beyond the glass wall to the blue horizon.

"Flags" of tiny lights drip from the ceiling. Waterfalls plunge to a lobby waterway where you can board a covered gondola to be transported outside and through streets of lagoons.

Even with the superb weather and glorious mountain views, having 900 rooms and suites to fill each night must have made the builders want a little extra good luck . . . the buildings are in the shape of a horseshoe.

Of the 400 acres, 27 are water. On land are the guest buildings, restaurants, boutique esplanades, nightclubs, convention quarters, and spa. There are acres covered with trees and flowers, thirty-eight holes of championship golf courses, sixteen tennis courts, swimming pools, Japanese bridges, and jogging and walking paths.

Room rates vary according to season. With spa packages you get an assigned room. Upgrading is always possible. If you've had a good year and can afford a few extra amenities and calories, request accommodations on the "Concierge Floor." A private lounge with complimentary fruit and hors d'oeuvres is one of the added pluses. Not that anyone lives poorly here. All accommodations offer a superior amenities package—mini-bars, private baths with separate tubs and showers, television, air-conditioning, radio, telephone, and balcony or terrace. Some rooms seem to be miles from the elevators. Our only problem was that the water in the lobby affected the humidity in our room. Because the rooms are large and pleasant but still ordinary, the most important requisite is a view of the pool and mountains or waterways and mountains.

The spa itself is efficient, extremely attractive, and reasonably intimate (although that is one word that could never be used to describe the whole resort facility). Overlooking lagoons, gardens, fairways, and mountains, every spa space affords a feeling of serenity.

Indoors, a superior staff makes sure that program participants get their share of pampering and reshaping. Men and women have separate areas. There are plans ranging from a half day (for

conventioneers) to seven days. All begin with a caring and helpful interview and offer the option for nutritional counseling, computerized body composition analysis, and in-depth fitness assessments. It's advisable to set up appointments and schedules in advance of arrival. A la carte spa-goers pay separately for everything, including entrance to the spa.

In addition to tennis, golf, and other team sports, spa exercise includes a brisk early morning walk, hiking in the Santa Rosa Mountains (with spa backpack, vans, and guides), classes (one or two per hour) in low- and high-impact aerobics, yoga stretching, water exercise, and dance. The octagonal classroom boasts a super-resilient floor, a fabulous sound system, and superb natural light. After these strenuous activities you can relax in the siesta room, steam room, sauna, whirlpools, or hot and cold plunges. Or, have a massage, facial, aromatherapy, hydrotherapy, herbal wrap, or loofah scrub, or climb into the "super space relaxer" (a dry flotation unit that apparently thrills everyone except those with the slightest tinge of claustrophobia).

Weight training and body toning go on all day in the fitness gym. In addition to twenty-two Universal stations, there are Lifecycles, rowing machines, tampolines, and treadmills. No one under eighteen is allowed.

Throughout the spa building the look is subdued (muted desert colors prevail) except for the striking beauty parlor with its black and white sophistication. Here, all beauty services are offered to both men and women.

Off the reception area, is the boutique for spa clothing. My guess is that

only the disciplined few can pass it by, even though the spa provides all the apparel needed for one's stay: a bathrobe, slippers, leotard, t-shirt and shorts, sweats. (You must bring your own socks and shoes.) They even provide pre-toothpasted toothbrushes!

Besides a nurse on duty, a doctor on call, and an affiliation with the Eisenhower Medical Center, there is a dietitian and spa chef. Meals are good. That's the bottom line. In fact, I thought they were better than the regular hotel food. The dietitian sees all diet-conscious spa-goers. A diet history is taken, tests are done, and a plan formulated to reach a healthy percentage of body fat. Some people need only education. Others require behavior modification. Each overweight person has a distinct underlying problem that is defined and addressed. While at the Marriott you can begin to enjoy a low-fat, low-salt, high-carbohydrate, nutritionally balanced diet. Extremely low-cal dieting or fasting is discouraged. Low-cal can lead to low energy, which undermines the exercise program. Minimum for women is 1000 calories, for men 1500.

Spa meals are served in the cozy spa juice bar–cafe, the hotel's "Lakeview Restaurant," and by room service. A typical dinner would be soup, salad, steamed bass, and homemade fruit sorbet.

Nowhere on the premises are a jacket and tie required. Of course, you have to judge the dress code of your group if you're with a convention.

Most of the people who come here strictly for pleasure are active types. In the winter, guests tend to be slightly older and more affluent. Yuppies gather round for summer fun *and reduced fares.* That's when you'll spy all the BMWs and Porsches in the parking lot.

As a rule, people don't come here for peace and quiet, even though the vistas are calming, as are many of the spas services and treatments. People like the Marriott's Desert Springs Resort and Spa because there's so much to do above and beyond the beautifying, reinvigorating, reducing aspects of the spa. They also like the pampering—for example, having staffers spraying the summer suntanners with refreshing mists of water.

You might find the hotel to be just too darned big. Still, the Marriott merits high points for many of its facilities, services, and staff members. It also melds the corporate and health worlds, giving businessmen and women a chance both to work and work out.

GETTING THERE

The Marriott's Palm Desert Resort and Spa is 13 miles southeast of Palm Springs and a 2½-hour drive from Los Angeles. A limo shuttle will pick guests up from the Palm Springs airport for a small fee. VIPs get real limos. Riding from the airport, you pass many streets named after the Hollywood celebrities that have homes and play the many golf courses in the area.

RATING

Overall: A good place to mix business, pleasure, and spa-ing

⊕   Variety; great views; competent spa staff; attractive spa space; great landscaping; golf; unusual lobby

⊖   Resort is too big and commercial

Main thrust: Beauty and fitness

Cost: Moderately expensive to expensive

The New Age Health Spa

NEVERSINK
NEW YORK

FOR THOSE WHO WANT TO flush out all the bad stuff from their bodies and minds, The New Age Health Spa might be just what the (homeopathic) doctor ordered. As you enter the 100-plus acres of this retreat cradled in the foothills of the Catskill Mountains, you are greeted by a placard requesting that all worries, cigarettes, alcohol, drugs, and candy be left "here"—in a large garbage can underneath the sign. Once you begin the program, you'll give up caffeine, sugar, salt, and all but a smidgeon of fats. To speed the body-cleansing process, enemas and colonics are offered to those who choose to go that route. Minds and psyches get a good airing not only by the mountain breezes, but also through zen meditation, yoga, T'ai Chi, and other, more American classes in aerobics, stretching, and toning.

Werner Mendel and his wife, Stephanie, the savvy owners of the spa, strongly suggest a trio of diet control, daily exercise, and relaxation techniques for true mind-body-spirit renewal. In reality, many guests cut corners, paying little attention to one or all of the above.

Hikers, rejoice! Wonderful walks and hikes ranging from two to twenty miles are offered every day, weather permitting. (For the long ones, bring your own canteen.) With the winter snow comes the opportunity for cross-country skiing and snowshoeing.

The white shingled main house, office and lecture quarters, spa building, and guest cottages are clustered together, with an outdoor pool and lounge area nearby. I thought the best guest rooms were in Neversink Cottage; however, no one picks The New Age for luxury living. Rooms are modest, but through the use of throw pillows, chintz curtains, and other homey touches, an attempt has been made to keep them from looking totally sterile.

There are no phones or televisions in guest rooms. In general, The New Age Health Spa is something of a spa camp. No one deep into glamour need apply! Those who do come seem to enjoy it, and the return visit rate shows that the directors are definitely doing something (no, a lot) right.

Going to classes, using the up-to-date exercise equipment, taking an indoor swim, and having a spa treatment entail a short walk to the Minisink Building. Pampering services include aromatherapy, massages, reflexology, loofah scrub, mudpack, facials, paraffin body treatment, and hair and nail care (you'll pay extra for most of them). One sauna and one steam room suffice for both sexes; some hours are coed, others males or females only. Changing rooms

ADDRESS
Neversink, New York
12765
TELEPHONE
1-800-NU-AGE-4-U
(New York)
914-985-7601
CREDIT CARDS
AE, V, MC

93

are outfitted with cubbies, hooks, and a couple of hair blow-driers. There are no lockers.

Here comes the X-rated part. Skip it if talk of "lower" body functions makes you cringe. However, if you're interested in serious inner cleansing through enemas and colonics, this is the paragraph (and the place) for you. Instruction is given in the self-administering of the enemas, and suitable paraphernalia is sold at the all-purpose boutique. Registered nurses help with the colonics, which are given in two designated rooms. Colon hydrotherapy involves controlled infusion of purified water through the rectum into the entire colon, assisted by some abdominal massage. Benefits are said to include increasing circulation and digestion; removal of all hardened waste, parasites, and gas; reduction of toxins; and a feeling of freshness.

Meals — plain, very bland food served in a spartan but pleasant dining room at several round tables — can be augmented by a visit or two to the excellent open salad bar at lunch and dinner. Diet options include (1) juice fasting, followed by a fruit and vegetable regimen; (2) a 450-calorie-a-day vegetarian diet; (3) a 950-to-1000-calorie-a-day regimen with some poultry and fish on occasion; and (4) unlimited food (entailing an extra fee). Much of the produce is grown in the spa garden.

After supper, a lecture on the healing qualities of herbs, nutritious eating, or other spa-related topics; television and video viewing; or bed and a book comprise the agenda.

Better pack *all* the necessities: shampoo, conditioner, alarm clock (a must!), rain/spa/seasonal/swim gear, Walkman, proper footwear, bathrobe, slippers, sweatsuit. No one dresses up. If you've forgotten anything, the boutique probably sells it. The big event of the weekend is the appearance of the shoe truck — the answer to your foot problems. Few can resist purchasing the perfectly fitted sports or walking shoe.

Fitness has definitely found a new home at The New Age. As a result, a few more men arrive each week and any reputation as a "ladies' fat farm" is fading. The guests are predominantly middle-aged and younger Easterners (and still preponderately female).

If luxury is a necessity for you, forget this one. But if you can be happy with a spa life devoid of fancy folks and frills, throw a few comfy things in a bag and take your frazzled mind, in-need-of-help body, and downtrodden spirit to The New Age Health Spa for a relaxing, invigorating, holistic experience.

G E T T I N G   T H E R E

I arrived at The New Age via the Redwood Taxi Company from New York City — door to door — with several stops along the way. The drive takes about 2½ hours. For self-drivers, The New Age will provide detailed instructions for arrival from most cities in the East, as well as limo information for transportation from New York and New Jersey airports.

R A T I N G

Overall: Pleasant dieter's spa camp with an emphasis on hiking and holistics

⊕ Hiking; supervised fasting; serene, noncompetitive Catskill Mountain environment; Oriental forms of relaxation and exercise; colonic body flushing

⊖ Unglamorous throughout; modest accommodations; no coddling or pampering

Main thrust: Weight control through diet, exercise, and the inner cleansing of body and mind

Cost: Moderate

New Life Spa

STRATTON MOUNTAIN VERMONT

ADDRESS
Stratton Mountain
Vermont 05155
TELEPHONE
802-297-2534
CREDIT CARDS
MC, V

THE STAFF AT NEW LIFE SPA may be small, but they more than compensate for their lack of numbers with the warm, welcoming atmosphere they've created here. Setting the tone is founder Jimmy LeSage, a short, bespectacled, enthusiastic, open-minded yoga devotee who presides over yoga lessons.

This is not a luxury spa by any stretch of the imagination, and the prices reflect this. Originally a ski lodge in the winter, the chalet-style guest quarters are simple and clean, with natural woods and bandanna prints in the rooms. There is no air-conditioning, but in this mountain setting a fan in each room is usually sufficient.

Massages, facials, manicures, sauna, and hot tub are available, but this is not a place to go for pampering. The emphasis is more on winding down in the bucolic surroundings, cleaning out on a carefully regulated Pritikin-style diet, and toning up on the spa's multiple-option exercise program. This is a spa where, though aided and abetted by a concerned, young, and friendly staff, the guests are expected to work the program themselves. In this sense, it is somewhat spartan. On the other hand, there is something quite pleasurable and reaffirming in taking responsibility for your own total well-being.

During the summer, all the guests (twenty to thirty-five people) at New Life arrive Sunday afternoon for a week's activities. Getting acquainted with one another is the priority of the first evening and seems fairly effectively accomplished by the end of it. Other first-day activities include weigh-in, measurement-taking, and body fat evaluation—all the usual leveling experiences of spa life. The tale of the tape will be repeated at the end of the week.

The welcoming night dinner eases you into spa fare by offering three courses. After that, only two courses are served. Less food consumed leads to more pounds lost.

The guests are not a chic crowd—this is probably determined by both the price (the price-value relation here is exceptional) and the lack of pampering—but they are generally a friendly and interesting group, ranging in age from twenty to sixty-five or so. Men make up about 20 percent of the visitors.

One of the best things about the spa is the hiking program, which makes full use of the surrounding rolling green farmland and mountains. Each day wake-up is at 7:00 A.M., followed by a brisk twenty-minute walk and breakfast. At 9:00, those who do not want to

95

go to exercise classes gather together for a hike that increases in difficulty daily. By the end of the week, those who can are climbing Stratton Mountain, several miles up and several miles back down again.

The afternoon activities include gentler walks, swimming, stretching and aerobics classes, and yoga. There are indoor and outdoor pools (the indoor one is Olympic-size), indoor and outdoor tennis courts, and a full sports complex. In the winter, there is skiing, both cross-country and downhill.

A tribute to Jimmy LeSage and New Life's program is the number of guests who choose to return year after year. Because the emphasis here is on quality of life rather than simple weight loss (although those who come to lose weight shed an average of five pounds in as many days), many people come back just to feel renewed and rejuvenated.

The food varies. Some meals are winners, others are not. Strict vegetarians can follow their diet without any problem, but there is always a choice of fish or chicken at night. There are desserts with every dinner, and by the end of the week some guests insist that the yogurt topping tastes like whipped cream.

The food regimen is based on more than 60 percent complex carbohydrates, a small percentage of protein, no animal fats, and as little vegetable fat as possible. Complex carbohydrates are considered the most efficient fuel for the body and keep the level of one's blood sugar steady. As a result, you are able to eat much smaller portions and still will not crave food in between meals. However, fruit is always available for snacking.

For those with a touch of cabin fever, a trip into one of the nearby towns can be distracting. Factory outlets abound, as do antique shops. Within thirty minutes' drive are several local movie houses, a summer stock theater, and bars with dancing. Hitching a ride with a newfound spa friend who has wheels is usually easy.

The spa seems evenly divided between guests who have come together—friends, husbands with wives—and those who come individually. Arriving with someone you know helps ensure a good time socially but is absolutely not a necessity. A group meeting at the end of the week confirms that most people—the men as much as the women—enjoy the New Life Spa experience. However, considering the male-female ratio, this spa clearly has advantages for single men.

It's important to bring hiking shoes, sweaters, jackets, and rain gear along with your usual spa attire, sports clothes, and casual evening wear.

GETTING THERE

You can fly to Albany, N.Y., and take a bus to Manchester, Vermont; or take an air-conditioned bus for the 4¾-hour drive from New York City's Port Authority Terminal. A van and driver will pick you up in Manchester.

RATING

Overall: Spartan, but special

(+) Weight loss program; hiking, bucolic beauty of Vermont; good value

(−) No pampering

Main thrust: Cleaning out, toning up, and winding down

Cost: Moderate

The Norwich Inn and Spa

NORWICH
CONNECTICUT

ADDRESS
607 West Thames
    Street
Route 32
Norwich, Connecticut
    06360

TELEPHONE
203-866-2401
1-800-892-5692

CREDIT CARDS
All major

WANT TO KNOW WHERE Manhattan's high society and high-styled crowd hide out wearing old sweats and sneakers? You guessed it . . . The Norwich Inn and Spa. Only two and one-half hours by car from New York City, The Norwich gets a big play from fashion luminaries such as Bill Blass and Mary McFadden—they, too, sometimes need to shed a few pounds, worries, and toxins. The roster is filled out by clientele from the Northeast. Ladies dominate, but the men who go there don't seem intimidated by the lopsided male-female ratio.

The Inn, a big 1900s red brick structure surrounded by trees and lawn, has been completely restored by owner Edward Safdie. A huge white Victorian birdcage housing two snowy doves adds a surprise element to the cheery floral chintz furnishings of the lobby. In the sprawling building are conference quarters, an antiques shop, ballroom, bar, restaurant with terraces overlooking the golf course, and a spa dining room screened off from the lecture/lounge alcove.

Guest rooms have a stylish rustic look. You'll find telephone, television, and private bath, but no amenities package and no elevator to take you up and down. It's not total luxury, yet it's a far cry from camping out. For top-of-the-inn living, ask for the Terrace Suite. Another option is a villa or condo on the property just past the "white wear only" lighted tennis courts.

Leave the Inn by way of the back door, walk down the semicircular brick stairway, and you arrive at the spa, the facade of which echoes the architecture of the main building. Inside, the mood shifts. The lounge is a modern, attractive, pastel-colored room with a welcoming fireplace. An open spa boutique is on one side, a refreshment bar on the other (help yourself to pitchers of herbal tea, potassium broth, mineral water, and the platter of fruit).

Mere sightseers or visitors are not allowed past the door leading to the work and play area. This well-conceived section is highlighted by an appealing, imaginatively tiled swimming pool surrounded by inviting sea-blue couches. Even when bustling with activity, this space maintains its serenity. Ethereally sponge-painted walls and classy classic urns add to the ambience of the adjoining men's and women's locker, changing, and wet areas (offering showers, steam, saunas, and whirlpools, and providing bathrobes, slippers, hair care products, razors, and shower caps). Other portals lead to treatment rooms for massages, body scrub, aromatherapy, thalassotherapy, facials, and waxing and to a beauty section where manicures and pedicures are done—without polish. (*An unofficial tip:* Bring your own nail lacquer; ask politely and they'll apply it for you.) Only women have the option of hydrotherapy in the sixty-jet tub, with or without minerals.

Flanking the pool are two glassed-in gyms. One is equipped with a Keiser Cam II machine, free weights, exercise bicycle, rowing machine, StairMaster, and treadmill. An instructor is always there to help you with these workout wonders. The other gym is for classes (stretch and tone, yoga, T'ai Chi, relaxation, and low-impact aerobics).

Once you've filled out the lengthy questionnaire and a legal release of responsibility, had your in-depth fitness evaluation, and gotten your schedule squared away, you can put yourself in the hands of the capable staff . . . or you can do your own thing.

The sad part is there are no spa programs offered on weekends. That means every service, treatment, and meal is a la carte. During the week, you can pick and choose from one- to five-day plans.

Although weight control is of major importance at The Norwich Spa, calories are not severely restricted. The idea is to eat less while exercising more, thus achieving permanent weight loss and avoiding the all too prevalent yo-yo syndrome. Generally women get 1000 to 1200 calories per day; men, 1800 to 2000. The chef follows U.S. Dietary Guidelines (high in complex carbohydrates and low in fat, sugar, sodium). Eating in the spa dining room gives you the advantage of sitting at round tables with fellow dieters wearing casual attire (sweats and slacks) and being right there for presupper crudités and post-supper lectures. Those who choose to eat (at no extra cost) in the far more attractive Grill, where ties and jackets are required, may order from the regular menu or low-cal fare. Reclusives may have a tray sent to their rooms. The food might not be as plentiful as you would like, but it is good.

If you have any questions about a personal diet, fitness program, relaxation techniques, or any spa-related problem, don't be reticent. Ask! With so many guests waltzing through, it's hard for the staff to concentrate on each one. However, they will respond fully and graciously to the serious spa-er.

The lectures, available to all, tend to be candy-coated pills, amusing and enlightening. After two talks that zeroed-in on weight and cholesterol control we left more cognizant of the importance of food composition as well as caloric content. Etched in our minds is the target-like diagram with its *best* foods, such as nonfat plain yogurt, skim milk, shredded wheat, most fruits and vegetables; *good* foods, such as low-fat yogurt, low-fat milk, whole wheat or rye bread, Grape Nuts, Nutri-Grain, or Total cereal, oatmeal, lean white meat chicken or turkey, tuna in water; *fair* foods, such as whole milk, fruit and vegetable juices, hard cheese, spaghetti; and foods that go directly from mouth to thighs. Included here are your favorites and mine—ice cream, cookies, hamburgers, butter or margarine, mayo, and so on.

Complementing the lectures are the spa tip sheets. Follow them and you win the health and fitness race. Of special interest to me were the handouts on negative indications for treatments most of us think of as totally harmless. For instance:

- Massage—(1) never with a fever; (2) not if you've had cancer or chemotherapy in the previous three months
- Thalassotherapy—(1) not for those with allergies to seaweed, iodine, or seafood; (2) never if hyperthyroid condition exists; (3) taboo for pregnant women
- Aromatherapy—(1) no alcohol for six to eight hours afterward; (2) no exposure to heat for two hours afterward
- Hydrotherapy—(1) may be dangerous for heart or blood pressure patients; (2) taboo for pregnant women
- Body scrub—(1) skin conditions may worsen
- Sauna and steam—(1) wearing jewelry can cause burns; (2) not advised for pregnant women

Diversions near the spa include a ride to Mystic Seaport and browsing in the numerous antiques shops that dot the Connecticut countryside.

Connecticut can get very cold in the winter and very warm in the summer. Pack seasonal clothes along with personal items, spa gear, and tennis and swimwear.

Northeasterners will find The Norwich Inn and Spa a quick and easy shape-up solution. As Bill Blass confided, "It's so close; why should I go farther?"

GETTING THERE

Take a train to New London or drive to Norwich, Connecticut.

Directions from New York City: I-95N past New Haven, off at Exit 76, onto I-395N, off at Exit 79A, onto 2A (east), off at Exit 32 (north), drive 1½ miles to Inn (on left).

Directions from Westchester: I-684E to I-84. When you get to Hartford, follow signs to Rte 2 East, exit onto 32 (south) and follow that to Inn entrance (on right).

It's also an easy drive from Boston and Newport.

RATING

Overall: A prime Connecticut entry in the American spa sweepstakes

⊕ Pleasant spa ambience; fine caliber equipment and classes; excellent food

⊖ Dicey weather; in-town site; standard rooms are not as luxurious as one might expect

Main thrust: Beauty plus weight loss through a combination of (not too extreme) diet and (doable) exercise

Cost: Moderately expensive

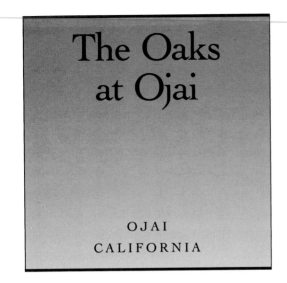

The Oaks at Ojai

OJAI
CALIFORNIA

FOR A LOW-KEYED, LOW-COST spa, The Oaks at Ojai is far more than adequate. The circular drive leads to a balconied stucco building filled with active, interesting women and perhaps a couple of men (many more during couples weeks). Particularly popular with L.A. ladies and minor starlets getting back in shape on a two-day to seven-day program, it also generally has one or two rather obese women in residence for six weeks or more. Reduced rates encourage a "heavy" summer season. Quite obviously founder Sheila Cluff's favorite (also hers: The Palms in Palm Springs), The Oaks benefits from the know-how of a strong, watchful management.

Situated on two floors of the main building, with some outside cottages, the rooms and facilities are clean and nice enough, but not at all extravagant or luxurious. Number 301-302, a big triple with sitting room, tops the list, but all accommodations have showers (a few have tubs), television, and telephone.

Walking past the fireplace, desk, and celebrity photos in the reception area, you immediately enter the spa. The exercise equipment (Paramount machines, free weights, exercise bicycles) are in a very wide hall-like area alongside the diet bar and lounge. (After seeing the rush of voluptuous vultures at the appearance of the crudité snack tray, we renamed it the lounge and lunge area!)

The well-executed aerobics classes (fourteen a day) appeal to both the out-of-shape and in-shape. Choices are water exercise, body dynamics, weight training, low-impact aerobics, dance, and yoga. Further conditioning comes in the form of mountain hikes, brisk walks, and nature walks.

The big heated pool with its delightful mountain views is the base for a lot of action (and inaction for the sunbathers).

A screen of glass separates the wet area (sauna, hot tub, shower) from the aerobics/yoga room. Rooms for massages and facials are dimly lit and quiet. Other beautifying services, each with its own *separate* space, are performed in bright, colorful, appealing new quarters. Services include hair care, waxing, nail care, makeup, and wardrobe and color analysis. Consideration is given to the total woman at The Oaks at Ojai— inner and outer. Sometimes a service or treatment seems unnecessary, but it's smart to take advantage of as many as you can.

Evening lectures run the gamut from

ADDRESS
122 East Ojai Avenue
Ojai, California 93023
TELEPHONE
805-646-5573
CREDIT CARDS
V, MC

Guidelines given by the staff may be followed rigorously or totally ignored, depending on your mood and self-motivation.

topics like plastic surgery (always well-attended), self-esteem, and nutrition to gems, history of the area, fashion, and contemporary art. Bridge, backgammon, and Scrabble games are also available.

I've saved the best for last: The food is great. Meals, served in regulated portions, are well presented and delicious to eat. Extra food prearranged by the nurse maintains those whose bodies need more than the well-balanced 750 calories per day usually served. Meals are eaten in the dining room or at the pool. A hot vegetable drink midmorning and that raw vegetable platter in the afternoon stave off hunger pains. Taboos: red meat, white flour, sugar, artificial sweeteners (honey and molasses are used), salt. If you hate the menu for a particular meal, an optional alternate meal stands ready.

By and large you make your own program here. Guidelines given by the staff may be followed rigorously or totally ignored, depending on your mood and self-motivation. It's fun to improvise a little and make use of the Racquet Club facilities nearby—for no extra charge.

Are you one of those who comes home from a big sale carrying several full shopping bags, boasting to your husband about all the money you saved? Me, too. Well, this spa's for you. The longer you stay, the more you "save." Spa plans ranging in length from a day to a month and offered throughout the year, range in price from moderate to a downright steal. There are special theme weeks—for example, aerobics, hiking, tennis, couples, mother-daughter. Of major importance is the twenty-one-day "Stop Smoking" program.

Pack your designer sweats (the ones

with the sparkles) for evenings. For the rest of the day, exercise and walking shoes, leotards, tights, swimwear, a warm-up suit, and robe will suffice. If you're inclined toward active sports, most of which are in the area though not at The Oaks itself, bring appropriate gear and a beach towel. Remember that evenings can be cool.

Ojai, a wonderful little town, offers an alternative to shopping at the in-house boutique. The arcade of stores there will charm you, but beware of losing your diet conscientiousness when you get to the ice cream and candy shops.

Mountains in the background enhance the serenity of the area, which has a reputation as a spiritual center.

If you don't lose weight at The Oaks, you've got to be cheating. Following the diet is totally uncomplicated. The menu is posted and unless you select the optional fare, you sit down and eat your meal without a choice in any category. As far as body toning goes, the facilities are there. Using them is up to you. Massages, facials, and beauty help certainly can't hurt. So all in all (especially for women), this spa scores very high on the charts in its price category.

Olympia Village Resort and Spa

OCONOMOWOC WISCONSIN

ADDRESS
1350 Royal Mile Road
Oconomowoc,
   Wisconsin 53066
TELEPHONE
414-567-0311
   (Wisconsin)
414-342-0414
   (Milwaukee)
1-800-558-9573
CREDIT CARDS
AE, V, MC, DC

YOU'LL PROBABLY SEE PEOple of all ages and types wandering around the 400-acre Olympia Village Resort and Spa in search of their next convention meeting or diversion. In the spa itself, the clientele tends to be mainly congenial Midwestern women who come seeking weight and measurement loss plus incentives for a better lifestyle. Some just want to shed their worries, relax, and be coddled.

The hotel is commercial but comfortable. To describe it, the manager used the term *rustic*. However, it does not have the charm implied by that word. Big and modern, it won't wow you, but neither will it intimidate you. All accommodations in the hotel (where the spa is located) have baths and showers, television, radio, and telephone. Their ambience is that of a good motel. Less mundane, but more expensive, are the villas.

One great advantage of the resort is the variety of activities available, which makes it ideal for family vacations. Fifteen tennis courts (some lighted), a large game room, on-site movie theaters, four restaurants, heated indoor and outdoor pools, a bar with live entertainment, bicycling, water sports, volleyball, racquetball, golf, hiking, and horseback riding should keep the rest of the gang busy while you're in the spa. In addition, there's cross-country skiing in winter, plus a 200-foot snow hill for beginners on downhill skis.

Soothing to tired minds and spirits, outdoor vistas include expanses of lawn and private lake surrounded by wonderful weeping willow trees. Rented swans (they get them in the spring and return them in the fall) grace the water.

Though the hotel is anything but intimate, the personal attention in the spa gets a star, and the spa space is surprisingly attractive. If you don't mind simple locker areas and multi-bedded massage, herbal wrap, and loofah rooms (there are divider-curtains), you'll find this area satisfactory. To clear your sinuses and pores and reduce puffiness, try the Eucalyptus Room, sauna, and steam cabins. For quick tanning, there is a sun bed. Some guests love to mingle with one another in the Roman pools, while others prefer the seclusion of the individual whirlpool baths with body shampoo containing oils and trace minerals. You'll relax like a 1930s movie star amidst the bubbles.

NOTE: Men do not get loofah scrubs or mineral baths.

Coed quarters include the weight room, exercise equipment room (with fifteen Global stations, Biocycle, tread-

mill, and Exercycles), and gyms (where yoga, low-impact aerobics, stretching, and spot reduction are offered). Servicing all resort guests, the beauty salon provides professional facials, hair care, manicures, pedicures, hot wax treatments, and makeup application. Sprucing up before returning home helps the ego.

Most spa days begin with a 7:00 A.M. brisk walk in the clean, country air. After breakfast in the spa restaurant, it's time for classes, treatments, and services.

Measurement rather than weight loss determines the diet program, which provides an intake of from 600 to 1200 calories, according to your needs. Two-, four-, and seven-day packages include personal evaluations and individualized regimens by a nutritionist. On the "Weight Loss Plan," guests check in, weigh in, and get measured on Sunday. Body cleansing on a liquid diet seems appropriate for blue Monday followed by restricted diets chosen from tasty calorie-counted menus. Meals, room, and exercise classes are included in the package fee, but pampering treatments are a la carte. "Burn-Out," a behavior modification plan, and various fitness and beauty options are also offered. Popular evening lectures on exercise,

wellness, and behavior modification are open to all guests.

White and brown sweats, leotard, bathrobe, and scuffs provided by the spa will be your Olympia uniform. Other than that, you'll need swimwear, athletic and walking shoes, tights, seasonal sports clothing (don't forget the Wisconsin winters get *cold*), and very casual lounging and evening attire.

In the midst of brewery, cheese, and lake country, this unsophisticated resort is a pleasant place for a first spa experience as well as repeat trips. It's nice to know you can bring the whole family and be sure no one will be bored.

Palm-Aire

POMPANO BEACH
FLORIDA

ADDRESS
2501 Palm-Aire Drive
    N.
Pompano Beach,
    Florida 33069
TELEPHONE
305-972-3300
1-800-327-4960
CREDIT CARDS
All major

THE STORY GOES THAT WHEN Elizabeth Taylor decided she was going to shed multiple pounds (yet another time) at Palm-Aire, she flew her own decorator down to Florida to decorate her suite in mostly mauve silks and such. We were fortunate enough to stay in that suite (#467) and were somewhat disappointed to see that the new owners, Mr. and Mrs. Gerald Katzoff, had changed it completely in their grand sweep redo. However, progress means change. Almost all the accommodations are now updated with cheerful cabana stripes, chintz draperies, and every amenity.

Palm-Aire is a large, busy place with lots going on. Coming here for absolute solitude would be an error. There is plenty of open space (lawn, trees, and a small lake), but there are also several buildings (among which a conference center, the hotel, the spa), thirty-seven—count 'em, thirty-seven—tennis courts, five eighteen-hole courses (plus practice and putting greens), boutiques, squash courts, pools, a par course with many exercise stations for joggers, and more.

The stunning dining room and bar (not for dieters) are off the "Palm-Aire green"-and-stone lobby. Less elegant, but healthier, is the garden-like spa dining room. There are several other places to eat, including your own room or terrace. The spa menu is calorie-counted.

For the spa program guest, individual recommendations from the medical, nutrition, and fitness staff follow a medical checkup and a fitness evaluation. These suggestions take into account your strengths and weaknesses and the realities of your life.

More women than men take part in the spa plans. Although this is not a super-expensive resort, the clientele knows and cares about looking good. Dieting is generally paramount, but beauty treatments are a close second and fitness is edging up.

Updated and swanky, the spa facility gets a gold star. Separate but equal (almost), the men's and women's spa areas connect at the main pool. Other coed areas are the exercise equipment room (complete with the latest word in exercise machines and weights) and the aerobics classrooms. Incidentally, a couple of the aerobics rooms have specially constructed floors for high-impact aerobics and choreographed dance.

The reception lounges, locker areas (complete with every possible product), and full service beauty salon and barber shop are efficient and look good. Available treatments are massages, facials, salt-glo loofahs, herbal wraps, and (for

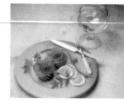

women) tanning beds. Wet areas include hot and cold plunges, sauna, steam, Swiss needle showers (for men), exercise pools, whirlpools, and thalassotherapy baths. Massages can be had in cabins or al fresco. Walled-in areas provide privacy for nude sunbathing. We were told that men love the daily water volleyball game, played all together in the altogether. I'm too basically Victorian even to try to visualize that one! Once a year men arrive from all over the world to join in the fun of the big (nude) volleyball tournament.

One way or another, everyone seems to have a good time. In fact, 80 percent of the guests are repeat customers, for which the management is deservedly very proud. Part of their success is due to the caliber of the staff. They are qualified, helpful, caring, and full of vitality.

Lectures and consultations on stress reduction round out the services, and a smoking cessation program is available. All cigarettes must be snuffed in the spa area.

There are several packages of varying time lengths offered. The most intensive plan is for fourteen days, geared to changing lifestyle through education, treatments, exercise, and realistic planning. Choices for shorter stays combine sports or beauty programs with spa workouts and diet regimens.

Because it is close to Fort Lauderdale and Miami with their big-time night life and shopping, action is always only a car ride away. Even nongamblers enjoy the harness racing just across the road. For something different, take an expedition to the Everglades.

If you play tennis and golf, bring appropriate attire. You might want to include something pretty for dinner. Keep it fairly casual. Even with the sprinkling of celebrities that are sometimes in residence, this is not the sequin and feather group. Packing for the spa program is no problem—a bathing suit and exercise and sports shows are all you need. The spa provides everything else. It's a good feeling to get into the uniform and be part of the Palm-Aire team.

GETTING THERE

Pompano Beach is only 15 minutes from the Fort Lauderdale airport. Palm-Aire will provide a limo to pick you up there and take you back. Other choices are the Miami International Airport and West Palm Beach Airport.

RATING

Overall: A well-run, big, and busy place to get beautiful

⊕ Staff; new spa decor; sports

⊖ Lack of serenity and intimacy

Main thrust: Dieting, beauty, relaxation, sports

Cost: Moderately expensive

The Palms at Palm Springs

PALM SPRINGS
CALIFORNIA

ADDRESS
572 North Indian
  Avenue
Palm Springs,
  California 92262
TELEPHONE
619-325-1111
CREDIT CARDS
V, MC, AE

THE FACADE OF THIS LAZY-looking hacienda on Palm Springs' main drag belies what's happening inside. Once through the portal, topped with palm trees carved out of wood, you realize that some serious fitness work is going on and that the clientele (mostly women thirty-five to fifty-five years of age) are thoroughly enjoying their stay. The majority come for a week or so to achieve fitness through diet, aerobics classes, and clean living—or just to relax. There is little doubt in my mind that a few, overwhelmed by the thought of checking into the nearby Betty Ford Center, come here to dip their big toe into the pool of detoxified water.

The red tile flooring and roof of the two-storied main building combine in interesting fashion with its white facade and blue trim—sounds like the Fourth of July, but it works for every other day as well. Some guest accommodations are in the main house (many with balconies), while others flank the pool and lounge area. The pool, though shallow, is good for laps and water aerobics; choose your petal and cool your heels while you warm your body in the flower-shaped whirlpool portion. The rest of the facility consists of a dining room, combination aerobics–exercise equipment room, and the separate sauna, locker, and shower areas for men and women.

Spa capacity: eighty-four people sharing forty-three rooms. Guests arrive together or are teamed up by assignment. If you prefer to be alone, that's fine—just pay the singles supplement. The other side of the coin is to share a bathroom with three others (in two bedrooms) to reduce the cost. For the occasional man who wants a single (with shower—no tub), there are two available. Don't expect anything even vaguely ritzy. Guests live in rooms of good size with standard furniture, air-conditioner, television, telephone, and, with the exception noted above, private bathrooms (tub with shower).

The railing on the second-floor veranda serves as a stretching barre before the hikes and brisk early morning walk. I liked that—it seemed a homey touch. Incidentally, there is also a pleasant leisurely walk scheduled every morning. Inside, you will find a lounge-lecture area with working fireplace and kitchen. Here you might watch a movie, listen to someone speak on such vital subjects as health, nutrition, fighting an addiction, and readjusting your love life, or just hang out and sip the ever present coffee, decaf, or tea.

Facial and massage stations with

extremely capable and knowledgeable massage therapists are situated near the lounge. Beneath the lounge you will find a small boutique, but Saks has so much more and is *so close!* The same consideration applies to the beauty salon.

Spa programs (minimum stay of two nights) are for those sixteen and over.

Policing oneself is the policy here. The understanding is that you are aware of the potential hazards of a fitness program for anyone who has physical problems or has had recent surgery. You must sign a medical release to this effect. Classes in aqua exercise, orientation to fitness, walking aerobics, strength training, yoga, body toning and conditioning, and other related subjects are offered throughout the day. Beginners through advanced participate together during aerobics sessions. Your pulse is taken three times per class. There is little personal attention, although the instructors are good. Guests fill in the exercise hours by using the two weight stations, Lifecycles, free weights, or rowing machine if they feel energetic.

Facials, massages, manicures, pedicures, hair care, makeup sessions, and hot wax treatments are available at extra charge. Private fitness consultations, nutritional counseling, and body fat analysis can also be arranged.

The interaction between guests at meals is a plus. So is the food. Natural products are used exclusively. The diet program suggests an absolute minimum of 750 calories and prefers 1000 to 1100

The climate works in favor of the "I hate to pack" folks. It's usually somewhere between excellent and divine.

in order to ensure sufficient intake of complex carbohydrates. Athletes' portions are double. You must sign up for your food choices a few hours in advance. Simple but tasty (no salt, no sugar) homemade snacks and meals keep dieters and nondieters satisfied. Incidentally, a registered nurse will consult with you each day if you so desire. Some people like to review their diet with every pound lost. (This used to be a true fat farm, but now fitness is making inroads and new friends for The Palms.)

Because it is small and confining, the locker area does not get much play. Guests change in their rooms (a few steps away from any activity) or just wear the same thing all day. Warm-up suits are fine for dinner. In addition to those, you'll need the usual spa attire, gym shoes, walking shoes, robe, beach towel, swimwear, a jacket or wrap for the evening, and possibly sports gear. The climate works in favor of the "I hate to pack" folks. It's usually somewhere between excellent and divine. Well, it does get a bit hot in the summer, but the rates drop when the temperature rises.

Palm Springs is in a desert setting with mountains in the background. Shopping is sophisticated, but culture is minimal. Although all those high-powered celebrity golf tournaments and houses owned by bigwigs have put the city on the map and made it sound like a glamorous destination, the downtown area is visually disappointing.

It was surprising to me to see walls in The Palms at Palm Springs covered with celebrity photos. Obviously, the owner, Sheila Cluff, loves them. For a place so unpretentious, the display seems incongruous. The dieters and fitness seekers here are a totally unassuming crowd, making it an unintimidating choice for the shy, first-time spa-goer. Cutting down on food intake, liquor, cigarettes, or stress is dealt with compassionately and informally. Women relax, let their fat hang out, and learn better living habits. The Palms has helped many a shaky hand, rattled mind, and unfit body pull it back together.

GETTING THERE

For a fee, there is a limo that will take you to and from the Palm Springs Airport three times a day. Ontario Airport has the same service for less, because it's closer. Driving from Los Angeles takes about 2½ hours.

RATING

Overall: A good place for those who want to chew the fat or drop it, give fitness a go, and keep the family fortune intact

⊕ Helpful stress-free ambience for the too-full figure; value; well-devised, though small, fitness classes

⊖ Unimpressive facilities

Main thrust: Fitness over fatness, plus rest and relaxation

Cost: Moderate

The Phoenix Fitness Resort

HOUSTON
TEXAS

IN YOUR CRYSTAL BALL YOU SEE a trim, fit body; in your mirror you see a series of chins, bulges, and love handles. It's time to give fate a helping hand at The Phoenix Fitness Resort in Houston, Texas.

With the knowledge, caring attitude, and motivational guidance of this intimate (sixteen guests, generally women only) spa, clouds lift, inches fall, and fitness becomes a realistic part of your future. Fine-tuning and toning the mind, body, and spirit, plus giving each client *tools for post-spa living* are the raison d'être of The Phoenix.

If you are looking for a retreat that provides extremely gracious living or divine little touches such as tables set with fine bone china and candles, you must continue your quest. Don't get me wrong. There's nothing spartan about the setup. It's just that glamour and luxury are not paramount here. Fitness is.

Being part of a larger, more formal complex known as The Houstonian (with a hotel, medical clinic, and health club on twenty-two acres of ground) qualifies The Phoenix as a spa resort. Spa guests sleep in a special wing of The Houstonian Hotel. A covered walkway connects that with The Phoenix house, a charming but ungrand manor where guests eat, lounge, change clothes, etc. Classes are held in The Phoenix gym, part of The Houstonian Health Club. Facilities at the club enhance the spa's offerings; mind-boggling exercise equipment, an indoor walking-jogging track, full service beauty salon, boutique, sauna, steam room, Swiss showers, and whirlpool. Then there are the courts for the rugged sports, racquetball and basketball. (Of course, that does mean there are times the spa people interface with Houstonian guests and club members.)

Another plus is The Houstonian Medical Clinic, first of all because of the thorough and highly professional medical and fitness profile ascertained for every week-program person. Then, too, it affords the opportunity for extra medical assistance to spa-goers who need preventative medicine or help with eating disorders, smoking cessation, foot care, postoperative procedures, or other health concerns.

The property includes three swimming pools (one for spa guests exclusively), tennis courts, and a fantastic cushioned outdoor one-mile Astroturf track that takes the lucky walker and jogger through The Houstonian's woodlands.

Spa plans, including a few "couples sessions," are available from a day to a

ADDRESS
111 North Post Oak
   Lane
Houston, Texas 77024
TELEPHONE
713-680-1601
1-800-548-4700 (out of
   state)
1-800-548-4701 (Texas)
CREDIT CARDS
V, MC, AE

114

week. Obviously, the longest stay gets the best results. It begins with arrival on Sunday, via limousine pickup from Houston Hobby or Intercontinental airports. A liquid diet is suggested for that night; tests, interview, and personal planning take place the next morning.

Then, with breakfast, lunch, dinner, and snacks at appropriate intervals, the daily routine commences:

1. Early morning brisk walk (two miles or more on that bouncy outdoor Astroturf track)
2. One and a half hours of stretching, toning, and low-impact aerobics classes in the spa gym
3. Circuit training on the state-of-the-art equipment of The Houstonian Club
4. A one-hour massage
5. A one-hour water exercise period
6. A forty-five-minute beauty treatment (facial, hair, makeup, aromatherapy, cellulite treatment, or nails)
7. Back to the gym for one hour
8. A show and tell lecture (on lifestyle management, self-defense, art and decoration, investments and business, hypnotherapy, or other topic)

In case you didn't notice, that adds up to *five hours of scheduled exercise per day.* The saving grace is the excellence of the classes, the resilience of the walking track, and the wonder of using the "twenty-first century" equipment. The Powercizer machines are the most sophisticated pieces of exercise equipment I've ever used. You begin your workout at the "master coach" station by entering your vital statistics in the computer. Then the fun begins. Moving from machine to machine, you are guided by name by the various computer "coaches" (each with his own personality), whose words appear on a screen, instructing you and encouraging you all the way. Each "coach" works a different set of large muscle groups. Don't be too surprised if one asks for your phone number when your performance is particularly laudable! Scores are kept in the computers' memory banks and are recalled to advise you of progress at each subsequent sitting.

But enough about exercise. Let's move right along into the dining room, where delicious meals (about 1000 calories a day) of low-cal, high-impact food keeps spa-ers fortified. During lunch and dinner, the chef-nutritionist answers questions, promises recipes (which she delivers), and imparts important nutritional nuggets of wisdom. Guests sit at round tables, chatting and eating what is put before them. You have no choices, but individual food preferences and allergies are taken into consideration.

Lockers and lounge abut the dining area, making daytime hours uncomplicated. Wearing a spa robe, your own sweats, or leotards, you go from activity to eating to resting to showering. No one wears makeup or jewelry. When you return to the hotel at night, there's no need to traipse through the lobby — The Phoenix has its own entrance.

When I was there, one guest had just gone through rather extensive liposuction and a face-lift. We were fascinated to see the black and blue fade and the contours change at each mealtime. She took it easy, but most spa-goers performed the full program with determination. Ages ranged from thirty to sixty. The motivated mothers and professional women came from as far away as Hong Kong. Friendships sprang up

between guests and the staff. No unwarranted coddling was noticeable, but camaraderie flourished, making it easier to go that extra step (or forego that extra calorie).

At the end of each week, those who have successfully completed thirty to fifty "miles" of aerobic activity (walking, swimming, Exercycling, etc.), receive a prize Phoenix Fitness Resort t-shirt, the color varying according to the mileage. These winners get applause, but there are no losers. Everyone departs with inches gone, a packet of enlightening and reinforcing information, self-knowledge, and a new makeup and hairdo. All appear ready to step more confidently into the big arena of the real world.

GETTING THERE

Fly to Houston. By prearrangement, a car or limousine will meet you at the airport. The charge, competitive with cab rates, appears on your bill at the end of your stay. There are two airports in Houston, so be sure to let them know at which one your plane is scheduled to arrive.

RATING

Overall: An excellent choice for those whose priority is on fitness rather than frills

⊕ Excellent fitness program; professional beauty services; expert medical care; cushioned Astroturf outdoor track; sophisticated exercise equipment; casual, congenial atmosphere

⊖ Lacks glamour and pampering; in-town site

Main thrust: Fitness for now and forever

Cost: Expensive

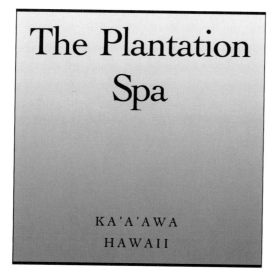

The Plantation Spa

KA'A'AWA
HAWAII

ADDRESS
51-550 Kam Highway
Ka'a'awa (Oahu),
Hawaii 96730
TELEPHONE
808-237-8685
808-955-3727
CREDIT CARDS
V, MC

ALOHA—THE VERY WORD CON-jures up visions of swaying grass skirts and palm fronds, waterfalls and serene secluded beaches, life in the slow lane. You won't find this idyll fulfilled everywhere in Oahu. Nearby Honolulu is now a big city, built-up, crowded, pulsing with tension. So it's particularly lovely to escape to the "old Hawaii" (with a new twist—the spa) that exists at The Plantation.

A spiritual aura pervades this rustic retreat, replete with exotic birds, tropical trees and flowers, splendid mountains, hypnotic waterfall, and a legendary Hawaiian beach along the ocean.

The first thing you spot as you approach the spa is a beautiful wood gate; just past that is a large "bulletin board" of charming three-dimensional figures depicting the spa week. A comfortable, secure feeling relaxes you and stays with you throughout your visit.

Bodil Anderson, the attractive Swedish guiding force of The Plantation, combines enthusiasm with inspiration. She and her husband, Dave, working with a small committed staff, make the place and the program work effectively in a manner that appears effortless.

There is no weigh-in, no fat-percentage-determining pinch, no medical checkup. People who go to The Plantation are basically healthy adults from all over the world who yearn for the solitude of nature and a week of rejuvenation.

The living is easy, but not really luxurious. Simple rooms in simple cottages keep the real world out. You won't find a personal television or telephone. Tropical breezes take the place of air-conditioning. In the lovely, stylish main cottage, you will dine, listen to lectures, and lounge amid delightful wicker furniture, Balinese fabrics, and handwoven rugs. Of course, much of your time will be spent in the great outdoors.

Teaching that healthy living results from the proper combination of exercise, attitude, and diet, the spa expounds a balancing act of physical and psychological health and harmony.

Here's how body, mind, and spirit thrive under the tutelage of the Bodils:

Body: The emphasis is on healthy eating, walking, jogging, hiking, aerobics, and swimming. Yoga and aerobics classes are scheduled to meet the requirements of the guests in residence. Manicures, pedicures, hair care, herbal wraps, massages, and facials are performed as part of the program.

Exercise equipment is unimpressive. The raves go to the water sports (espe-

ble garden and fruit trees, the chef serves primarily natural foods.

About fifteen minutes away is the Polynesian Cultural Center, where old villages of the Pacific Islands are re-created and crafts and quilt-making can be viewed. Other scenic side trips to places with names like Crouching Lion Rock and Chinaman's Hat Island delight everyone.

Open year round to fourteen guests at a time, The Plantation is at its best in March through June and September through early January. February brings rain; July and August are very hot.

At the spa boutique, you'll find well-designed spa t-shirts, robes, sweatsuits, island jewelry, backpacks, books, herbs, and oils. Bring the rest: good walking shoes, swimwear, an evening wrap, ultracasual clothing, personal items. Be sure to pack a sunhat and sunglasses.

The Plantation Spa gives the nerves a break and teaches the techniques of enjoying a healthy life. In addition, you'll learn to do the hula-hula!

cially the canoe trip down the Kalana River), the beach walks, and the two-and-a-half-hour hike to Sacred Falls.

Mind and spirit: The emphasis is on tuning into nature and yourself. Positive thinking gets a lot of play. Guests learn how to organize their thoughts into ideas and then map out a plan of acting for solving a problem. This leads to a "take charge, can do" attitude.

Relaxation is part of the picture, as is contemplation and concentration. Opportunities to unwind are found in bird-watching, enjoying the outdoor pool, gazing at the mini-waterfall, lazing in the outdoor whirlpool, or simply contemplating the endlessness of the ocean.

Neither smoking nor alcohol is allowed on the premises. Diet, a prominent component in The Plantation's holistic health equation, is basically lacto (dairy)/vegetarian, though guests do have the option of a special juice-and-broth fast. With their own vegeta-

---

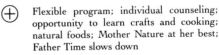

GETTING THERE

Fly to Honolulu International Airport. From there, take a cab or drive along Like Like Highway and onto Kamehameha Highway until you see the sign directing you to The Plantation.

RATING

Overall: Isolated, innovative, inspiring

⊕ Flexible program; individual counseling; opportunity to learn crafts and cooking; natural foods; Mother Nature at her best; Father Time slows down

⊖ No air-conditioning; small guest rooms; can be lonely

Main thrust: Healthy rejuvenation plus getting in touch with oneself and nature

Cost: Moderate

Regency Health Resort and Spa

HALLANDALE FLORIDA

ADDRESS
2000 South Ocean
Drive, Suite P
Hallandale, Florida
33009
TELEPHONE
305-454-2220
CREDIT CARDS
None

THE REGENCY MAY BE MIS-named, but it's not misplaced. Ocean frontage and a sandy beach make this spa resort a restful, peaceful spot to engage in healthful activities. So what if it's not so regal?

This place fills a need, and it serves its clientele well. Every Sunday, women (mostly) who are "fifty-nine and holding" unpack for one week to several months of renewal, confident that their limited incomes are being invested in better living, better health, and caring companionship. Look past the plastic flowers and you see real people having a real good time.

Having been there for a quarter of a century, the manager recognizes almost everyone. Many guests have been coming year after year. They arrive from all over, but New York accents predominate.

Twin-bedded with walk-in closets, television, mini-fridge, radio, telephone, air-conditioning, and bathroom, the fifty-five accommodations are adequate. Guests spend most of their time in the restaurant, boutique, spa, or on the beach anyway.

Whether you choose to follow an individually programmed diet or eat the Regency way is up to you. Meals are simple, making calorie counting almost unnecessary. Watch the pounds melt off. Fresh and nutritious foods (mainly vegetarian) lead the way to a cleaner inside and a more attractive outside. The full board plan is the only way to go (it includes an afternoon and bedtime snack).

In addition to the no-extra-fee spa treatments (massages, sauna, whirlpool), beauty parlor services can be had a la carte. The makeup class is especially popular and teaches many tired but willing hands to apply less rouge, choose a lighter eyebrow pencil, and to blend it all in. Even though the exercise equipment is sympathetic to hardening arteries and the aerobics space is in the same room, enough body toning is available to make total lethargy a bit of an embarrassment. When misery wants company, the daily class in aerobics answers the call.

On returning from a game of shuffleboard or a swim in the Olympic-size outdoor heated pool, you can try a little yoga to get out the mental and physical kinks. They'll show you how.

Golf is available and free three times a week for those on a two-week or more program. The fairway is not too far away.

At night everyone enjoys the dancing and live entertainment. Popular, too, are the evening card and bingo games.

119

Surrounding Hallandale are shopping areas that beckon browsers and buyers alike. Miami is a half hour away in one direction, Fort Lauderdale a half hour in the other.

Even if you're eighty years young, bring your leotard and bathing suit along with casual and evening wear. For dinner, men must wear jacket and ties; women deck out in dresses rather than slacks.

Cutting out the toxins (including liquor) while de-stressing in the company of a completely homogeneous group could be a very practical, rewarding, and enjoyable vacation. If you're right for the Regency, it will be right for you. Go in good health.

GETTING THERE

The choice is yours—fly to Fort Lauderdale or Miami. In either case, take a cab to the Regency (about a half hour ride).

RATING

Overall: Short on its own style, but long on a healthy lifestyle for guests

     Warmth; fresh, nutritious diet food

⊖   Commercial decor; only for a 50 + clientele (which could also be a plus)

Main thrust: Holistic health, relaxation

Cost: Moderate

Rosario Resort and Spa

EASTSOUND
WASHINGTON

ADDRESS
Orcas Island
Eastsound, Washington
  98245
TELEPHONE
206-376-2222
1-800-562-8820
  (Washington)
CREDIT CARDS
V, AE, MC, DC,
  Discover

THE SAN JUAN ISLANDS ARE nowhere near Puerto Rico, neither in location nor in mood. They lie in Puget Sound, where Americans and Canadians have found a healthy playground Northwest Pacific style. There on the shores of Cascade Bay in the town of Eastsound on Orcas Island, the Rosario Resort and Spa plays host to spa-goers, athletes, business groups, families, and nature lovers, many of whom just can't get enough of life on the water's edge.

At the Rosario, mood and decor lean toward the understated. Beautiful wood paneling in the turn-of-the-century mansion (which is the main house) adds a touch of formality. However, in general, everything is very, very casual. Several two-story complexes house the guests—up to 179 of them. If you don't have a car and wouldn't enjoy a half-mile walk to the mansion, ask for a room near the main action. Some accommodations have kitchens and fire-

places, but don't expect anything remotely fancy. In fact, a little sprucing up throughout the Rosario wouldn't hurt. Still, it *is* homey. Rooms come with all the necessities—television, telephone, coffee pot, shampoo and hair conditioner. Many offer a view of the bay and a balcony for watching the sun rise or set. If you miss these attractions from your *little* (and I use that word advisedly) nest, try the large multi-windowed dining room for spectacular vistas of boats and water, snow-capped mountains, forests, and some of the other San Juan islands.

On the grounds are a marina, a small grocery and sundries shop, a dockside open cafe eating area, and an outdoor pool. For indoor swimming, the spa pool suffices. A further option in good weather is a dip in the lakes of the public parks a short drive away.

The spa spreads out on the lower level of the mansion. Classes consist of stretching and toning, low-impact and aquatic aerobics, yoga, and relaxation therapy, all geared to spa novices and vacationing athletes who just want to keep up with their workouts. Technique is not given a passing thought, nor is what you wear.

Nautilus equipment fills a small room of its own; Exercycles, treadmills, and trampolines share space in the classroom gym. Sauna and whirlpool, facials, nail and hair care, waxing, body wraps, salt-glo, and many different kinds of massages (including a Japanese chair massage) make up the pampering and preening roster.

The spa is open to all on an a la carte basis, but money-saving spa plans are available throughout the year except

121

during holidays. These one- to four-day programs do not include meals.

The crowd at Rosario is hard to type. Are they basically McDonalds or Maxims? Who knows? Who cares! They are a diverse group; independent, secure, athletic, and unpretentious. Many come with kids in tow to enjoy the plethora of water sports, bicycling, hiking and walking in Moran State Park, golf, and tennis, in addition to the spa activities and a browse through the fine crafts shops of Eastsound.

How you pack depends on your activity level, but in general, you'd be wise to bring aerobics, water, hiking, and sports attire (including appropriate shoes), plus personal items and casual wear for dinners.

For a healthy, laid-back spa experience, the Rosario Resort and Spa rules the Northwestern roost.

GETTING THERE

Getting there can be half the fun if you take your own boat directly to their marina. Those of us who must resort to public transportation have three options: (1) *By car:* Take the Washington State Ferry Service from Anacorts. Drive onto the ferry or park car at Anacorts. Rosario will provide transportation to and from the ferry for a small fee. (Anacorts is 2½ hours from Seattle or Vancouver). (2) *By air:* Fly to Seattle-Tacoma Airport; take San Juan Airline to Orcas Island; prearrange transport to spa by spa van. (3) *By seaplane:* Take Lake Union Air from Seattle direct to the Rosario marina.

RATING

Overall: A simple "you're on your own" spa that takes advantage of the glories of the San Juan Islands

⊕   Seascape; landscape; private marina; a certain appealing quaintness of the mansion; family oriented; numerous water sports; untaxing physically and mentally for the neophyte spa-goer.

⊖   Old plumbing, pool, etc.; spa program needs more structure; living quarters without charm

Main thrust: Lowering the stress level while rejoicing in nature's wonders

Cost: Inexpensive to moderate

122

Safety Harbor Spa and Fitness Center

SAFETY HARBOR

FLORIDA

ADDRESS
105 Bayshore Drive
Safety Harbor, Florida
   34695
TELEPHONE
813-726-1161
1-800-237-0155
CREDIT CARDS
AE, V, MC

SAFETY HARBOR SPA HAS HAD a rebirth and in its new life has added the words *and Fitness Center* to its name. It has not added *just* the words, but also the equipment and staff to back them up.

Five natural mineral springs clustered together on the east shore of Old Tampa Bay dictated the site of this tried and true health haven. The spa retains the dignified seaside resort exterior that it had years ago when my mother- and father-in-law and all their friends from New York made a yearly winter foray there. However, in the *new improved* version, the 230 guest accommodations have been spruced up and a new wing has been added.

Fortunately, the feeling of unadorned comfort that has long been a trademark of the spa remains. Only the suites have kitchens, but all rooms have bath, shower, direct dial telephones, and television, and you can request a mini-fridge. The public spaces are decorated with soothing, upbeat murals.

Safety Harbor is casual both in atmosphere and in dress. When Rosalyn Carter went there for a few days, she arrived ready for dinner in a trim pants suit, but with a quick glance she absorbed the personality of the place, excused herself for a few minutes, and reappeared in the dining room in a maroon sweatsuit to mix, meld, and just be comfortable.

These days, when you check in, you fill out a questionnaire that will help determine your needs and wants. An orientation hour is set aside for neophytes—some guests come without a clue as to what to expect and feel much more confident having taken this tour. After a medical screening, a plan is devised for your stay there . . . and thereafter. Safety Harbor's goal is to help you begin to change your lifestyle for the better and send you home equipped to carry on their regimen on your own.

Offered each day are the popular two-mile walk, water aerobics, exercise and stretch classes, weight training, low-impact aerobics, rhythmics, and jazzercize. You can also work out on body-improving equipment of outstanding caliber. The ten treadmills are built right into the floor and have computer read-outs that tell you everything but your age. Exercising arms and legs at once is actually fun on the stationary Schwinn bikes, with left and right handlebars that move separately. Other equipment includes Nautilus, Paramount and Universal machines, free weights, climbing machines, and trampolines.

There is an outdoor pool for sun lovers and an indoor pool and Jacuzzi

filled by the "Springs of the Holy Spirit" for those who want to take advantage of the area's therapeutic waters. Back to the great outdoors for tennis (seven courts), a four-hole golf course and putting green, croquet, basketball, volleyball, biking, shuffle-board, and brisk morning walks. Rafting and fishing can be arranged, as can a golf game on a nearby eighteen-hole course.

Around the spa area, you'll see men and women wearing white towels and relaxed expressions. The massages (Swedish), loofah scrubs, herbal wraps, and Lancôme facials are done by experts. Followed up by a little time-out in one of the saunas or steam rooms, these treatments make up a major part of the Safety Harbor stress reduction routine. Lectures on behavior modification are another essential component.

The calorie-counted spa menu is recommended for health and weight conscious guests. On the 900-calorie-a-day plan, the food is quite good, though the portions are small. Meals are eaten in what was previously an old domed mineral bathhouse and is now an attractively designed dining room. Making the rounds each mealtime is the head nutritionist, who will answer questions and give advice. Box lunches are provided each day for anyone who wants to eat on the pier, viewing lots of peaceful blue sky and clear water.

Two fully qualified doctors (one a cardiologist) are on site full-time for consultations and care.

A la carte stays are one option, but there are also more economical "Safety Harbor Fitness Plans" of varying duration. A fitness profile, some sports opportunities, classes, treatments, beauty care, and diet plan are included along with meals and rooms. Especially

noteworthy are the low-rate summer package and a one-on-one smoking cessation program featuring hypnosis.

Safety Harbor Spa and Fitness Center is in the small town of Safety Harbor. Nothing to shout about there, but down the road a piece (about an hour and a quarter drive) is the Epcot Center and even closer are Busch Gardens and its African game park. Tours can be arranged by the hotel. For theater and dance, check out the Performing Arts Center, which is very close. Otherwise, evening entertainment generally consists of excursions to nearby malls and movies.

Comfortable, easy clothing is worn throughout the year (but you might want to pack party clothes for the Christmas season). You'll need your own bathrobe, slippers, exercise and sports clothes and shoes, sun hat, and sweatsuit. For summers, concentrate on fabrics that breathe (cottons, linens).

As the place has changed, so has the clientele. The group tends to be younger than in the past. Some business people now come to use the conference as well as the spa and fitness facilities. Summer rates and programs bring families, though anyone under sixteen is not allowed to use the spa facilities.

GETTING THERE

Tampa International Airport is 20 minutes from Safety Harbor by limo, taxi, or rental car. The resort will provide return transportation to the airport.

RATING

Overall: A safe harbor to tie into for a thorough overhaul

⊕ Natural mineral waters that might be curative; excellent beauty treatments; relaxed style; fine exercise equipment

⊖ Humidity, flat terrain

Main thrust: To change unhealthy habits

Cost: Moderate

Sonesta Sanibel Harbour Resort and Spa

FORT MYERS

FLORIDA

ADDRESS
17260 Harbour Pointe
    Drive
Fort Myers, Florida
    33908
TELEPHONE
813-466-2156 (spa)
813-466-4000 (hotel
    reservations)
CREDIT CARDS
V, MC, DC, AE

SONESTA MEANS PERSONAL service. Guests at the Sonesta Sanibel Harbour Resort and Spa are grateful for the high caliber of personal service there that offsets the less than intimate ambience created by the size of the hotel building. The 280 rooms bustle with conventioneers in addition to pleasure and health seekers.

The resort's condominium buildings offer a perfect setup for a family or two couples traveling together. Every unit has a kitchen, living-dining room, two baths, and two bedrooms. They are fully equipped, comfortable, and have daily room service. Decorated by the owners, each accommodation has its own personality. The two buildings themselves are prosaic, but each sports a pool and Jacuzzi. Although only adults over sixteen are allowed in the spa, all ages are welcome in the condos and hotel, and there are activities to keep the youngsters busy.

At the core of the Sonesta Sanibel Harbour Resort and Spa is the famed Jimmy Connors U.S. Tennis Center. Tennis doesn't get much better than this: There are twelve well-groomed and lighted courts (eight Har/Tru clay and four composition), plus a *dazzling* center court that seats 5,500 tennis buffs. Obviously, the tournaments here are spectacular in terms of setting and play.

But save some applause for the spa. It deserves it.

The three- to six-day programs begin with a complete physical evaluation by the staff. Included are an assessment of general fitness, cardiovascular condition, weight needs, target heart rate, and percentage of fat tissue you have in relation to muscle and bone structure. Thereafter, you'll follow a prescribed schedule that will include exercise, proper meals, and delightful beauty services. Summertime is bargain time due to the oppressive humidity during that season.

Beneath the circle of the stadium are the enormous men's and women's spas, which offer a remarkable range of facilities. Among these are

- Excellent racquetball courts (two for men, two for women)
- A knock-out aerobics room with tiny twinkling lights that dance with the music (coed classes)
- An attended exercise room that has state-of-the-art equipment: fifteen different Keiser (air-pressure) machines with ultra-smooth resistance, which work every possible part of the body, plus the best of stationary bikes, StairMaster, abdominal flexers,

The beauticians who do the facials and the waxing and perform head-to-toe minor miracles, including fantasy nails, are true experts. *My* fantasy is to spend the day with them once every week for a century or so.

Available on the terra firma are basketball, volleyball, and handball courts, golf, and an "exercourse" with thirty-six stations. If you're a water buff, you have your choice of sailing, kayaking, wind-surfing, or fishing.

Casual dress is fine for day or night, but no silky tennis shorts, please. Tennis shirt and shoes are required on the courts. Spa guests receive bathrobes in their lockers.

World famous for its seashells, Sanibel Island is fun to explore. You're sure to return home with seahorses and starfish along with the obligatory t-shirt.

and a workout machine that has a safety feature for catching the weight bar and also keeps your body in perfect alignment

- A separate body building room for the real animals (I mean this is tough stuff!)
- Well-equipped wet areas, featuring several male and female whirlpools of varying sizes, a large inviting coed pool (a better place to socialize than the local bar), salt-glo loofah bath cabins, scotch showers, saunas, and steam rooms
- Massage cabins and herbal wrap rooms

Decorated with taste and pleasant in every way (to say nothing of all the freebie products at everyone's disposal), the locker and shower areas are great.

GETTING THERE

The Sonesta Sanibel is a 25-minute drive by car or cab from the South West Regional Jetport in Fort Myers, Florida. Sunlite and Apple shuttle taxis stationed across the path from the baggage claim area charge reasonable fares to the resort.

RATING

Overall: Surprisingly superior fitness spa off the beaten Florida track

⊕ Equipment; massages; beauty care; tennis; personnel

⊖ Hulking buildings; summer humidity

Main thrust: Body toning, relaxing tensions

Cost: Moderately expensive

Sonoma Mission Inn and Spa

BOYES HOT SPRINGS
CALIFORNIA

MAILING ADDRESS
P. O. Box 1447
Sonoma, California
  95476
SPA ADDRESS
18140 Sonoma
  Highway
Boyes Hot Springs,
  California 95416
TELEPHONE
707-938-9000
1-800-862-4945
  (California)
1-800-358-9022 (rest of
  U.S.)
1-800-358-9027 (rest of
  U.S.)
CREDIT CARDS
All major

WHY HERE? THAT WAS MY first thought when we drove into the circular driveway of the Sonoma Mission Inn. This enclave of serenity and beauty, with its charming pink stucco buildings, gardens, and courtyard, seems to have been plunked down without a thought in the big middle of nowhere—no pretty scenery, no quaint little town.

Inside the complex, relaxation comes with the territory. Adhering to the style of the old 1927 building, the new spa, conference, and guest buildings blend in well, as do the gardens, pool area, and tennis courts. Colors are muted; hues change gradually as the sun rises and sets. High wooden-beamed ceilings, Mexican-tiled floors covered with pink and gray carpets, and a giant wood-burning fireplace flanked by two buffets with cornucopias of seasonal fruits embellish the lobby. The Grille dining room echoes

the very informal, comfortable yet sophisticated decor. A more casual restaurant with a wine-tasting bar and a boutique called "The Big 3 Market" is across the courtyard. Nothing about the Sonoma Mission Inn complex is grand or pretentious, but charm abounds.

Guests accommodated in the newer, more expensive "Wine Country" rooms can wind down in front of their very own wood-burning fireplace, enjoying a sip of the complimentary Sonoma red wine or mineral water. (The best part is that these fireplaces are cleaned and set up each day.) Room #180 is one of the top-of-the-liners. "Mission Inn" rooms (in the main building) cost less and are rather spare. "Garden Court" #233, with its butcher block type furniture, is architecturally unusual: One rounded wall overlooks the garden courtyard. In all, 170 guest rooms provide comfortable, quiet, but far from elegant refuge.

The spa building itself boasts a stunning entrance, replete with a pink marble fountain and a grand arrangement of colorful flowers. Facilities are coed except for the locker areas. The focus here is on relaxation through major pampering, a dose of stress management, and the option to work out as much or as little as you desire—a program that appeals primarily to people from ages thirty-five to fifty-five who are not looking for a "fat farm."

Spa treatments offered include indoor and outdoor massages, hydrotherapy, herbal wraps, facials, aromatherapy, fango (mud) packs, reflexology, seaweed-based thalassotherapy, whirlpool, sauna, and steam. You can tone up on the nine Keiser Cam II machines, the exercise bicycles, inversion ma-

131

chine, mini-trampoline, and by using the free weights. Each day's schedule features classes in water aerobics, low-impact and comprehensive aerobics, yoga, tennis, introduction to equipment, and stretching. The brisk morning walk takes you into the mesa for an hour and a half.

A doctor and psychologist preside over stress management workshops. Their relaxation program incorporates biofeedback and physical exercise. The self-hypnosis instructor introduces guests to an unusual method for taking control of their own lives; and for believers in a bit of the occult, there is a Tarot card reader who demonstrates the use of cards to learn more about the psychic causes of personal stress and how to diminish tensions.

Because the Sonoma Mission Inn is in the heart of vineyard country, it comes as no big surprise that the dietitian approves of a limited consumption of wine. "It is good for you in moderation," she explains. "Wine is relaxing, thins the blood, and lowers the cholesterol level." No need to be a closet nipper here.

Fruits and vegetables grow in the immediate vicinity of the spa, so the food is appealing and fresh. No one goes hungry. The spa meals are ample. If one is not on a program but wants to diet, he or she can order the dishes marked with an asterisk on the menu (low in calories, sodium, sugar, and cholesterol). Spa guests check their choices in advance on the 1000-, 1200-, or 1500-calorie menus.

The spa can be used a la carte, but several programs are offered. A five- to seven-day program includes room, full

board, treatments, use of facilities, and consultations with the nutritionist and fitness expert.

Bathrobes are provided in the spa. Bring leotards, swimwear, sweats, proper shoes, tennis clothes, slacks, and shifts. Ties and jackets at dinner are not required but are often worn by the conference crowd. Northern California can be chilly any time of the year, so be prepared for a drop in temperature.

Obviously, wine tours to the fifty or so vineyards in the area remain the most popular extracurricular activity and provide fascinating fun. Less appealing (even boring) are the balloon rides. For those who crave the big city, San Francisco is about an hour away.

Keeping the Inn filled seems to be the major thrust of management at the moment. To accomplish this, tour groups are welcomed, and I worry that this trend may lower the standards. So far, the resort maintains its reputation as a charming, upscale inn and spa.

GETTING THERE

To get to the Sonoma Mission Inn, fly to San Francisco International Airport. The drive from the airport takes 1¾ hours. Sonoma Airporter service is frequent and takes you door to door for a fee. It's best to prearrange this transportation.

RATING

Overall: A low-key attractive spa in the wine country, with many choices available (among them, red or white)

⊕ Architecture; the wine country; beauty services, freebies in your room (hair products, loofah sponge, wine, mineral water)

⊖ Immediate surroundings; rooms are not as well appointed as one might expect; limited spa space

Main thrust: Beauty and relaxation

Cost: Moderately expensive to expensive

Southwind Health Resort

CARTERSVILLE
GEORGIA

ADDRESS
632 Old Allatoona
Road
Cartersville, Georgia
30120
TELEPHONE
404-975-0342
CREDIT CARDS
V, MC, AE

DON'T EXPECT *GONE WITH the Wind* when you fantasize about a spa experience in the Georgia countryside. Southwind has many very impressive features, but it is more like the House by the Side of the Road than Tara! The clapboard Victorian home with veranda and requisite rocking chairs is by no means a fancy manor. There are generally no men at all, much less footmen. Your bags are carried by the young women on the staff or by the owner, Doreen MacAdams.

The house does in fact sit by the side of the road, home to a comfy, cozy establishment run with care. Yes, tender loving care—Southern style. I'm beginning to think that the Civil War was called that because the South is so darned *civil*. Everyone, including guests, at this spa seems to have had genteel manners bred into them.

Next to the house sits an old railroad car, which serves as an office. The former Cartersville general store (brick inside and out) is now the gym and lies just a hop, skip, and jump away. Swimming in the big outdoor pool stops when the air turns cold, but the hot tub soothes tense bodies year-round. Surrounded by enough lawn and trees to give the feeling of real country, Southwind Health Resort is a relaxing, rejuvenating, unintimidating retreat graced by the nearness of Lake Allatoona.

Inside the three-story house, the furnishings, though modest, show good taste. Five tall arches allow entry to the dining room from the living room, hall, and kitchen. On the second floor, you'll find most of the bedrooms and a wonderful little sun room. The eight to sixteen (twenty-two in a squeeze) guests are assigned rooms, which are generally shared.

All accommodations are very clean and attractive, though simple (no telephones or television). If you prefer a private bathroom, a quiet bedroom, or one that is particularly warm or cool, mention it when making your reservation. As part of a nineteenth-century house, the rooms vary in size, attributes, and drawbacks.

Relaxation of a different sort reigns on the third floor, where daily massages and facials plus end-of-stay make-overs are performed. There is one station for each of these services.

Except for the Christmas closing, day, week, and weekend programs are enjoyed by Georgians, other Southerners, and a sprinkling of Yankees. Occasionally a "couples week" is scheduled, but generally Southwind is a women's haven. Most are grateful for the chance to shift gears and change habits without men around.

It is amazing how much gets accomplished with such minimal facilities. Everyone who works here is a pro, and Doreen MacAdams keeps the place running smoothly and efficiently. She believes that an important factor in lifestyle change is education.

Lecture and seminars on such subjects as nutrition, physical fitness, mental health, or self-image are straightforward, fascinating, and easy to comprehend. Most helpful is the fact that guests are encouraged to ask questions and solicit advice.

The seminar on preventing cardiovascular (CV) disease made quite an impact. We were all amazed to learn that:

- Every year one million people in the United States have a heart attack.
- 300,000 of those don't even make it to the hospital.
- 200,000 die within months of having the attack. *(More people die from CV disease than any other cause.)*
- 50 percent of people don't know they have a CV problem until they have a heart attack.
- Perhaps as many as 90 percent of all CV problems can be prevented: (a) by *treating hypertension* (high blood pressure), (b) by *controlling cholesterol levels* (buildup of cholesterol inhibits blood supply to the heart and can actually act as a tourniquet), (c) by *cutting out cigarette smoking* and *secondary smoke inhalation*—the heart specialist said that if he could be President for only two minutes, he would enact one law: to prohibit smoking—(d) by controlling the "soft risk" factors: *overweight, sedentary lifestyle, stress,* and *alcohol indulgence.*

It is important to remember that physical exercise is vital to a healthy heart, but should you have palpitation or pain when exercising or immediately afterward, it's a sign that should be investigated.

From the physical therapist came these invaluable pearls:

- When you sit, knees should be higher than hips.
- Knee problems stem from the ankles.
- Have your chin in and your back straight when working at a desk. (A raised work area helps.)
- Carrying small free weights in hand and pumping them while walking can cause problems.
- Carrying heavy shoulder bags can make you weak on one side and tight on the other, causing skeletal problems.
- Thirty to forty-five minutes of brisk walking three or four times a week, starting slow and increasing in rapidity, is fine aerobic exercise.
- Any "interrupted" exercise is not an adequate aerobic workout. (For instance: a doubles game of tennis doesn't qualify—you aren't moving continuously.)
- Proper exercise not only keeps the heart going, but also prevents cramping, enhances endurance, keeps the joints "oiled," and controls weight.

The "Creative Visualization" lecture gave new meaning to the power of thinking positively. *"Fake it* till you *make it!"* The idea is to visualize your goals and expect them to become reality. Have faith in yourself, breathe deeply, relax, and enjoy the small gains that lead to the big ones. Positive words generate positive feelings, which in turn allow us to love ourselves and lead to positive responses from others.

The daily schedule includes a delightful nature walk, aerobics, stretching and toning classes (mostly without equipment, because there are only a couple of exercise bicycles, rowing machines, and trampolines), beauty treatments, cooking demonstrations, and seminars. Twice-weekly field trips to the nearby "Sport Court" (which offers saunas, steam rooms, an indoor pool, and many exercise machines) add to the fun.

Everyone agrees that the food is delicious. Eight hundred to 1000 calories per day are allotted, and you make your menu choices in advance for the multi-course meals. Tables are laid in charming manner, with napkins folded a unique way each night using Japanese origami techniques.

Here's a sampler of meals for one day:

Breakfast: One low-cal egg, grits, orange juice, and coffee
Lunch: Corn chowder, Italian salad, lemon chicken, baked potato, banana mousse
Dinner: Pita triangles, romaine and artichoke, shrimp scampi, broccoli with red peppers, fresh fruit

Pack light. You'll live in your sweats and exercise clothes. Dinner dress is casual. You'll need socks and walking shoes and a jacket or sweater for winter hikes. Bring all personal needs, including swimwear, a robe, slippers, and reading material. There is no shop on the premises.

When you leave Southwind, you take with you a cookbook, exercise manual, fitness evaluation, a little less weight, and lots of knowledge about how to lead a healthier, happier life. This site, where the historic Battle of Allatoona was fought, is a terrific spot to begin fighting your own battle of the bulge.

GETTING THERE

Southwind is located 45 minutes by car from the Atlanta airport and 35 minutes from the city. Complimentary transportation is provided via the Southwind van. If you're driving, take I-75N to Exit 122, turn right at the bottom of the exit. Bear left at the fork and cross the tracks. Continue one mile and you'll see the sign: Southwind Health Resort.

RATING

Overall: A small, unassuming spa that serves up delicious low-cal food, a doable fitness program, helpful information, and a dose of Southern comfort

$\oplus$ Relaxing, low-key, country atmosphere; nurturing staff; fine seminars

$\ominus$ House sits too close to paved road; unimpressive exercise equipment; no glamour or excitement

Main thrust: Laying the groundwork for healthy habits

Cost: Moderate

Spa Hotel and Mineral Springs

PALM SPRINGS CALIFORNIA

AS A GUEST OF THE NEWLY renovated Spa Hotel and Mineral Springs in downtown Palm Springs, you are one step away from the relaxation of a natural thermal mineral whirlpool bath and one block away from heavy duty shopping. In addition, what better tonic could there be than breathing the clean desert air and gazing at the San Jacinto Mountains?

Whereas the spa building has a very open, ultra-modern, almost clinical appearance, the tone of the hotel is soft, elegant, and comfortable. Both aspects seem appropriate. There are 230 guest rooms and suites, uniformly well decorated and equipped with telephones, air-conditioning, sound-proofed walls, mini-bar, color television, and a nice amenities package. Some have balconies and kitchenettes.

All public rooms are tastefully decorated with comfortable furniture and Southwestern colors. There's indoor and patio dining, and the food both diet and regular is good California fare.

The hotel and spa abut the three swimming pools, one of which is Olympic-sized and filled with fresh water. The others contain *agua caliente* natural mineral water. Suntanning around the pool is popular year-round; for clothes-shedders, the roof solarium is the hot spot.

Water is what the spa is all about, and the real guts of the place is the wet area. There are an incredible number of separate rooms for individual hot mineral whirlpool baths, all lined up in a row. When the doors are all open, it's rather like a chorus line of sparkling, dress-up bathtubs ready to do their stuff. Individual changing rooms add to the luxury. Spacious and efficient, with a fastidious and helpful staff, these areas also offer eucalyptus rooms for vapor inhalation, sun beds for overall tanning, saunas, rock steam rooms, loofah wrap, massage rooms, and a huge "cooling room" containing many beds, where a thoughtful matron covers your eyes so that you can drift off into a peaceful rest.

The air in the separate male and female spas is smokefree. Coed classes are held in the aerobics salon and the weight-training gym, which features Paramount equipment, exercise bicycles, free weights, and more. Passive folks can hang out in the imposing Ilona of Hungary Beauty Salon. Skin care is its forte, but you can count on a good job with any of the many esthetic services available.

For tennis buffs, there are three lighted courts. Other activities nearby

ADDRESS
100 North Indian
    Avenue
Palm Springs,
    California 92262
TELEPHONE
619-325-1461
1-800-472-4371
    (California)
1-800-854-1279 (out of
    state)
CREDIT CARDS
MC, V, AE, DC, CB

There are an incredible number of rooms for individual hot mineral whirlpool baths. . . . When the doors are all open, it's rather like a chorus line of sparkling bathtubs ready to do their stuff.

include golf, horseback riding, and a mountain train trip.

A la carte use of the spa (with free entry) is possible for all hotel guests and Palm Springs residents age sixteen or over. In fact, you are likely to run into a lot of townies using the facilities and services for diversion and quick revitalization. Packages available include one for five nights/six days. This consists of deluxe room, three spa meals a day (1000 calories suggested), lectures, use of all spa services, plus a facial, massage, scalp treatment, herbal wrap, loofah scrub, manicure, pedicure, brisk morning walks, and exercise classes.

Sweatshirts and bathrobes are provided. Bring resort wear along with your swimsuit, slippers, socks, aerobic and walking shoes, tights and leotards, sweatsuit, jacket, personal items, and sleepwear.

The Spa Hotel and Mineral Springs is a handsome, fine place to unwind. The thermal mineral water feels so good and possibly has curative powers. If you like in-town hotel living and a spa experience without too much stress on a strenuous fitness regimen, this should do it for you.

GETTING THERE

The ride from Palm Springs Municipal Airport is a swift 5 minutes. The spa will send a courtesy car to transport you.

RATING

Overall: Beauty in the salon and bathing in the sun and soothing mineral water

⊕ Natural thermal mineral water; good air and climate

⊖ Too few classes, city sidewalk site

Main thrust: Relaxation, whirlpool-style

Cost: Moderately expensive

Sun Spa

HOLLYWOOD
FLORIDA

ELDERLY WIDOWS CAN TURN into steamy "red hot mamas" at the Sun Spa on the ocean in Hollywood, Florida. Other guests simply continue their quiet, refined way of life with an added dash of splash. It may be all wrong for you, but many takers have been grateful for a few weeks every year with blue skies, the beach, and the pleasures of an old-fashioned Florida spa. Add the security of a homogeneous guest list and life-long staffers and what a woman coming here gets is what she wants. There are men who love it, too, but they are vastly outnumbered by the ladies.

So, what's new? Well, practically the entire decor. Sparkling with beveled mirrors, the lobby now makes the guests' diamond brooches seem even livelier. The dining room has been transformed with new chandeliers and gray and mauve decor. The starlight roof over the dance floor makes danc-ing with the four dance instructors every night more fun. And everyone does seem to have fun, decked out in their finest clothes.

Entertainment doesn't depend on your dance card being filled up; there are also movies, bingo, shopping excursions on the Sun Spa minibus, and cards, cards, cards. When women get older, many seek the comforts of the card table over all others. Games of poker, bridge, canasta, and mah-jongg go on and on.

The accommodations are clean but minimal. Most important, in each of the 174 guest rooms and suites, there is a safe for stashing valuables and a magnifying mirror to ease the strain of applying mascara without the mishap of a corneal abrasion.

A doctor and a nurse are available to provide t.l.c. and real medical aid. Also at your beck and call is a dietitian who will put you on any specialized diet you need and help you stick to it. She guides you in your daily menu choices if you're one of the 40 percent who are on a regimen. The guests rave about the quality of the food. As the proprietor pointed out, "With our food, you could gain a hundred pounds." Obviously, a kindly watchdog is necessary. Meals can be taken in the dining room or private quarters.

It's show time downstairs and spa time upstairs. The gym equipment room is geared to those who want to keep fit but aren't looking to enter the triathlon. The weights, exercise bikes, and jogging machines do nicely. You can take any of four aerobics classes daily—two in the lovely outdoor pool. Saunas, whirlpools, nude sunbathing, massages,

ADDRESS
3101 South Ocean Drive
Hollywood, Florida 33019
TELEPHONE
305-944-9666 (Dade County)
305-921-5800 (Broward County)
1-800-327-4122 (outside of Florida)
CREDIT CARDS
None

facials, body wraps, and beauty services are in demand. Men's and women's areas are very similar. The gals get it together surrounded by red and white, and we all know that blue is for boys.

Golf and fishing can easily be arranged. Sports activists don't hang out at the Sun Spa.

This is one place where management has defintely got the hang of it. Guests return year after year, never staying less than two weeks at a clip; many stay months. In fact, a few have moved in permanently. And why not? The price is right, the food is good, the ocean is warm, the spa facilities are well kept up, and life is short even if you've lived long.

Sun Spa is open from October until April, and they have to turn down guests each season.

GETTING THERE

The Sun Spa, 15 minutes from Fort Lauderdale International Airport and 30 minutes from Miami, offers no transfer transportation. Taxis are easy to find at both airports.

RATING

Overall: A secure island in the sun for ladies and gents of a certain age who want to get a little leaner and have a little fun

$\oplus$ Location; friendliness; caring staff

$\ominus$ Not chic enough for many spa-goers

Main thrust: Relaxation and rejuvenation for folks whose minds are more active than their bodies

Cost: Moderate

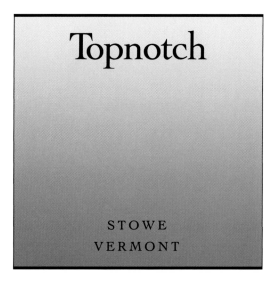

Topnotch

STOWE
VERMONT

ADDRESS
Mount Mansfield Road
P. O. Box 1260
Stowe, Vermont 05672
TELEPHONE
802-253-8585
1-800-228-8686
  (Canada)
1-800-451-8686
  (Eastern U.S.)
CREDIT CARDS
MC, V, AE, DC, CB,
  Discover

TOPNOTCH IN STOWE, VERmont, just added another notch to its belt by building a 20,000-square-foot spa. It was planned by a husband and wife team well trained by years at the famed Canyon Ranch and Doral Saturnia spas. For many years, the Topnotch on Route 108, away from the main drag, has enjoyed a reputation as one of the Northeast's finest ski and tennis resorts. The rustic quality of the public rooms, combined with fireplaces and old Oriental rugs, continues to have appeal, even though time has taken its toll on the furnishings. My guess is that management will spruce it up a bit to better complement the clean newness of the spa. Guests may opt for one of the 100 or so rooms and suites or a condo or townhouse. Television, air-conditioning, telephone, and the amenities package found in every accommodation make life at the Topnotch comfortable.

With 120 acres, there's lots of room to spread out. Along with the hotel (providing conference center facilities), you'll find indoor and outdoor tennis courts (the Tennis Clinic gets raves from the locals); riding stables and trails; hiking, jogging, and cross-country skiing paths; fishing streams; swimming pools; and ice skating pond. The itch to shop can be soothed by a stop in the tennis and ski shop or the gift and sundries shop.

Then, of course, there are wonderful mountain views from just about everywhere. For those who desire a view from the top, the ski lifts and runs of Mt. Mansfield are a short ride away. Or, are you ready for mountain biking? They're ready for you!

The spa at Topnotch promises to be a winner. The spa building is separate from the hotel, but a glass-enclosed walkway shelters health and beauty seekers from both winter winds and summer rains. Men and women enjoy their own wet areas with steam, saunas, and Jacuzzis. The sexes merge for water classes and low-impact aerobics, stretching and toning, yoga, and weight-training classes. In the two gyms, floors are cushioned and the equipment is high-quality. Salt-glo loofah scrubs, hydrotherapy, massages, and facials are performed in small, cheerful private rooms, and a water cascade awaits those interested in a do-it-yourself hydro-massage. A full-service beauty salon looks after hair, nails, and makeup.

Each spa program participant has the opportunity for a fitness assessment or, for a fee, one-on-one consultations. Seminars on nutrition, stress management, and other holistic health topics come with the territory. Although spa services and treatments are available on an a la carte basis to the townies and the hotel guests, those on a spa plan get penciled in first for these.

Two unusual program offerings are (1) an art studio where you can de-stress through artistic expression and/or learn a hobby that will take your mind off of work, (2) the option in the winter to participate in an early morning su-pervised cross-country ski run rather than the brisk wake-up walk.

The "formal" restaurant in the hotel is romantically dark; the spa restaurant is realistically bright—you can see the calories going down! Topnotch food is good enough to keep you wanting more, which you can always get if you're not a weight-watcher.

Spa plan rates vary according to the time of the year. A fabulous period (for the non-budgeter) to change one's lifestyle here is the enchanting season of the changing of the leaves in the fall. For two weeks or so, the countryside is virtually ablaze with indescribable reds, yellows, and oranges that every artist's palette yearns to duplicate.

Pack according to the requirements of the season. Winter can be beastly cold, and part of summer might be baking hot. With the right clothing, it won't matter—the air is so sweet and the thermostats so handy. Certainly bring spa and swim clothes, tennis and ski gear if you enjoy those sports, proper footwear, personal items, pro-tective cream for skin and lips, and casual après-spa wear.

Stowe captivates everyone. Pictur-esque and well looked after by its proud population, the village boasts historic buildings, cozy shops, and delightful crafts. In addition, its Green Mountains have kept skiers and hikers enthralled for many a year.

GETTING THERE

Fly to Burlington International Airport, then shuttle via Clark, Sullivan's, or Russell's taxi companies (45 minutes). Greyhound and Vermont Transit buses de-liver you right to Stowe from far-flung places. By car, New York City means 6½ hours on the road; Boston, 3¾ hours; Albany, 3½ hours; Hartford, 4 hours; Montreal, 90 minutes.

RATING

Overall: Brand-new spa—clean as a whistle and worth one

$\oplus$ New equipment; lovely view; clean air; lure of the mountains; tennis and skiing; quaint village

$\ominus$ All the little kinks of a new facility, which will take more time to work out than you will

Main thrust: "Cream and steam" for the sports-minded

Cost: Expensive

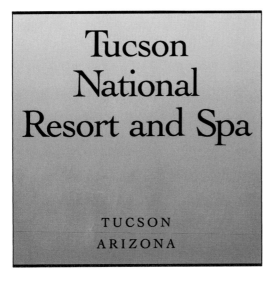

Tucson National Resort and Spa

TUCSON
ARIZONA

ONCE A GOLF AND COUNTRY club, the Tucson National Resort and Spa has now developed into a fine beauty and health oasis—simple, straightforward, and pleasant as can be. It is graced by the Santa Catalina Mountains (grand for viewing and hiking), the proximity of the city of Tucson (twenty miles away), the remarkable climate (at least for three seasons), and air perfumed by cactus and mesa.

A Southwestern combination of Indian, Mexican, and gringo styles using massive carved rock for unusual accents sets an attractive, though not elegant, stage for entrances and exits into the public areas of the resort. There are wide covered walkways replete with arches that abut the meeting rooms and one of the two dining rooms. Everything is casual and navigable without a map or chart. The 167 modern, appealing guest accommodations have fridges, wet bars, television, tele-

phone, radio, nice bathrooms and closets, and patios. Some have fireplaces. When I was there, about 150 other guests were somewhere on the premises, a handful of whom were spa program people and many a la carte spa users. The resort and spa seemed amazingly quiet and peaceful.

Spa facilities and staff are highly professional. Although the spa area is not grand in size, it corrals a happy herd of health-conscious people who prefer a hassle-free, competition-free beauty and fitness program. In fact, it sometimes seems to be each guest's private spa, with at least one staff member focusing attention on her or him.

For those on the spa plan, proposed schedules are drawn up in advance of arrival. Conventioneers can also prearrange services and treatments. The Tucson National offers spa plans from one day to one week, plus a la carte participation.

Men's and women's facilities are separate but basically equal, although the men's has a scotch shower plus a Russian bath, and the women's has a Swiss shower plus sauna and steam cabinets. Other treatments are salt-glo and loofah, inhalation therapy, herbal wraps, massages, sun-bed tanning, facials, and all beauty services. Hot whirlpools, cold plunges, and pools relax and refresh on command.

There is a "ladies only" Panthermal room, which houses a machine and a control board. One lies down inside this other-worldly contraption, with head protruding. It may give you a moment of apprehension; the good news is that it will give your cellulite cells the double whammy. Invigorating and relaxing

ADDRESS
2727 West Club Drive
Tucson, Arizona 85741
TELEPHONE
(602) 297-2271
1-800-528-4856
CREDIT CARDS
All major

A Southwestern combination of Indian, Mexican, and gringo styles using massive carved rock for unusual accents sets an attractive stage. . . .

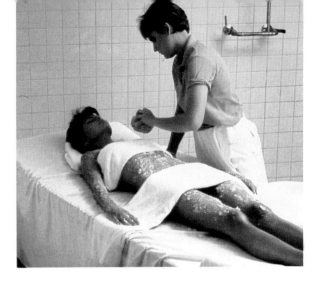

at once, the chamber is preheated to 100 degrees. At the command of the control panel, negative ions fill it up, resulting in positive reactions; some pure oxygen is sent in for good measure; a seaweed and algae lotion is dispensed; and then a lukewarm rinse prepares your body for re-entry. You'll find yourself thinking, "Hey, no sweat," in this 1990s version of the steam cabinet.

Fitness seekers can spend leisure hours on the six lighted tennis courts or the twenty-seven holes of golf. The exercise program consists of classes in aerobics, T'ai Chi, stretching, and water workouts. Each sex has its own equipment room with Cybex machine, free weights, Lifecycles, rowers, jogging machines, and trampoline. Early morning walks are for everyone. With the help of technology, the staff is able to determine complete fitness profiles for everyone.

The sports psychologist helps people reach peak performance through visualization and imagery. For instance, try to see in your mind's eye the perfect golf swing and assume you can do it. Imagination and affirmative thinking result in a better reality. The same technique is used for stress reduction.

Diet meals are served in the informal Fiesta Cafe, a few steps below the main reception area. Weight watchers eat there alongside regular diners (and smokers). There is always the option of being served in your room.

A jacket is requested in the more formal restaurant, but casual clothing is all that's needed anywhere else anytime. A bathrobe and slippers are complimentary for one's stay.

Weekends bring live entertainment. For anyone interested in extracurricular activities, a side trip to town is fun. Tucson still has some of the vestiges of the Old West. Arts and crafts abound. Nearby Nogales, Mexico, is another fascinating place for sightseeing and shopping.

Although the Tucson National Resort and Spa depends upon convention business for revenue, the spa is a serious part of the overall operation. So, if you need a helping hand to relax or shape up, put 'er there, pard!

GETTING THERE

The Arizona Stagecoach will transport you between the Tucson airport and the resort. It's a half-hour trip and quite reasonable.

RATING

Overall: A soothing, well-run, healthy home on the range

⊕ Attractive, separate male and female spa areas; fine air; Southwestern desert sensibility; golf

⊖ Convention-oriented resort

Main thrust: Overall fitness in a friendly atmosphere

Cost: Moderate to moderately expensive

The Spa at Turnberry Isle

NORTH MIAMI BEACH
FLORIDA

ADDRESS
19735 Turnberry Way
North Miami Beach,
  Florida 33180
TELEPHONE
305-932-6200
CREDIT CARDS
All major

BIG, BEAUTIFUL AND SPLASHY-flashy, Turnberry appeals to high-flying fast laners with plenty of spending money.

A full resort on Florida's Gold Coast, Turnberry consists of several tower buildings with guest accommodations, a country club, a yacht and racquet club, twenty-four tennis courts, two golf courses, and the spa. The grounds are well manicured (as are the hands of the guests), and the public spaces are decorated to a fare-thee-well. The fun and games go on year-round. The disco, the large comfortable bar with its model boat collection, the restaurant (where regular menus and calorie-counted spa menus are offered), the appealing pool, and the pebbled poolside area are favorite stomping grounds for the bulls and the bears. It almost goes without saying that there is a full band and entertainment each night—above and beyond the diversion provided by people-watching.

Accommodations leave little to be desired. The gracious rooms are well decorated with top quality furnishings and bathrooms boast whirlpool bathtubs for two. Beds are covered in inviting flowered linens, and all rooms have safes so you can sleep without anxiety. The fact is, security gets a big star here. At the entrance to guest rooms is an emergency switch that sets off an alarm in the security office.

All rooms have a water view as well as a patio or terrace. Spa room #425 and suite #430-1 are especially snazzy. The penthouse suite has its own roof hot tub.

For guests who choose to bring their own accommodations, the 100-slip marina can handle yachts up to 150 feet.

Although the conference center is what brings in the big bucks here, the spa is also considered serious business by those who avail themselves of its excellent facilities.

Adjacent to the pool and rec area, Turnberry Spa caters (and I use that word advisedly) to a small privileged group. There are separate women's and men's areas. The ladies' vanity area is pink and flattering. Herb tea is served at the bar. Facilities and services for each sex include sauna, steam rooms, plunge pools, massages, facials, body wraps and peels, hot wax and permanent hair removal, manicures, pedicures, hair care, makeup, vita baths, aerobics classes, supervised exercise equipment room, whirlpools, nude sunbathing, bicycling, accompanied brisk walks, and nutrition/diet programs.

Before spa guests come to Turnberry,

they are contacted by telephone for information on their likes and dislikes, general health, and condition. On arrival, the nutritionist does some body fat-to-muscle ratio testing. The doctor examines for vital statistics and takes medical history. The physiotherapist checks you out. Then you check in.

The standard diet plan allows 900 calories a day, with an emphasis on fruits, vegetables, and whole grains to ensure that you maintain muscle and lose fat. Three copies of your diet are made; one for the dining room, one for you, and the third for the dietitian, who sees people every day at lunch and acts as the gentle policeman.

Weight loss is the goal of most of the clients. This is accomplished through diet and exercise, and a six-day program is recommended for those intent on learning new habits. The nutritionist is very forthright and open, easy to talk to, and manages to make believers of his disciples.

Individualized programs make it possible for sedentary people to enter an exercise regimen in progressive stages. Sometimes a client is simply introduced to activity. Classes are scheduled for all levels in exercise and aerobics. Boasting one of the strongest water classes in the country, Turnberry

has fortified that area with fine aqua equipment.

All resort guests may use the spa and pay daily admission plus fees for services, but those on spa plans get preferential treatment.

Obviously, if you're going to hobnob with the likes of Madonna, James Caan, and Lionel Richie, you'll want to bring some spiffy duds for evenings. Daytime wear is casual and spa attire is provided by the resort. Only at the Yacht Club is a jacket required.

The character of the cast of characters I cannot attest to, but the character of the place is *la dolce vita* on the water.

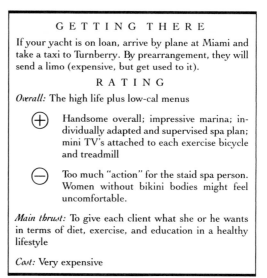

GETTING THERE

If your yacht is on loan, arrive by plane at Miami and take a taxi to Turnberry. By prearrangement, they will send a limo (expensive, but get used to it).

RATING

Overall: The high life plus low-cal menus

⊕ Handsome overall; impressive marina; individually adapted and supervised spa plan; mini TV's attached to each exercise bicycle and treadmill

⊖ Too much "action" for the staid spa person. Women without bikini bodies might feel uncomfortable.

Main thrust: To give each client what she or he wants in terms of diet, exercise, and education in a healthy lifestyle

Cost: Very expensive

Two Bunch Palms

DESERT HOT SPRINGS
CALIFORNIA

ADDRESS
67-425 Two Bunch
    Palms Trail
Desert Hot Springs,
    California 92240
TELEPHONE
619-329-8791
1-800-472-4334 (So.
    California only)
CREDIT CARDS
MC, V, AE

TWO BUNCH PALMS IS ONE OF the well-guarded secrets of the spa world—well guarded literally as well as figuratively. To get past the sentry at the grand impenetrable gates leading to the property, you have to prove yourself a verifiable member of the Two Bunch bunch. That means you have an appointment, a reservation, or you work there. Opt for the reservation. Two Bunch Palms is so indescribable that I can't wait to describe it.

Through the centuries this site has been home for native Indians, Spanish conquistadores, American explorers, and the U.S. Army scouts who charted the two bunches of palm trees on their maps. Two Bunches of Palms later officially dropped the "-es" and the "of," becoming Two Bunch Palms—the name even sounds like a perfect laid-back retreat.

Reputedly, Two Bunch Palms has also had its moment of infamous glamour, serving as a hideaway for Al Capone, his henchmen, and any number of peroxide blondes. Even they felt secure here!

All these phantoms of past eras linger on, creating an atmosphere of intrigue and adventure that is also strangely peaceful. This is the perfect place for self-absorption, self-indulgence, and escape. You can come here alone or with your spouse, friend, paramour, or the guru of the moment. You can bring your grocery bag, your karma, your flask, or your bicycle. No one will bat an eyelash at your choice—except the staff, who will close one eye or both while making you feel completely relaxed and wanted. Still, your privacy is never disturbed.

Rustic, casual beyond casual, Two Bunch Palms covers twenty-eight acres of land. The integrity of the land has not been destroyed by the flagstone walkways that lead to the small office/ boutique, guest quarters, fountains, meditation benches, sun bins, picnic tables, barbecue pit, restaurant, lighted tennis courts, gazebo, duck pond, pool area with its thatched umbrellas, "lakes" of natural hot mineral water, Jacuzzis, and spa. Palm and tamarisk trees abound. A lot of river rock has gone into the walls. Victorian and Art Deco furnishings lend a mood of borderline funkiness. The fact that there is no cohesive look adds to that. All rooms seemed scaled down. You'll probably feel like pushing the walls out a little, but the charm compensates for a lot. Plus the vista of the mountains gives the feeling of wide-open space.

Al Capone's (supposed) private bungalow is now rented out to VIPs (supposed and real). The "lookout roof" is now used by guests who only have to look out for ultraviolet rays. The tunnel leading from there through the property to the gate is not used at all, but it's fun to know it exists. The rest of the 100 guests reside in forty casitas or bungalows with patios and villa rooms, each with its own distinct personality. "Casablanca" units are desert-style, and four of these face their own pool or adjoining Jacuzzi. Casita #122 in the older area typifies the general look—a rose-colored bed with an overstuffed bench at its foot, a mirrored wall to give the *illusion* of space, Art Deco touches, a kitchenette, bathroom, and patio. Many of the rooms have cooking facilities; all have a shower or tub, television, radio, and telephone with a coded number. Two nights is the minimum stay; eighteen the minimum age.

With many good restaurants nearby, you may choose to eat only your breakfast in the Two Bunch restaurant (once a casino). That is the one meal that comes with the room rate. Many guests buy or make a picnic lunch and eat it somewhere on the property that they find special. Not only is there no diet plan, there is a real live bar serving intoxicating beverages in surroundings of stained glass and Victorian furniture. The whole place is so intoxicating that I can't imagine the need for artificial stimulants or relaxers.

The plan here is no plan at all. You are allowed to take advantage of what's available, but doing absolutely nothing is a viable alternative. Much emphasis is put upon the waters. Magical? Curative? Who knows? It comes from the depths of Miracle Hill and flows hot and mineral-laden to the "lakes" and Jacuzzis of Two Bunch Palms. Maybe it helps people with rheumatism, arthritis, gout, and neuralgia. Perhaps it rejuvenates. One thing is sure: It relaxes and soothes. Most who come here are healthy anyway.

Walking and hiking are major sports. The lovely trails, the clean air, beautiful sunrises and sunsets, and great weather make this form of exercise particularly rewarding. Then there are the two tennis courts and a stable not too far away. Spa-goers can use the sauna, mineral water showers, pools, and sun bins for nude sunbathing as they wish. Fees must be paid for aromatherapy (using essential oils to stimulate or sedate body functions), reflexology (to promote healing by massaging the hands and feet), facials, hair treatment, salt-glo and herbal steam (a treatment that involves hosing with warm mineral water, a gentle salt rub, then an herbal steam bath using tamarisk, yucca, lavender, mullein, sage, rosemary, and peppermint). The several types of massage done by experts are also a la carte. Unusual, to say the least, is the Shiatsu Massage Room—unless you're used to a mattress on the floor over an Oriental rug, with Tibetan bell music playing in the background. It is soulful and soothing, capable of transporting your mind to another level of consciousness. If you have some money left when you leave, you might purchase some of the mineral water beauty products.

As you wander around the premises, you'll see guests taking it easy in the

sun or pools. Others will be meditating and doing yoga alone, on their way to the spa building for a little pampering, or looking for a soupçon of exercise. In many cases, they'll be in the same bathing suit that they've been wearing all day long. Movie luminaries almost always make up part of the getaway gang that seeks a haven at Two Bunch. People from all walks of life fill in the balance of the roster. The staff and natural surroundings make everyone feel equally at home. (As we were leaving, the Ralph Lauren group arrived.)

My daughter, Nancy, loved this place. No wonder—it's a combination of Robert Louis Stevenson and a 1940s B movie. You can let your hair down, put on your sarong, and wait for your man Friday to tiptoe in. The area is called geothermal, the valley is called Coachella, the black cat mascot is called Misty, and I call the whole place strangely wonderful. In a way, they

get away with murder (not the Al Capone brand). There's no bellboy, no room service, no structured exercise program, no calories counted. Yet the offbeat appeal is amusing and the atmosphere so pleasantly relaxed.

GETTING THERE

Guests from Los Angeles generally drive the 2½ hours to this resort. Desert Hot Springs is very near Palm Springs, a favorite fun spot for the celebs and golfers, so they know the way. If *you* don't, fly to Palm Springs and take a cab or drive, taking Freeway 10 to the Palm Drive exit. Take a left off the freeway. Go to the second stop, which is Two Bunch Palms Trail, where the resort-spa is located.

RATING

Overall: A rustic spa retreat for would-be wood nymphs . . . and you and me

  Back-to-nature ambience; hot natural mineral waters; privacy; security

⊖ No cohesive look; lack of amenities; no diet or exercise program

Main thrust: Relaxation and rejuvenation with wonder water

Cost: Moderately expensive

The Westin Kauai—Kauai Lagoons

LIHUE

HAWAII

ADDRESS
Kalapaki Beach
Lihue (Kauai), Hawaii
  96766
TELEPHONE
1-800-228-3000
1-808-245-5050
CREDIT CARDS
All major

FOR ONCE YOU CAN BELIEVE the travel brochure. The beauty of "the Garden Island," with its lush, tropical greenery and mountain walls that rise dramatically out of the Pacific Ocean, remains relatively undisturbed and truly breathtaking. Clever of the Westin group to stake out this site for a lavish Las Vegas–type resort–conference center–spa. Some will enjoy the razzmatazz; others will find it too touristry and flamboyant.

The Westin Kauai delivers what it promises. The only problem is that it delivers it to so many. Even though the enormity of the space precludes running into crowds, 850 guest accommodations means lots of bodies. Fortunately, only a few of them are at the spa. The spa is small, but special.

Guests are housed in imposing tower buildings. The resort hotel rooms (smoke-free accommodations are available) are decorated in muted earth tones. Balconies and windows overlook the pool—the largest in Hawaii—or the 800 acres of gardens and lawns.

With two Jack Nicklaus golf courses, eight tennis courts, and an easy-to-follow jogging path—not to mention the magnificent Pacific—the outdoor attractions are the big attention-getters here. The hotel arranges island excursions, including snorkeling and scuba-diving for underwater enthusiasts, and also surfing and deep sea fishing.

The Westin's extensive and excellent art collection adds panache to the somewhat glitzy decor in the public areas. Indoor facilities include twelve restaurants and lounges, a discotheque and supper club, ballroom, boutiques, and a complete conference center.

Inside the spa building, serenity reigns. The area, tropical blue and pink in decor, is clean and classy. The size of the gym (small) and amount of weight equipment (minimal) let you know right off where the emphasis lies. Blissful pampering seems to be the name of the game. Massages, facials, and body skin treatments bring relaxation, even slumber. In both the men's and women's spa areas are a sauna, steam room, and whirlpool to further reduce tensions and extract impurities.

Those who take part in the spa program begin each day with a refreshing walk along the beach. This is followed by classes in aerobics, toning, stretching, and water exercises. These are offered a few hours daily and generally draw from four to ten guests. You'll find the instruction amazingly good for a non-action-oriented spa.

In the spa building at the "Wellness Center," those on a spa program receive a fitness assessment, nutritional

The resort is spectacular in its own way, but the island is the thing. . . .

analysis, blood tests (cholesterol and such), health risk and lifestyle appraisal, and fat analysis. Based on the results, the staff will devise a personalized improvement plan to ensure a healthier existence. These tests and the use of the spa are also available to all hotel guests and a limited membership on an a la carte basis. Spa packages of one-half day to one day are being expanded to longer time spans, and a spa meal plan is in the works. Spa cuisine served in "The Terrace Restaurant" draws nutritious, low-calorie food from the area. If you've never tasted *ahi* (bluefin tuna), *mahi mahi* (dolphin fish), or *ono* (local mackerel), get your taste buds ready for a treat.

It's difficult to get an accurate reading on the guest list of such a large place, but don't expect many young adults—except for honeymooners. Middle-aged, middle-of-the-road Americans, conference people, and family groups predominate. For a couple with one partner who wants to spa and the other who doesn't, it's a spot to consider.

Don't forget to bring several bathing suits. That's the daytime uniform. Also pack sports clothes and footwear, personal items, sunglasses and sun hat, shoes for spa/beach/walks, dinner clothes (both casual and semi-dressy),

plus a shawl or jacket. The spa provides fluffy bathrobes and exercise clothes.

The resort is spectacular in its own way, but the island's the thing. Even spa people tend to spend a good percentage of their time on excursions to view the beauty of Kauai by automobile, boat, and helicopter.

On the resort grounds, a fleet of colorful horse-drawn carriages transport guests from place to place. Romantic Venetian boats are ready to take you on the island waterways. A sleepy lagoon, a tropical moon, and you on an island . . . If you're totally swept away by the mood, there's even a wedding chapel at water's edge.

GETTING THERE

To get to this Westin Wonderland, fly to the Kauai, Hawaii, airport from whence you will be whisked away by a white stretch limousine, compliments of the hotel. The ride lasts only a few minutes.

RATING

Overall: Opulent, sprawling sports and conference resort with a small, appealing spa geared for relaxation

(+) Weather; spa pampering; scenery; gigantic pool; sports; art collection

(−) Minimal weight equipment and gym space; no feeling of intimacy except at the spa; overwhelmingly large

Main thrust: Pampering the lotus (and pineapple) eaters

Cost: Moderately expensive

157

The Wooden Door

LAKE GENEVA
WISCONSIN

D O YOU LONG FOR THE good old days of 4-H Camp, when you made up your own bunk but not your face . . . when you thoroughly despised and yet totally enjoyed being "scheduled" . . . when, grateful for every morsel and ecstatic with the thought of peanut butter and cottage cheese extras, you ate what was on your plate without thinking of turning it over to see the markings? The Wooden Door awaits you!

Obviously, the name is a take-off on the posh Golden Door of California. But this does not even offer a golden doorknob. It is super-rustic and without amenities. Yet it works.

The aim is for the guests (inmates, campers—take your choice) to be mindless and mindful at the same time: mindless of all the anxieties and frustrations back at that remote place called home and mindful of taking advantage of the information and self-help opportunities offered here. Go with the flow and let the pounds fall where they may.

Surrounded by seemingly untamed foliage on three sides and a lake on the fourth, the Wooden Door takes advantage of the property of the Covenant Harbor Bible Camp and the wonders of Mother Nature. Healthy living seems only appropriate in this atmosphere. No one should dare light a cigarette and disturb the pristine air, although smoking is allowed outdoors.

Consistent in atmosphere, decor, outlook, and tone, this place reduces life to the essentials. Everything is supremely simple—and wooden (including the door, of course). There is a clubhouse divided into office, eating room (*restaurant*—even *cafe*— are far too fancy words), and lounge area (which has a big window overlooking the lake and "wilderness," a fireplace, and large paintings of Jesus). A walk away (uphill), you encounter the many porched wooden cabins. Don't expect too much—bunk rooms and closet stalls are shared, as are the bathrooms. You've got to "love thy neighbor." Space is at a premium, so don't bring much. In addition, the self-help begins the moment you arrive with your unloading your own gear.

Although the place feels as though it's miles and miles from civilization, it's actually a short walk into town. If you want that walk to be on the wild side, you can check out the infamous Sugar Shack, a male striptease parlor one-half mile away. Antiquing in nearby Richmond attracts the more demure ladies.

The attractively paneled country-style gym and exercise studio provides

ADDRESS
Highway 50
Lake Geneva,
  Wisconsin
HOME OFFICE
P. O. Box 830
Barrington, Illinois
  60010
TELEPHONE
312-382-2888
CREDIT CARDS
V, MC

It is super-rustic and without amenities. Yet it works.

a certain amount of comfort for those taking classes in aerobics, stretching, dance, and weight-lifting. Yoga is offered on the lakefront when weather permits—indoors if the weather doesn't.

No one is forced to do anything, but most clients avidly exercise for the five- to six-day stay, taking classes, hiking (year-round), swimming, canoeing, water-skiing and sailing (in the summer), cross-country skiing (in the winter). The action begins at 6:00 A.M. By 7:00 P.M. you're ready for the untaxing make-overs and fashion consultations, movies, or lectures.

Getting in shape so often means fighting the food habit, and that's also true at The Wooden Door. It's not that you don't eat here; it's just that you don't eat a whole lot—900 calories a day of low-salt and low-fat, high-carbo-

hydrate, and high-fiber cafeteria meals may seem barely enough to get you through the exercise regimen and leave you enough energy to scrape and stack your own dishes at the end of each meal! The plus side is that you'll be minus about five pounds when you leave. The required eight glasses of water per day replace the sweat and tears. (You'll need your doctor's okay for the diet.)

Frills? Forget it! There's no television, *one* pay phone, and no maid service. However, a bit of pampering is not out of order, just an out-of-pocket expense. For an additional fee, you may sign up for massages, facials, pedicures, and manicures.

On-site with you and wearing many hats (or leotards in this case) are the three owners. Others on the staff include a cook, waterfront director, and instructors in exercise, yoga, and cross-country skiing.

The Covenant Harbor Bible Camp facility is occupied by religious groups at various times through the year. The Wooden Door spa weeks are sprinkled in between. Sessions accommodate up to ninety-seven women (no men) from ages eighteen to "old and bold." (Believe it or not, some return again and again.)

Clothing should be comfy and utilitarian: sweats, leotards and tights, gym shoes, walking shoes, and seasonal clothing (swimwear in summer, cross-country ski wear in winter).

If this brand of basic living in the woods is your thing, you'll probably love The Wooden Door; otherwise you're likely to find the Outward Bound ethic too spartan.

When you leave The Wooden Door, you'll surely feel glorious about your weight loss and your ability to cope with (and actually enjoy) life without luxury. What price glory? Not much! It's one of the few well-run bargain basement spas.

GETTING THERE

The Wooden Door is in Lake Geneva, Wisconsin, on Highway 50. From Chicago's O'Hare Airport, you can drive the 90 miles, taking I-94N to 50. There are limo-buses to Lake Geneva twice a day from O'Hare. If you're driving from Milwaukee, the trip will take less than 1 hour.

RATING

Overall: A "bare bones" refuge where the staff helps you to help yourself reduce weight and stress

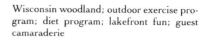 Wisconsin woodland; outdoor exercise program; diet program; lakefront fun; guest camaraderie

⊖ Minimal amenities; lacks sophisticated exercise equipment

Main thrust: Diet program, fitness, and personal "regrouping"

Cost: Inexpensive

II

SPAS OUTSIDE OF THE UNITED STATES

Badrutt's Palace Hotel— Acapulco Spa

ST. MORITZ SWITZERLAND

ADDRESS
CH 7500 St. Moritz
Switzerland
TELEPHONE
011-41-82-21101
(direct dial)
212-838-3110 (Leading
Hotels of the World,
in NY)
1-800-223-6800
(Leading Hotels of
the World, outside
NY)
TELEX
74-424 PALSM CH
CABLE
Palace St. Moritz
CREDIT CARDS
DC, EC, VS

IF LIFE HAS BEEN GOOD TO YOU and you want to give yourself a big treat, put down your Hermès attaché case, gentlemen; grab your Leonard leotard, ladies; and fly to the good life at Badrutt's Palace in St. Moritz, Switzerland, where the scenery and the service are guaranteed to dazzle you. Here you will rejuvenate in true luxury. "Tradition at its best" is the hotel motto, and this lives up to it.

The elegant, though dark, lobby of the Palace has a panoramic view of St. Moritz, its lake, and the Alps. Spectacular! There is a main dining room that can seat 400 people and has a certain grandeur softened by abundant flowers. In general, the food is haute cuisine and delicious. There is also a la carte dining in several other rooms, each with its own appealing ambience. The Renaissance Bar is cozy and the King's Club is the important local disco.

Most of the 240 guest rooms are decorated for those who think "fast food" means caviar on toast points. However, you must be sure to stay in the main hotel. The rooms in the Beau Rivage are old and slightly delapidated. All rooms have television (with CNN from the United States), telephones, radio, and mini-bar. I was intrigued by the four-button push panel in my room. Like an echo from another era, its purpose was for summoning the valet, maid, waiter, or one's personal servant residing in another part of the hotel.

The spa complex is called The Acapulco and can be reached directly by elevator from each floor, so you can wear a bathrobe covering your swimsuit or leotard. There are lockers and changing rooms, if you prefer. Conceived as a replica of a 1930s ocean liner by the hotel owner, Mr. Badrutt, and executed by an Italian shipbuilder, the spa is very spiffy with its highly polished mahogany and teakwood.

In the spa bar-cafe-lounge area adjacent to the indoor pool, one can choose from a diet or regular menu. The diet menu is much simpler than the one prepared for weight watchers in the main dining room.

The indoor pool is heated and large enough for serious swimmers; the outdoor pool is rather small. The Acapulco also houses Jacuzzis, showers, massage rooms (where several types of massages are offered), sauna, squash court, an indoor golf practice room, and two gym rooms, one with body building and muscle toning equipment and the other for stretching and exercising. Both gym rooms have resilient floors. There is no assistance with the use of the equip-

ment unless prearranged, but exercise bicycles, mini-trampoline, Nautilus, punching bag, free weights, and a rowing machine are at the guests' disposal. Available to all guests are stretching and toning lessons with music and an able instructor. Another free class is water gymnastics.

This is not a heavy-duty aerobics place. It is, however, very sports-oriented. Tennis is available on well-kept lighted courts at the hotel in the summer and at nearby indoor courts in winter. Hotel courts become an ice skating rink when temperatures drop.

The main winter event here is, of course, skiing (and après-skiing). The ski room in the hotel is fully equipped. This is the place for anything you want to buy, borrow, or have fixed that has to do with the sport. The guests' ski lockers are here, too—no traipsing on the Oriental carpets with drippy ski boots.

It is for good reason that the owners, Messrs. Andreas and Hansjurg Badrutt, are so proud of the hotel built by their great-grandfather in the appealing town of St. Moritz. As Hansjurg Badrutt explained, "We've managed to find the balance between old tradition and new ideas in combining the grand old hotel and the sleek, new Acapulco Spa." I agree.

GETTING THERE

To get to Badrutt's Palace, fly to Zurich and then take a commuter airline to St. Moritz. Or you can take a train directly from the airport or drive. It takes about 3 hours to motor from the Zurich airport.

RATING

Overall: More of a treat than a treatment

⊕ Luxury; service; sports

⊖ Weak aerobics program

Main thrust: The good life and recreational fitness

Cost: Very expensive

Grand Hotel Beau Rivage — Belmilon Beauty and Fitness Spa

INTERLAKEN
SWITZERLAND

ADDRESS
CH 3800
Interlaken
Switzerland
TELEPHONE
011-41-36-216272
(direct dial)
TELEX
923-122
CREDIT CARDS
All major

RECENTLY RENOVATED AND housing an intimate health and beauty spa, the Grand Hotel Beau Rivage would be a good choice for a week's respite after (or during) a European trip. It is situated between the amazingly clear lakes of Interlaken in the Bernese Oberland.

The hotel is attractive inside and out. Service is efficient and cordial. A lot of velvet and a touch of class have gone into the 100 rooms and suites. Up-to-date with modern bathrooms, direct-dial phone, mini-bars, and television with individual video systems and a film selection, most accommodations come with a view you'll want to take home with you. Looking out from the front rooms, you are face-to-face with the north wall of the Eiger or the majestic Jungfrau. In some rooms, such as #502, the owners wisely left the original wooden beams when they reno-vated. What an unusual room divider they make!

The hotel boasts two restaurants, a bar, a snack area (on the spa level), conference rooms, and a ballroom. *One quick tip:* Whether you're on the bed and breakfast plan, half board, or full board, *don't* have the continental breakfast in your room—enjoy the delicious buffet in the main dining room.

For those guests who do not wish to sign up for the "Beauty and Fitness Programme," there is a chance to partake of all good things on an a la carte basis, assuming the time slots are not all taken. In the Belmilon spa area, you will find a masseur, beautician, hairdresser, indoor swimming pool (big), sauna, solarium, and a fitness room (small but with adequate equipment). Nearby the hotel are tennis courts, golf, horseback riding, sailing, hiking, windsurfing, and skiing.

To welcome those taking part in the spa program and to facilitate interaction between the guests and the staff, there is a get-together party on the night of arrival. At that time you are given an idea of what's ahead.

The first day of pampering begins with a private consultation with the head beautician, who analyzes your skin, makes suggestions, and helps determine a program that will meet your specific needs. Included in the week's fee are three complete facials, dyeing of eyebrows and lashes, back peeling, manicure, pedicure, three massages, a hair wash, supervised daily gym exercises, and use of the swimming pool, sauna, and fitness room. The rose-colored robe you wear will be changed each day. Room and full board

. . . it is a sweet and gentle week for any woman. Maybe we owe ourselves that kind of thing at least once in our lifetime.

(diet or regular meals) are part of the spa plan. Also available are cellulite treatments, waxing, permanent hair removal, herb baths, body wraps, and lymph drainage.

In the spa program, clients are not pushed to maintain a regimen unless they themselves request it. Says directress Miss Gabriella, "We have a small operation, but very intimate. Maybe that's our big plus—it is very personal and friendly. A lot of people come here for a week every year.

"I have a lot of special equipment, but I am of the opinion that a machine cannot replace a practiced hand."

Although the hotel is called the Grand Hotel Beau Rivage, this is a small-scale operation. Still, it is a sweet and gentle week for any woman. Maybe we owe ourselves that kind of thing at least once in our lifetime. In addition, spouses and children are welcome and are certain to enjoy the pleasures of the area.

There is no dress code, but ties and jackets for men are preferred in the hotel dining rooms at dinner. For spa wear, pack a sweatsuit, exercise gear, shorts and slacks, plus appropriate shoes. Be prepared for unseasonal weather.

Go into Interlaken for delightful shopping, walks, and closer views of those clean, clear lakes; hike in the mountains. Or, take an exciting rail ride up and through the wonders of the Jungfrau, where you will be enchanted by the ice palace, waterfall, and the vistas. For that trip, you'll need warm clothing and sunglasses no matter what the season. Should you want further exercise, golfing, riding, surfing, sailing, tennis, and skiing can be arranged. Relaxing on the Lake Brienz paddle steamer is still another option. If you happen to be there in the summer, catch the William Tell Opera and the Swiss Open Air Museum.

GETTING THERE

Road and rail links make the Grand Hotel Beau Rivage easily accessible from Zurich, Berne, and Geneva airports.

RATING

Overall: A small spa (in a big hotel) oriented to healthy ladies who need to relax

⊕ Individual scheduling; tender loving care; idyllic setting

⊖ Small staff; scales heavily weighted on the beauty treatments side and light on fitness

Main thrust: Beauty

Cost: Moderate

Brenner's Park-Hotel and Spa

BADEN-BADEN
GERMANY

O H, YOU'RE BAD, BADEN-Baden. You make everyone's hometown seem so crass, so stressful, so dirty! We must live where we live, but we can choose where we visit. I choose genteel, relaxed, clean Baden-Baden, at the edge of the Black Forest in Germany. Splendid Brenner's Park-Hotel and Spa is right in the middle of town, situated in a beautiful park with a gurgling river. A memorable time awaits you there—all you need is a week to spend, money to burn, and good luck with the weather.

As you settle into the lap of luxury, you'll enjoy impeccable service, unique spa treatments, and the hotel's elegant public rooms, including a salon with wood-burning fireplace and live piano music, the dining room, a cozy piano bar, and the beauty salon.

Accommodations go from faultlessly decorated "normal" rooms (each differ-

ent) to a monumental royal layout. If your budget will bear it, ask for one of the suites that comes with an enormous bathroom replete with a sybaritic tub and real gold fixtures (including johnny mop), innumerable mirrored closets, antique furnishings, and your own safe. Insist on a panoramic view of the park and river. After a great night's sleep between the freshly pressed linen sheets and under a sumptuous down comforter, you'll awaken to the delights of the electronic control buttons for the usual calling of servants and the less usual raising and lowering of window louvers and awnings. Slipped under the door, you'll discover, is the "Suggestions of the Day" sheet, a poetic accounting of special events and attractions, the general spa classes scheduled, and menus for lunch and dinner. Outside the door you'll retrieve your newly shined shoes, left out the night before.

Reigning over your stay will be Brenner's debonair director, Herr Richard Schmidtz. He takes great pride in his realm—especially his own brainchild, Brenner's Spa, comprised of the Lancaster Beauty Spa and the Villa Stephanie–Black Forest Clinic. All buildings are connected, making for easy access from your rooms (with you possibly attired in one of the hotel's fluffy terry robes).

Once upon a time, Napoleon III stayed at the Villa Stephanie. Now it houses a mansion-like clinic known for its painstakingly complete medical checkups. Hydrotherapy, fango (mud) packs, oxygenation, massages, and medical treatments of all kinds are given there. The distinguished in-house doctors are assisted by capable aides

ADDRESS
Schillerstrasse 6
D7570 Baden-Baden
Germany
TELEPHONE
011-49-7221-3530
   (direct dial)
212-838-3110 (Leading
   Hotels of the World,
   in NY)
1-800-223-6800
   (Leading Hotels
   of the World, outside
   NY)
TELEX
0781261
TELEFAX
353-353
CREDIT CARDS
AE, DC

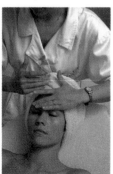

and up-to-the-minute technology. Plastic surgeons and other specialists are on call, and cell therapy is available. Clients live in the Villa or the hotel.

Personalized spa plans for beauty, fitness, and weight control (six or seven days) at the Lancaster Beauty Farm (again, this is in the hotel) consist of lodging, full board, and three hours of treatments or services each day: facials, body and face lymph drainage, manicure, medical pedicure, body massage, brush massage, makeup session, relaxation exercises, sauna, cellulite treatment, and/or water exercise (in the big indoor pool). After consultations, spa people receive a personal weekly schedule card.

In terms of space, decor, and equipment, the beauty rooms are fine. Unfortunately, the exercise rooms need more

equipment and the space is inadequate and unattractive.

Energetic spa-goers enjoy the tennis and nearby riding, golf, and hiking along scenic mountain trails—the icing on the Black Forest cake!

Other delights are horse racing, concerts, excursions to local vineyards, and buying the latest styles in fashion and jewelry. No one should miss the Casino, a Belle Epoch edifice of overwhelming proportions and knock-out decor. If you should lose your shirt, tie, and jacket (those, your passport, and a nominal fee get you in), you can always pop *au naturel* into one of the two public bathhouses—both very clean, with de-stressing, ache-reducing, fun-providing thermal mineral pools, whirlpools, and more. Swimsuits are required in some areas, but all *is* nothing at all in others.

I'm amazed at men and women who can be nude together and blasé at the same time.

You may ask, "Why is this ultimate hotel in Baden-Baden?" The answer, of course, is because of *the water*. Two thousand years ago, those clever Romans harnessed the radioactive mineral hot springs of Baden-Baden to whoosh and wash them into shape, easing the embarrassment and pain of obesity, rheumatism, arthritis, and other aches or maladies. Their grottos are still visible.

The mineral water is also delicious to drink, and what better food with which to drink it than the haute cuisine of Brenner's! For dieters, a "reduction menu" consisting of 1000 calories per day satisfies taste buds and appetites. *Sample lunch:* weight watchers' portions of melon cocktail, turbot on fennel, potatoes, salad, stewed apples. *Sample dinner:* consommé with herb dumplings, saddle of lamb with tarragon, French beans, mixed salad, raspberries. To cut down on everything but eliminate nothing is the philosophy of the dietitian. For special diets, an in-house doctor calls the shots.

High season starts in April and runs through November; there are no spa package plans for the end of August or the Christmas season. The hotel is open year-round. If you can't make it for the cherry blossoms and magnolia trees of spring and summer or the fine plumage of the high-toned guests of autumn, how about spending a white Christmas with nonstop festivities at the edge of the Black Forest?

By anyone's standards, Brenner's Park-Hotel and Spa guests rank way up there. An aura of wealth sweetens the air. Closets get filled with morning clothes, afternoon frocks, and evening outfits in addition to spa and sports wear. Safety deposit boxes bulge with jewelry and cash. The hotel (in fact, the whole town) has a reputation for drawing older people, but there is now a big push for younger fitness-and-fun seekers. I was amused to hear that the hotel keeps a computerized daily average of guests' ages.

For those who like to hear the guest list before accepting the invitation, Brenner's might include a repeat visit by a Rothschild or Gabor, Charles Percy, Brooke Astor, Madame Pompidou, Frank Sinatra, or European royalty.

There is so much to be said for Brenner's Park-Hotel. Reducing it to the ABC's of spadom:

A is for the overall mark it gets (add a " + ").
B is for beauty farm, Black Forest, and baths.
C is for care, "cure," cuisine, classy, nearby castles, Cuckoo Clocks, and the Casino.

GETTING THERE

Many roads lead to this last resort of grace and charm, the fastest being the Autobahn from Frankfurt (100 miles away) and Stuttgart (65 miles away). Strasbourg, France, lies 50 miles away.

RATING

Overall: Beauty treatments, water therapy, and more in a divine setting with every elegance

(+) Natural thermal mineral water; ambience; private park; beauty treatments; fine physicians and clinic (in-house); staff; proximity to the Black Forest

(−) Inadequate gyms and exercise equipment; needs more young blood

Main thrust: Relaxation, rejuvenation, and beautification of one's inner and outer landscapes

Cost: Expensive to very expensive

Champney's Health Farm

HERTFORDSHIRE ENGLAND

ADDRESS
Tring, Hertfordshire
HP23 6HY
England
TELEPHONE
011-44-2-86-3351
(front desk)
011-44-2-87-3155
(reservations)
CREDIT CARDS
AE, DC, Access, BC

HAD I SEEN HENRY HIG-gins' sweater, Mary Pop-pins' umbrella, Lady Win-demere's fan, Princess Di's tiara, and Sherlock Holmes' cap hanging together on the hall coatrack, I wouldn't have been surprised, because this place is such a wonderful melange of people, styles, architecture, and activities. Champney's at Tring—an old Rothschild mansion that looks as if it got caught in a time machine—now whirs and whirls with all kinds of Space-Age health, beauty, and exercise goings-on. No one here need worry about what the neighbors are saying: 170 acres of English countryside keep all outsiders at bay.

During the long, relaxing drive from gate to portico, the first thing that comes into view is the well-worn Victorian brick edifice. Unhappily, a second look reveals the new, architecturally uninspired wings. But not to worry. Ivy will soon cover those barren walls and add to the serenity of the typical English gardens and lovely old trees.

As soon as you step in the door, you feel comfortable here. The soft leather couches, beautiful wrought-iron stairwell, and high ceilings have the feel of home—or at least a dear friend's home.

There is a cocktail bar in the drawing room, completely set-up and tended. But guess what it doesn't serve. Right! The nonalcoholic frolic goes on until 11:00 P.M.

Meals, pleasant and delicious, are served in the simple, cheerful dining room, with a movable "wall" screening off the slim folk from those who are working at it. (Even the regular menu is calorie-counted.)

To the rear, an inviting terrace looks onto the gardens. A touch of surrealism is added by a gigantic chess set on the lawn. It's like something out of *Alice in Wonderland*. The pieces are two feet high, and one could square dance in the squares.

In the mansion, the guest accommodations (on the second floor) have high Old World ceilings and four-poster beds with long side drapes. The regular rooms in the new wings are very like everyday modern hotel rooms. For budgeters, lesser quarters without private bathrooms are available. Big spenders should ask for suite #56. The extra-large rooms there consist of a living-dining area with pink moire walls and plum carpeting, a bedroom with an elaborately draped bed, a sumptuous carpeted and marbled bathroom with a whirlpool tub, and a second bathroom with a stall shower. My guess is that this is better than your master wing back home. All eight suites and sev-

enty-two rooms fill up in summer, late spring, and early fall. The rest of the year is less busy.

If you are in the "stop smoking" program, you are assigned a nonsmoking guest room—no *ifs* or *ands*, and certainly no butts!

Down a corridor or two from the lobby, one finds the spa facilities. The big glassed-in pool is ideal for water exercise classes, and the whirlpool is a good place for relaxation. There are two excellent squash courts with ultra-resilient floors. Twelve pieces of Nautilus-type equipment are in the exercise room, in addition to free weights, a jogging machine, and exercise bicycles. There is always supervision and training assistance in the gym. A fitness assessment sheet with comprehensive data on progress made is kept on file for each guest.

Plenty of lights, music, and action make the classes in the extra-large aerobics room fun for all. There is even a portable floor for tap dancing sessions.

Men have their own wet spa area. Impressive and sequestered, it provides saunas, steam rooms and cabinets, baths (seaweed, pine, or Epsom salts), plunge facials, and massages of all types (including "slendertone," using an electrical current to relax and tone). Then there are high- and low-intensity solariums and reflexology, acupuncture, and chiropody treatments.

The new ladies' area is stunning. Between the beauty parlor offerings and those of the spa, name it and it's yours: manicures, pedicures, hair care, waxing, tinting, ear-piercing, aromatherapy, and all the services mentioned on the male spa list. Breast exams and Pap tests are also given.

Available to quench your thirst in all

Champney's— an old Rothschild mansion that looks as if it got caught in a time machine— now whirs and whirls with all kinds of Space-Age health, beauty, and exercise goings-on.

areas is Champney's special spa water.

In addition to the swimming pool and squash courts, sports enthusiasts will find three tennis courts, badminton, croquet, volleyball, a putting green (an eighteen-hole golf course is nearby), billiards, Ping-Pong, darts, guided hiking, brisk walks, and a "Start Jogging Safely" program.

For those who want to slow the pace, an artist reigns over daily painting, drawing, and pottery classes.

The mental health program consists of lifestyle consultations, lectures, yoga, and stress reduction sessions.

Aiming for prevention rather than cure, Champney's philosophy of positive health emphasizes a balanced mixture of exercise, relaxation, correct diet, and therapeutic treatments in a relaxed atmosphere.

Special two- to seven-day courses include: (1) "Lifestyle Planning," (2) "Stop Smoking," (3) "Self-hypnosis," (4) "Health and Beauty," (5) "Health and Fitness," (6) "Back Care."

On arrival, guests see a nurse-consultant and often a dietitian. A personalized daily program is devised that ensures no one will run the risk of doing the wrong things or overdoing the right things. Individual appointment cards are hung on the guest room doors each night, indicating the following day's fun and games.

Year-round, many people travel from all over the globe and go directly to Champney's from the London airports, somehow resisting the pull of the big city. However, if you can arrange to have the best of both worlds, take time for nearby London's theater, shopping, museums, monuments, and the changing of the guard.

Rain gear is essential in England, as are jackets and sweaters. One thing you don't have to bring to Champney's is rubber boots. They have many old pairs available for a walk on the wet side. In general, clothes are a secondary consideration. It is so relaxed no one will bat an eyelash if you wear your own bathrobe and slippers to dinner. Pack spa and swimwear, a sweatsuit, and exercise shoes.

GETTING THERE

The best option is to fly to London and have Champney's arrange for a car to pick you up. (Taxis are very dear, and drivers tend to get lost.) The drive takes over an hour. The (inexpensive) train ride from London takes you to Berhamsted station, and a car can pick you up there for a minimal fee for the 10-minute ride.

RATING

Overall: A finely tuned operation geared to make you that way, too

⊕ Aerobics and treatments; tap dancing; crafts room; good mix of people; atmosphere

⊖ Unstable weather

Main thrust: Weight loss and fitness program to prevent mental and physical deterioration

Cost: Moderate to expensive, depending on room and program

Hotel Des Iles Borromées — Centro Benessere

STRESA ITALY

STRESS TAKES A HOLIDAY IN Stresa.

There you are standing on your own little balcony of room 506 at the Hotel Des Iles Borromées in Stresa, Italy, looking out at the incomparable beauty of Lake Maggiore and the fairy-tale Borromean Islands. Then your gaze lingers on the snowy peaks of the Alps, a mere twenty minutes away. The sight is breathtaking, the clear air both relaxing and invigorating.

This Ciga chain hotel is run in exquisite fashion; the premises are impeccably kept. In the lobby the elegant seating areas, each with its own hue of blue, yellow, or wine brocade, centered on fine old Oriental carpets, overlook the glorious lake and the garden with trees pruned by talented landscape artists. The rounded etched glass windows reflect the sparkling sconces and chandeliers, white and gilt European mirrors, and marble floors that have felt the foot of many a dignitary and now know the soft step of sneakered spa-goers. A card room and a bar are at either end of this gracious area.

Guest accommodations (many with balconies) come with amenity packages, tasteful furnishings, television, mini-fridge, direct dial telephones, baths and showers to make the living easy. An elevator transports guests from room to spa, a delightful area with up-to-date machines and equipment.

Interviews with the "Centro Benessere" spa medical team and beautician initiate the week's program. (It is a good idea to bring your blood test results from home, thus saving the time it would take to have the test done there—these are serious people who insist on knowing your physical and behavioral status and patterns.) A very personalized fitness/beauty program and menu can then be worked out for you. From that point on, no decision-making is necessary on your part. You go at your own pace, following the schedule for each day, which is placed in your mailbox the night before. They even let you know what to wear for each activity! (The bathrobe and stylish green and white sweatsuit they supply will get lots of use. The sweatsuit is yours to keep.)

The typical spa day includes: *one and a half hours of physical activity* (aerobics, walking, stretching, and water exercise); *one and a half hours of beauty treatments* (personalized to include such needs as cellulite control, attention to special areas such as eyes or neck, massages, facials, beauty salon services, body wraps); *one-half hour of water treatments* (hygienic baths, Turkish bath, sauna, hydromassage).

ADDRESS
Corso Umberto 1, 67
28049 Stresa (Novara)
Italy
TELEPHONE
011-39-323-30431
  (direct to hotel)
011-39-323-32382
  (direct to spa)
1-800-221-2340 (Ciga
  hotels)
CREDIT CARDS
All major

174

Swimming (in indoor or outdoor pools), tennis, golf (nearby), hiking, skiing, water sports, jogging, special medical treatments, shopping, sightseeing, and lounging fill the noneating hours.

Thirty spa-goers can be accommodated, along with a la carte participants from the hotel.

Because most of the guests seem to be interested in beauty treatments, unwinding, getting a start on a healthier lifestyle, and enjoying the surroundings, you may find the aerobics classes sparsely attended. But then, there's something to be said for one-on-one training.

Weight control is part of the program for guests who desire to leave lighter. For those, temptation is lessened by emptying the guest's mini-fridge. So that dieters will not constantly be

counting pounds instead of calories, the scale is also carted away from the bathroom. Weighing in and out is enough, and at the end of the week the verdict is generally a good one.

Meals are available through room service or in the spa portion of the lovely dining room. Every weight watcher finds supplemental vitamin

pills and individually prepared menus at each meal—typed up, delicately framed, and personalized by name. Look around. The surprise is that everyone is eating something different. Perhaps once or twice a week, *lunch* will include meat, fish, or chicken. A sprinkling of yeast is always offered to help your digestion and complexion. Only at breakfast is coffee available; mineral waters and the soothing house "tea" suffice thereafter. You will be eating superbly creative, delectable meals served by handsomely uniformed waiters with a flourish and a smile.

Though it is open year-round, high season (that means higher prices) is the time to go—May, June, July, August, September (concert month), and October. Everything looks brighter when the sun shines. That's when you'll find the upper crust Continental types and celebrities (Ben Gazzara, assorted

Rockefellers and Vanderbilts, Sylvester Stallone—he loves those weight machines).

What to pack? Attractive resort clothes, jackets for men, swimwear, exercise and sports duds, personal items, and seasonal outerwear. Otherwise you'll be fine in the hotel bathrobe and spa sweatsuit.

One hour from Milan by car and one good clean breath away from Stresa shopping, the Hotel Des Iles Borromées–Centro Benessere ("Fitness Center") whispers, "What is your pleasure?" The staff will do its best to make you healthier and happier. They begin with loaded dice: the expansive, serene lake; the majestic Alps in view; superb hotel-spa facilities; proximity to Switzerland and the Lake Como region. *Bellissimo!*

GETTING THERE

From outside Italy, fly to Milan's Malpensa Airport. It will take about an hour to get to the hotel by car or cab. The drive is a delightful one through quaint villages and along the banks of what might be the most beautiful lake in the world. There is also train service from Milan to Stresa.

RATING

Overall: Lakeside hotel-spa with many special attractions, all good!

⊕ Staff; environment; ambience; beauty services; medical expertise; food; location

⊖ Not deep into aerobics, though they are available; not all technicians speak English.

Main thrust: A regimen for rejuvenation and healthy living under the expert eye of a fine medical and beauty team

Cost: Expensive

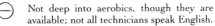

Grayshott Hall Health and Leisure Center

SURREY ENGLAND

ADDRESS
Grayshott, near
  Hindhead
GU26 6JJ
Surrey, England
TELEPHONE
011-44-42-873-4331
  (direct dial)
CREDIT CARDS
DC, AE, V, MC

A S ONE ENTERS GRAYSHOTT Hall, the words over the portal exhort *"Pax Intrantibus"* (loosely translated: "Peace to all who enter"). Leaving, one reads the motto *"Salus Exeuntibus"* (loosely translated: "Health to all who leave"). Those words are the core of Grayshott Hall's philosophy. To make sure no evil spirits gain entrance, there are gargoyles adorning the facade. You can feel assured that this is a protected and protective place.

Sitting serenely on 47 acres of lawn and gardens abutting 700 acres of National Trust land, this lovely spa is a mecca for those who seek peace and/or a healthier lifestyle. Here you can be as active or as inactive as you like. Formerly the home of Alfred Lord Tennyson and his wife, this old English mansion does make one want to wax poetical. The entry, nonsmoking and smoking parlors, and wood-paneled, leathered snooker room all have the look of genteel English country living—nothing flashy but lots of understated style. From the inside, one views the putting green, the par 3 golf course, the croquet and badminton areas, the formal English gardens, and the truly magnificent trees. As you go on to the spa area and the new wings, modern times set in. Although the architecture is sterile, the guest rooms are very comfortable and utilitarian—almost all have television, radios, direct dial telephones, and a private bathroom. A few guests still must use the shower down the hall. To put you at ease about your valuables, there is a wall safe in each of the eighty guest rooms and junior suites.

In the front parking lot, you are likely to see Rolls-Royces, Mercedeses, BMWs, and an occasional Jaguar or Porsche sitting alongside more plebian automobiles. This tells you a lot about the guest mix. Most guests come for five to six days; some just want to crash out for a few days without liquor, cigarettes, and the pressures of business and entertaining. About one-third are on a diet; fitness and health are the concern of the rest. All year round, young and old, men and women find Grayshott Hall to be a haven for concentrating on their own needs.

On arrival, you see a health consultant, who explains the routine, takes your history, blood pressure, and weight, and finds out why you're there. A personal program is then determined from the numerous services, treatments, and classes available. (Those on a severe diet will see a consultant each day thereafter.) A record card is kept on all guests, and individual program sched-

All year round, young and old, men and women find Grayshott Hall to be a haven for concentrating on their own needs.

ules are hung on guest room doors every night.

A wide range of medical attention is at your beck and call. There are visiting doctors twice a week, a psychiatrist on call, an osteopath and a physiotherapist there almost daily. That's above and beyond the capable resident staff.

Posted in the hallway is a sign-up board for golf (nine holes), tennis (one court), Ping-Pong, badminton, bridge, chess, croquet, and snooker. Other activities include excellent horseback riding, bicycling, hiking, and jogging. Doing laps in the indoor pool and then lazing in the whirlpool are still other options.

Unlike many American spas, the prevailing attitude in Grayshott's gym is noncompetitive. But it is a superb place for getting fit, and a highly popular spot. The minute you check out the equipment, you know why. There is a well-cushioned jogging machine with an angle upgrade feature, three exercise bicycles that constantly measure the rider's pulse rate, mini-trampoline, dumbbells, and six Hydra fitness machines. These are incredible! Working with hydraulic cylinders instead of weight stacks, they each stimulate opposing muscles simultaneously and the six apparatuses cover the body: (1) leg extension, (2) biceps-triceps, (3) seated leg press, (4) ab/ad for hips, (5) the butterfly for chest and back, (6) shoulder press. There is an instructor to show you how to use the machines. Super-sophisticated and user-friendly, these are great fitness tools that develop tone rather than muscle unless specifically programmed for the latter. Best of all, since your capabilities dictate the action, they're safe and simple.

Men and women instructors alternate for the classes in the gym and in the large, carpeted dance and stretching classroom. Along with instruction, encouragement is freely given, making everyone feel at least adequate.

On to treatments and beauty: Aromatherapy is a big thing (full body massage with essential oils on the acupuncture points for relaxation or stimulation), and reflexology is not far behind in popularity. Then there are seaweed and mud wraps, sauna, steam cabinets, cold water plunge, massages, facials, manicures, pedicures, hair care, makeup, sitz baths, blanket heat treatments for older bodies, hot wax and permanent hair removal, plus the *pièce de résistance*, the new-type solariums (tanning machines), which have "burners" rather than tubes. Though it sounds ominous, they are many degrees safer. As you can surmise, there is room after room designed just for pampering.

One large area is set aside for physiotherapy, where treatment is given for back problems, post-operative rehabilitation, and many illnesses.

Help for the unhappy: The stress reduction program is carried out by a well-trained and very caring medical staff. It has been structured by the highly regarded Stress Syndrome Foundation of London, whose clients include Margaret Thatcher and many members of the cabinet. The course takes three days and is an extra expenditure—but aren't you worth it?

The food at Grayshott is good but not great. There is a diet menu in the diet dining room, and there are calorie-counted choices in the main dining room. If you are on a diet program, you *must* eat in the diet room, where individualized, prescribed meals are served.

For evening pleasures, numerous board games are available, and there are interesting lectures on everything from feelings to futures. For other diversions, the surrounding area offers three major theaters, Windsor Castle, and Hampton Court. Sometime before, after, or during your visit, you'll want to stay in London (an hour's drive). After all, as those antique mugs say, "If you're tired of London, you're tired of life."

Dress at Grayshott Hall is very casual. Bathrobes take you everywhere within. Outside, you'll need sweaters, jackets, and rain gear. (This is England, you know.) Warm clothing is a must in winter (though, hallelujah, all rooms—public and private—are well heated). Casual wear and gifts can be purchased in the boutique.

It would be hard to imagine a guest leaving disgruntled. The director of the spa puts it this way: "Our program is totally flexible; each person is catered to individually. You can do as much or as little as you want, but we do have discipline if you desire it . . . Americans like to be programmed. We try to work it so the guests get the best out of their time here." How nice! How true!

GETTING THERE

Fly to London. Let the staff prearrange for a car service to pick you up at Heathrow for the hour-long trip to Grayshott. Or rent a car and drive. Don't take a cab—that'll take too many of the wrong pounds off of you.

RATING

Overall: Low in profile; high in performance

(+)   English countryside; large, well-trained staff; snooker; multifaceted program

(−)   No gourmet food; iffy weather

Main thrust: Healthy living through exercise, diet, and relaxation

Cost: Moderately expensive

King Ranch Health Spa and Fitness Resort

KING CITY, ONTARIO CANADA

ADDRESS
R.R. #2, King City, Ontario L0G 1K0 Canada
TELEPHONE
1-800-263-3272 (from U.S.)
1-416-833-8332 (outside U.S.)
CREDIT CARDS
MC, V

WITH THE DIRECTORS OF the famed Canyon Ranch as project consultants, the Koffler family of Canada undertook a grand and glorious enterprise—the building of an "international health resort" in Ontario. They amassed $38 million and, voilá, a formidable new entry into the spa sweepstakes appeared.

King Ranch Health Spa and Fitness Resort has a lot going for it. The well-rounded fitness, nutrition, and stress reduction programs operate on 177 acres of hills and meadows in low-slung modern buildings topped with silvery cedar shake roofs and interconnected by covered walkways. As seasons change, so do the opportunities for outdoor sports.

The 182,000 square feet indoors house the following facilities:

Clubhouse: Built for dining and "hanging out," the Clubhouse will ease you into a gentle mood with stone fireplaces, wood beams, and slate floors. Canadian crafts fill the nooks and crannies. Added attractions include the International Waters Bar (where you can drink the spring and mineral waters of the world), a demonstration kitchen, music room, theater, and boutique.

Guest accommodations: Featuring balconies or terraces, the 120 rooms and suites offer stylish, simple country comfort.

Spa: A remarkable 70,000-square-foot facility houses exercise studios; weight room; racquetball, squash, and tennis courts; swimming pool; and running track. The options for pampering include massages, herbal treatments, inhalation and relaxation treatments, steam room, sauna, whirlpools, skin care, and beauty salon services. Men and women have totally separate wet, locker, and lounge areas but share classrooms and pool.

The different seasons require different clothing, so come prepared for the weather. Always on the packing list: appropriate footwear for the various activities plus spa and swimwear, casual evening clothes, and sports gear.

Being close to Toronto allows for a quick excursion or two into town for a change of scene and a taste of Canadian city culture. On the way, you'll enjoy fascinating village antiques shops and local arts and crafts.

Whether you seek a spa experience for total relaxation of mind and body, to shape up (in both those categories), to get rid of bad habits and extra weight, or for pure play (tennis, cross-country skiing, etc.), the staff at King Ranch will help you without intruding.

My feelings about this spa are very positive. As the guest list and the programs grow, King Ranch Health Spa and Fitness Resort is sure to blossom into a beauty.

Grand Hotel & La Pace

MONTECATINI TERME
ITALY

ADDRESS
Viale della Torretta 1
51016 Montecatini
   Terme (Pistoia)
Italy
TELEPHONE
011-39-572-75801
   (direct dial)
212-838-3110 (Leading
   Hotels of the World,
   in NY)
1-800-223-6800
   (Leading Hotels
   of the World, outside
   NY)
TELEX
57004
CREDIT CARDS
All major

WHO SAYS YOU CAN'T have it all? Certainly not the residents of Montecatini Terme, Italy, resort spa of the czars and stars. They think they've got it, and they're willing to share it! The "all" is the H$_2$O—the magical, mystical waters that bubble up, hot and healthy, from deep within the earth, spewing forth rejuvenation, "natural medicine," and jolly good fun. The water is the top attraction. The Grand Hotel & La Pace (simply La Pace to those in the know) is the premier hotel, *the* place to be seen, and the only hotel in Montecatini that boasts its own in-house spa. They open April 1 and close October 31. If you go, try for September, when the fancy folks hang out.

What do you expect to find in a grand old European hotel? Elegant red and gold carpeting running down the marble staircase? This hotel has it! Intricately carved and frescoed ceilings in the dining room? They're here! Bathrooms the size of parlors? Just take a look. Real antique furniture patinaed with use and care? Yes, that too! The charm makes up for any little non-modern inconvenience one may encounter. The smartly appointed Old World lobby, indoor and outdoor pool, gardens, unusual guest rooms, and helpful staff with their courtly ways make life at the Grand Hotel & La Pace a joy. Only those who insist on antiseptic modern quarters might find fault.

Taking the waters—drinking and "bathing" in this unique resort town—has seduced people from all over for many centuries. Here the *public* drinking (water) houses and baths intrigue even the most stand-offish of the hotel guests. A short walk from the La Pace (which is right in town) takes you to three notable establishments: (1) The Excelsior—huge, new, spic-and-span modern—has every conceivable rejuvenating facility using water, volcanic mud, machines, ozone, etc.; studies indicate helpful effects on digestion, arthritis, liver, and body aches; (2) the Istituto Grotto, for extreme medical problems; (3) Tettuccio, a city in itself, devoted to drinking the healthful, toxin-purging waters, with seven fabulous fountain areas. Each elaborate station at Tettuccio dispenses four different waters of varying strengths. Miles and miles of Italian marble terraces, hundreds of imposing columns, restaurants, shopping arcades, a casino, manicured parks, a children's playground with attendants, frescoes, and fresh air boggle and soothe the mind at once. It is gorgeous! You must dress properly—no shorts or jeans. The water cure here is

183

While we were there, we ran into Sheik Ahmed Zaki al-Yamani of OPEC fame—and my mother told me that oil and water don't mix!

taken very seriously, and the government holds tight reins on the public "waterworks." Under no circumstances do you take too much, too little, too late, or too soon. That means everyone carries his prescription with him.

Bring your blood test results from home. They can do the tests here, but you'll lose a day—no one receives water-mud therapies without a blood analysis.

Called "The Natural Health Centre," the spa at the Hotel La Pace offers a week-long program that includes room, board, medical and diet conferences, the special drinking waters, exercise and stretching classes (very few takers in this category), tennis, plus one health or beauty treatment a day from the list that follows:

- *Underwater treatments:* massage, ozonized bath, mineral bath, mud bath, sauna, algae treatment, Jacuzzi
- *Manual treatments:* body and facial massages, beauty treatments, makeup, facial and body peels
- *Mud therapy:* complete mud bath (using the volcanic mud of Montecatini), anti-cellulite treatment, anti-psoriasis treatment, skin cleansing

In addition to this seven-day "Health and Fitness" plan, one can opt for a fourteen-day complete body flushing and pampering program.

Unfortunately, the spa space is unimpressive and practically devoid of decor. However, the technicians are capable and kind.

Diets are under the aegis of the nutritionist, who makes out personalized menus for each day, keeping in touch with every spa-goer throughout the week. Weight loss results from proper diet, certain naturally laxative waters and herbs, and loss of fluid through body wraps, which cause one to sweat out toxins. Excellent food (diet and otherwise) makes mealtimes totally enjoyable, whether you take them indoors, by the pool, or in your room.

Most guests are happy to drink the prescribed water, eat the designated food, and exert as little energy as possible. The staff will pat your back and rub your tummy while you diet, de-tox, stop smoking, and relax.

If you want to switch gears from inner needs to outside attractions, you might take a quick sightseeing trip to Florence, Siena, Pisa, Lucca, or Elba Island. The concierge will gladly make arrangements. However, why leave Montecatini? It is charming and pretty. One feels so safe there. Even the elderly (and there are many) stroll alone in the rolling parks or on the shaded sidewalks, surrounded by an invisible blanket of security.

Clothing considerations: Bring swimwear, personal items, seasonal resort wear, a sightseeing outfit and shoes, sports gear for tennis and golf (the Montecatini golf course overlooks Leonardo da Vinci's boyhood home). A bathrobe and sweatsuit are provided by the spa.

Many famous people have graced the halls of this hotel—Sophia Loren, Stephanie Powers, Saudi sheiks, suave Europeans, heads of state, recipients of trust funds. . . . While we were there, we ran into Sheik Ahmed Zaki al-Yamani of OPEC fame—*and my mother told me that oil and water don't mix*!

Mr. Pucci, the beguiling director of

La Pace, told me, "We specialize in personalization of treatment. We have to do it because, as you know, everyone is different. Something that is good for you may not be good for me." That kind of attitude, supplementing the incredible graciousness of the hotel, makes it a favorite of ours and the rest of the world. The Grand Hotel & La Pace is an extraordinary place where special people gather for extra-dividend water.

So . . . let it flow, let it flow, let it flow.

GETTING THERE

Fly to nearby Pisa or Florence. Complimentary transfers to the hotel take the stress out of arrivals and departures between La Pace and the airports.

RATING

Overall: Put a little spring (water, that is) in your step, especially if you are in the autumn of your life.

⊕ Wonderful hotel and spa staff; Old World ambience; delicious food; tension-reducing, health-giving natural thermal mineral water; the beauty of the Tuscan surroundings

⊖ Spa decor and size

Main thrust: Rejuvenation plus purging of toxins and worries

Cost: Moderately expensive

186

Clinic La Prairie

MONTREUX SWITZERLAND

ADDRESS
CH 1815 Clarens/
    Montreux
Switzerland
TELEPHONE
011-41-21-643311
    (direct dial)
212-772-8470 (in NY)
1-800-821-5254
    (outside NY)
TELEX
453172
CREDIT CARDS
None (and no personal
    checks)

A FRIEND OF OURS FROM Zurich raved about Clinic La Prairie. He had spent two holidays there to be pampered and to relax and revitalize. When asked why he had decided to go there, his wife (number two) replied, "Because he married me and I'm so much younger than he!" (We chuckled, but it had the ring of truth.) Our friend went on to tell us that he felt a great difference in his vitality and energy level for about five years after each visit. He is a very down-to-earth, credible person, so that's food for thought. However, I am far from convinced.

Founded by Dr. Paul Niehans about fifty years ago, the Clinic La Prairie has opened its doors to about 65,000 people from all over the world. Most come to drink of the fountain of youth, with high hopes of retarding the deterioration of their minds and bodies, increasing sexual vitality, and diminishing disorders of the respiratory and cardio-vascular systems. La Prairie accomplishes this (or tries to) with t.l.c. and C.L.T. (cellular living therapy).

Here's how it's done: Various organs of specially reared black sheep's fetuses are collected; cells from these are prepared in suspension; the ones from the organs you need are injected into a big muscle mass (generally your buttock). This is said to make your own cells in those organs regenerate, thus slowing down the aging process. Cell regeneration begins about four to eleven days after the injections, and the therapy generally attains its optimal effect three to four months later and lasts two to five years. "This is the unique action of fresh cells from the Clinic La Prairie. It remains the one biological and natural method of human revitalization," reports renowned heart transplant specialist Dr. Christiaan Barnard.

The difference between this technique and other cellular therapy methods is that here fresh and living cells are used—freeze-dried is taboo at La Prairie. There has never been a case of shock symptoms (though you may be experiencing one now) or allergic intolerance to the therapy, which is always given by a highly qualified medical team.

The course of treatment runs from Wednesday of one week to Tuesday of the next. However, for two days before that you must be around for a checkup, medical diagnosis, and procedure plan. Then on Wednesday you check into your room at La Prairie and have a consultation with the doctor. Thursday, fresh cells are prepared, allergy tests are given, and the cells are injected—all

Small and intimate, Clinic La Prairie is something between a charming hotel and a hospital.

this is done in your room. Friday and Saturday are devoted to rest and pampering by the staff, complimentary treatments, and visits to the beauty specialist for care of the face and body. On Sunday you bathe or shower, take a little walk, and do more of the above. The final tests are done on Monday; a complete survey is taken and advice given on how to eat and what to do for the next three months. Departure day is Tuesday. Added attractions available are acupuncture to refresh you and diminish wrinkles (no pain involved), a weight loss program, discounts on La Prairie products and chiropractic treatments—all in tandem with the injections.

Most people who come to La Prairie are healthy, though some do have specific health problems that they hope to cure. The treatment has been given to the young and the old. (It even seems to help retarded children). A ninety-year-old man had just finished his week of revitalization when we were there. Many return after a few years for more of the same. The ratio between men and women is about 50:50.

Small and intimate, Clinic La Prairie is something between a charming hotel and a hospital. It has a small terrace and garden and can dispense its treatment to twenty-four people at a time. The medical staff is excellent. In fact, everything seems high caliber; even the maids speak at least three languages so that they can help provide a friendly,

comfortable atmosphere while keeping the premises sparkling. Double rooms are available for couples or friends. Beautiful Swiss white-on-white bed linens are used. As you lie there between those crisp, clean sheets you can watch four movies a day in English on your television set or read the papers and magazines of your choice.

Meals are elegantly served and the choices are tempting. Bring your own nighties, robes, slippers, and resort wear.

By the way, for those two days after arrival and before the shots begin, there are many activities in the Montreux area to keep you entertained. Among them, the casino, shopping, cultural events, and architecture, to say nothing of the delights of Lake Geneva.

GETTING THERE

To get to Clinic La Prairie, fly to Geneva and then take a taxi or train to Clarens/Montreux. The La Prairie limousine service is available by prearrangement.

RATING

Overall: Elegant private hospital spa dispensing shots and high hopes to intrepid seekers of renewed youth

⊕ Pampering; knowledgeable medical staff; good beauty products; the possibility of slowing down the aging process and revitalizing your whole being

⊖ It costs a bundle; no proof the treatment actually works (not approved by Food and Drug Administration of the United States)

Main thrust: Rejuvenation of body and mind through live cell injections

Cost: Very very expensive

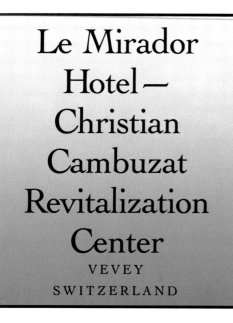

Le Mirador Hotel — Christian Cambuzat Revitalization Center

VEVEY

SWITZERLAND

LE MIRADOR HOTEL AND Christian Cambuzat Revitalization Center sits high on Mount Pelerin and seems to be watching over the entire Vaudois, Valais, Savoy Alps, and lovely Lake Geneva. The vista alone is a hard act to follow.

Not only is Le Mirador a top hotel with fine service and good food, it is also a notable business conference center and, most important, a spa with a world-wide reputation for its weight loss program. Add to this a fine sports and fitness complex and the package is a tidy one.

The hotel itself has an elegant lobby suitable for high tea with the grandest of the grande dames. Each of the 150 guest rooms and suites is different, but the ones I saw were all decorated styl-ishly with lush French fabrics. Sixty-four of the rooms are in the annex and are decorated in a more contemporary fashion. Apparently, many people prefer staying there, but not I. All rooms are equipped with television, mini-bar, direct dial telephone, and radio. The hotel gets top marks in several categories, but the Lancôme freebies and the snuggly bathrobes especially rate gold stars in my book.

If you are not on your way to the lower-level spa and fitness center wearing your turquoise bathrobe, you will probably be comfortably dressed in relaxed sports clothing as you traverse all areas of the hotel and grounds. Ties and jackets are requested for men at dinner, but this is not strictly enforced.

Even if you opt not to make your reservation as a client of the Christian Cambuzat Revitalization Clinic, you can choose your meals from a diet menu, sign up for massages, beauty and hair care, and use the facilities of the sports and fitness complex. Outstanding is the indoor-outdoor pool with its see-through cupola that allows sun rays to tan you. There is a game room (table tennis, pool, electronic games, etc.), sauna, tanning machine, and separate men's and women's exercise rooms (where there are attendants, but no instructors). The equipment in the two rather small rooms is about the same: free weights, exercise bicycles, slant boards, rowing machines, and Nautilus. Whirlpool baths, showers, and lockers are in adjoining rooms.

Amazing to all who survey or use it is the intricate, sophisticated indoor golf-training setup under the tutelage of the clever Scottish pro Hugh John Lennon.

ADDRESS
CH 1801 Mont Pelerin
  Vevey
Switzerland
TELEPHONE
021-921-35-35
  (Switzerland)
011-41-21-51-3535
  (from U.S.A.)
TELEX
451-149
CREDIT CARDS
AE, MC, VS, DC, CB,
  Eurocard

No group therapy here— it is all individual, with a view toward long-term benefits.

It's twenty-first-century golf instruction, using electronic and computer gadgetry with video replay equipment. It will tell you everything about your swing—the good, the bad, and the beautiful.

The tennis courts are a short walk away from the main building, and a pro is available. For walkers, hikers, and joggers, there are many well-marked scenic paths.

If you are serious about starting a long-range weight loss program, determined to stop or at least cut down on smoking or drinking, or if you feel the need to be detoxified and rejuvenated, you might want to give the Christian Cambuzat program a try. The clinic is part of the hotel and boasts many satisfied clients.

The spa process begins with an advance questionnaire sent to you to be filled out. On arrival there is an in-depth consultation to determine possible causes of stress, weight, or other health problems. A plan is then proposed for diet (800 to 1100 calories per day, generally), treatments and/or services, and relaxation activities and techniques. During the treatment period, many more one-on-one consultations will be scheduled. Very comprehensive records are kept; in fact, a memo of all food ordered by dieters is sent to the clinic each day. Spa guests who do not have a weight problem are simply kept on a nutritious diet.

Each person is prescribed a menu of services and treatments. No group therapy here—it is all individual, with a view toward long-term benefits. Medications are never given. The treatments use natural products and are all of the pampering variety: facials, facial peeling, skin care, herbal wraps, underwater massages, and body massages. Of course, manicures, pedicures, waxing, tinting, and permanent hair removal treatments are also available.

For relaxation and detoxification, at least three days of the program is necessary. Slimming requires two weeks or more, though the clinic will accept clients for shorter periods.

One of the techniques used for the smoking cessation program is to serve a brew of tea with secret ingredients twice a day. No amount of pleading will influence the brewmaster to reveal the recipe.

The Cambuzat program does not incorporate much physical activity, which should appeal to more sedentary types.

At the end of your stay, you will be presented with a routine to follow for the next ten days. After that, the assumption is that your psyche and body will keep you on the primrose path.

Below the hilltop perch of Le Mirador is the town of Vevey, with its life-size statue of former resident Charlie Chaplin, who is buried there. The Castle of Chillon is another attraction worth visiting, perhaps on the way to the famous casino in Montreux. Shopping is good here, as are the many cultural events that go on year-round.

With every curve you take on the winding road up to the top of Mont Pelerin, you will distance yourself from the hustle-bustle and cares of everyday life.

GETTING THERE

To get to Mont Pelerin and Le Mirador, fly to Geneva. If you prearrange it, a limousine from the hotel will meet you—it is a 50-minute drive. There is also a train from the Geneva airport to Vevey, which is 5 minutes from the hotel. The drive from Lausanne is 15 miles; from Montreux, 8 miles.

RATING

Overall: Spectacular view; elegant, quiet hotel with a special kind of spa

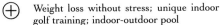 Weight loss without stress; unique indoor golf training; indoor-outdoor pool

⊖ No real aerobics program

Main thrust: Lifestyle change and weight loss

Cost: Expensive

Hotel Limmathof and Spa

BADEN SWITZERLAND

IF YOU WANT A SPA VACATION IN Europe and are on a bit of a budget, dump the blues (and the pills) and rejuvenate the natural thermal water way. The Limmathof in Baden, Switzerland, is a neighbor of the Veranahof/Staadhof (also in this book). It is also a good choice if you're wary of traveling alone; the place seems to give you a reassuring hug as you enter. I met a lovely American lady there who had just arrived for her fourth visit. She said she came back because she felt so welcome there, so unthreatened, and so peaceful—not a bad recommendation.

The outstanding physical feature of the Limmathof is the large outdoor terrace with its blue and white striped awning overlooking the Limmat River. Across the river is a charming building surrounded by masses of flowers. Sitting in a white lounge chair on that terrace at dusk, watching the lights turn Baden into a mini-wonderland, is an unforgettable experience.

The public rooms of the Limmathof are comfortable and cozy. They are also a little shabby. Time makes inroads on us all, unfortunately. If you can look past the worn upholstery you will see some beautiful antique tapestries and country furniture. The reception parlor area is large, but has an intimate atmosphere replete with flowers (roses when I visited). The dining room is small with walls decorated by well-carved cherubs and floral wreaths.

The guest rooms are nice, but far from spacious. If you go there, ask for an even-numbered room—they're on the river and the view is superb. That alone could make you feel better all over. Mrs. Boesch, the congenial assistant manager, was proud of the gifts that are given each guest: a lovely fruit basket and samples of Dr. Babor's makeup and natural skin products. When she showed me how to raise the electric bed for sitting up and reading, she beamed with pleasure. Every bed in the seventy-two rooms has this feature, with the control on the night table. Room 142 had a television, a bathroom with two sinks, and an authentic Biedermeier armoire.

The rooms can be had for a daily rate that includes continental breakfast, service, and taxes or with half board (two meals daily) or full board. All spa facilities are extra. The difference in rate for a twin-bedded room for two without and with full board is about $25 to $30 (U.S.) for each person.

The food at the Limmathof is more than adequate. It is tasty, there are enough choices, and the service is car-

ADDRESS
CH 5400 Baden Switzerland
TELEPHONE
011-41-56-22-6064
(direct dial)
TELEX
56088
CREDIT CARDS
All major

ing. There is also a diet menu available.

At least one visit to the very special (totally a la carte) *taverna* is a must. This is called the "Goldener Schussel Inn." History buffs and trivia gatherers will be interested to note that it was first mentioned in official records in the thirteenth century. Entering the *taverna* today is like a trip back in time. It is a wonderful room with beautiful wood, intricate paintings on ceiling panels, and superb historical touches.

The Limmathof Beauty Center is not spectacular, but it does offer Dr. Babor's natural makeup and skin products, manicures, facials, and pedicures.

The spa is reached by elevator from the guest rooms. There one has a choice of several thermal baths and a swimming pool. Each thermal bath is in a separate room or cubby: There is one for individual use, another for family use, one with jets, and still another with hot bubbling water. Massages, treatments for migraine and lesser headaches, and hydrotherapy (therapy using the thermal water as a tool) are given in other areas.

The hydrotherapy treatments fall into three categories: alternating hot and cold gushes, steam gushes, and flash gushes (for back and neck). If you're

still not sated and have some adventure in your soul, go for a fango pack, an ice pack, or hayseed pack (not just for country bumpkins). Last but not least are the Finnish and steam saunas.

Don't come here for aerobics. However, there is a sports center nearby for spa guests. The Limmathof can arrange for tennis games or instruction, badminton and squash, fishing, hiking, and horseback riding. You can enjoy concerts, lotto, and films in the hotel.

If you feel like leaving the hospitality and restful quality of the Limmathof for a while, take a shuttle bus or stroll to the old town of Baden. You'll find quaintness at every turn, and you'll enjoy perusing the boutiques, galleries, museums, and sidewalk cafes. If you're feeling touched by Lady Luck, stop by the casino. Just remember, the spa vacation should clean out your mind and body, not your bankbook.

The area near Baden offers many shopping and cultural opportunities. Zurich is just twenty minutes away. Also, there are half-day excursions available to other parts of Switzerland and the Black Forest in Germany. But even a walk along the footpaths of the Limmat River can be a delightful change of pace.

Don't expect to run into WWD's "Beautiful People" here. However, the clientele seem to be nice, genteel folks, mainly fifty and older, with a sprinkling of families.

Dinner is mildly dressy; the rest of the time casual clothes are worn. Don't forget your swimsuit and cap (required). Weather is tricky, so be prepared for chills in the summer on occasion, snow in the winter, and rain anytime.

The revitalizing and therapeutic effect of the natural hot thermal water is the main reason to choose this unpretentious spa-hotel with its special brand of charm.

GETTING THERE

The nearest airport to Baden is Zurich. A taxi, limo, or bus will get you to the spa from there in about 20 minutes.

RATING

Overall: A homey, comfy place to test the waters

⊕   Charm; water power

⊖   Not for the movers and shakers

Main thrust: Mineral springs—rejuvenating, revitalizing, relaxing, curative

Cost: Moderate

Hotel Nassauer Hof

WIESBADEN GERMANY

AMIDST CONCERTS, THEATER, opera, ballet, grand casino, summer festivals, and parks galore, the stately Nassauer Hof reigns supreme in the divine spa city of Wiesbaden, Germany. It beckons the business person and spa-goer interested in rejuvenation and prevention of deterioration with the help of water that bubbles up from the earth, laden with soothing, curative minerals—and is it ever *hot!* How hot is it? It's so hot that snow falling above the ground onto cement or marble around the springs does not stick for even a moment, making the winter cityscape reminiscent of a balding white-haired gentleman.

On the premises of the chic Nassauer Hof one encounters several restaurants (one rates a Michelin star), gardens, a pool fed by the hotel's own mineral spring, a full-service beauty salon, and a spa area that should be complete by the time you finish this sentence. I saw it in the bare bones stage, and it promises to be very handsome. The guest rooms and suites differ from each other, but all are outfitted for the sophisticated traveler.

Outside the hotel lie glorious parks to be enjoyed by walkers, tennis players, and joggers. (Every guest gets a charming jogging path card.)

While I was there, management expressed great enthusiasm about the innovative spa programs on the drawing board. Room and board (diet menus), beauty, aqua exercise classes, and treatments using the wonderful spring water, foot reflexology, massages, facials, lymph drainage, and use of the exercise room and equipment (minimal) will keep spa clients busy in a relaxed way for anything from one day to one week.

Sightseeing should be a part of every guest's schedule. The Rhine Valley trip is a must. Other options are shopping in the up-to-date boutiques or checking out the old section of town with its cobblestone streets and quaint public drinking well, where people come carrying pitchers to fill. Cultural events go on nonstop. That's true, too, of activity in the elegant casino. Then there's the Irish-Roman Bath House behind the hotel, with its huge pool and extensive massage and therapy facilities plus medical offices and staff—worth a look-see.

For Wiesbaden, you'll need sweats, swimwear, and city-type dinner clothes. What you forget, you can probably find in one of the shops that surround the hotel.

ADDRESS
Kaiser-Friedrich-Platz
3-4
6200 Wiesbaden
Germany
TELEPHONE
011-49-61-21-1330
212-838-3110
(Leading Hotels
of the World,
in NY)
1-800-223-6800
(Leading Hotels
of the World,
outside NY)
TELEX
4-186-847
TELEFAX
(06121) 133632
CREDIT CARDS
All major

GETTING THERE

Frequent trains and buses leave from Frankfort Airport to Wiesbaden stations. A cab will take you from there to the hotel (5 minutes). Driving from Frankfurt takes a quick ½ hour on the Autobahn. *A happy note to the business buff:* Keep this spa in mind as a place to stay if you have a trip planned for Frankfurt. The Nassauer Hof provides complimentary transportation to and from Frankfurt convention centers. Why not add a little water rejuvenation into your work schedule?

RATING

Overall: A captivating wonder-waterhole surrounded by a city of culture and style

⊕   Near the beautiful Rhine Valley; elegant hotel; fine staff; natural thermal mineral springs; classy city

⊖   Low mark in fitness program

Main thrust: Relaxation and revitalization using the earth's resources

Cost: Expensive

Grand Hotel Orologio

ABANO TERME
ITALY

ADDRESS
Viale delle Terme 66
35031 Abano Terme
Italy
TELEPHONE
011-39-49-66-9111
  (direct to hotel)
1-800-223-9868 (Utell
  reservations)
TELEX
OROROY 430254
CREDIT CARDS
All major

YOU NEED NOT CLUTTER UP your mind trying to remember what date it is when at the Grand Hotel Orologio in Abano Terme, Italy. Month, day, and year are spelled out charmingly in flowers in the sand garden in front of the entrance to this impressive colonnaded white structure with green shuttered windows.

Within its old and new wings (I preferred the old) are 260 guest accommodations, including one gigantic imperial suite, plus three restaurants, a bar with live music and dance floor, billiard room, card room, beauty salon (using all natural products), spa, three thermal mineral swimming pools, a par course, jogging track, two tennis courts, bicycle rental (tandem and regular), and convention facilities. However, fango (mud) is the featured attraction.

Abano's volcanic mud, mixed with its renowned natural thermal mineral spring water, simmers and matures behind the hotel in huge outdoor vats. After several months, it is used to heat away your body aches and pains. The treatment is called fango. Many guests feel spryer and younger as a result of the relaxing and sweating out of impurities.

For those who want to pay for the ultimate in privacy, thirteen suites have been fitted with incredible individual treatment rooms (in addition to wonderful modern bathrooms) fully tiled and equipped with sink, hydrotub, warming closet for towels and fango sheets, scale, a massage bed, and lots of valves, tubes, and hoses. The therapist comes to your suite and the routine begins:

1. Lie in bed fifteen minutes with fango pack applied.
2. Attendant washes you off with a hose.
3. Sit in ozone (bubbling) mineral bath ten minutes.
4. Rest on massage bed one-half hour (covered).
5. Luxuriate to massage by the therapist.

Whether you go through the procedure in private quarters or downstairs in the clinical-looking women's or men's spas, it must be done several mornings in order to get results. A doctor's prescription for the proper water and fango treatments (how much water, how long, temperature, etc.) is given to each guest after a consultation on arrival. Special equipment for (no shock) electrical therapy and cardiac treatment gets frequent use under the watchful eye of a specialist.

Afternoons can be spent in the spa taking inhalation treatment, a sauna, or steam bath; having beauty treatments; participating in sports activities; working out in the exercise equipment room; or shopping (for that exquisite piece of Italian jewelry).

Set back from the main street, the Orologio is an easy walk to anything Abano has to offer, but don't expect excitement . . . unless, of course, Sophia, Marcello, Silvana, or a delegation from the White House happens to be back in residence. (The soigné director of the hotel, Mr. Baccara, proudly showed us a delightful thank-you letter from President Ronald Reagan.)

Open from March till November, this fully air-conditioned hotel and spa has the added attraction of being close to Venice.

The Orologio has seven- to fourteen-day programs, which include room, two meals a day (the third is inexpensive), medical conference, and daily treatments. All esthetic services are available for a fee.

You might want to dress up a little for dinner. During the day, the bathrobe they provide plus your own swimming and sports gear will suffice. Bring a wrap and raincoat.

Why is the fango-tango music to some folks' ears? Supposedly, it relaxes and renews in addition to helping those suffering with arthritis, gout, sciatica, traumas from surgical operations, and many other afflictions. There are, however, contraindications—it's a no-no for pregnant women and people with certain chronic medical conditions. So it's not like chicken soup . . .

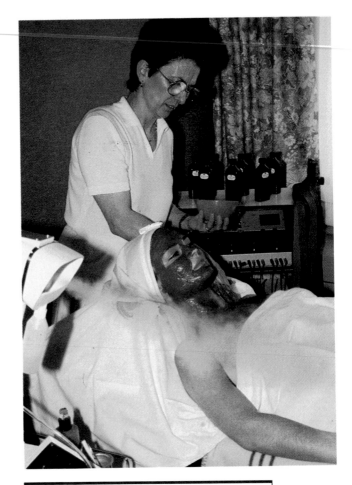

GETTING THERE

From Venice, Abano can be reached by bus and train. The drive takes about an hour.

RATING

Overall: A fancy fango establishment requiring time but very little physical effort

(+) Private water and fango therapy cabins in some suites; natural thermal/mineral water right from the source; treatments overseen by medical staff; Venice nearby; good value

(−) Not secluded; no aerobics program; not a lot of younger adults

Main thrust: Fango and hydro (mud and water) therapy for rejuvenation, relaxation, and release of pain

Cost: Moderate (unless you opt for a private treatment cabin)

Quellenhof Spa and Golf Hotel

BAD RAGAZ
SWITZERLAND

ADDRESS
CH 7310 Bad Ragaz
Switzerland
TELEPHONE
011-41-85-90111
(direct dial)
1-800-223-6800
(Leading Hotels
of the World)
TELEX
855897
CREDIT CARDS
AE

THE QUELLENHOF IS A FAIRY-land hotel-spa set in its own beautiful park at the foot of the Alps. One can easily visualize a royal carriage being met by footmen at the entrance. I was there in summer and found myself charmed by velvety grass, trees, flowers, and views; but even in the winter with a white blanket of snow, it must be serenely lovely. There is, in fact, a large winter garden—all glassed-in and a great place to lounge.

Although Germany's Chancellor Helmut Kohl had just been there prior to my visit and the Queen of Sweden was expected, the people we saw at the Quellenhof were not well known, but they were well dressed, well mannered, and probably well heeled. Most of them were fiftyish and older.

The public rooms of the hotel are quite grand. There is an elegant dining room with a fine continental menu and a diet menu, a cozy grill room, a bar, library, bridge room (which gets lots of use), beauty parlor, boutique (stodgy stuff), sauna, fitness room, solarium, thermal and regular swimming pools, conference rooms, and the adjoining therapeutic spa. A few steps away are the red clay–surfaced tennis courts and the hotel's renowned golf course. Jogging or walking in the hotel's private park is a must. Other choices for physical fitness are biking, mountaineering, and hiking, and for winter guests, downhill and cross-country skiing. The Quellenhof is open year-round.

Of all the sports, the main focus is on golf. The eighteen-hole course gets a standing ovation. Lovely to look at, delightful to play, it lures people from all over the world. And it's right there on the hotel grounds. Three golf pros are available for private lessons. In the winter, the course becomes a haven for cross-country skiers.

Because the hotel was built in 1869, it has the classical facade of the nineteenth century. Each room is distinctive, modern and efficient. You would be especially lucky to get a room like #318, a large corner room with a lovely view of the church spire and mountains. All of the 135 rooms and eight suites have television on request, radio, mini-bars, and direct dial telephones.

Everything about the five-star Quellenhof has an aura of elegant serenity. Manager Pierre Barrelet explains, "We are sort of an island. We try to give quite a lot of service in the traditional way of hostelry: modern in management, but in the old tradition." This is done with a staff of 140.

In the therapeutic department, early

morning exercise is open and free for all guests. Other activities have fees. Here's what's available: treatment pool and gymnasium, cardiovascular rehabilitation, first-class massages, passive physical therapy (including heat treatments for melting away subcutaneous fat layers (medical permission is required), fango and other body wraps, speech therapy, and pedicure. In addition to the thermal (34°C) and regular swimming pools, there are rooms for individual thermal baths. Natural therapeutic water seems to be especially helpful for rheumatism and various related complaints, but it is also used for prevention of ills and for general revitalization. If you are wary of any of these treatments, it might help to know that you are in very experienced hands. The special diagnostic departments, modern labs, and X-ray facilities are strictly no-nonsense. The medical team of fifteen doctors and attendants is impressive; the facilities squeaky clean and inviting.

Dress at the Quellenhof is quite proper: daytime dresses and slacks outfits for women, golf wear and jackets for men. Ties and jackets are the ticket

"We are sort of an island. We try to give quite a lot of service in the traditional way of hostelry: modern in management, but in the old tradition."

202

to the dining room at night. Of course, bring bathing suits, caps, and robes for the spa center.

There is no minimum stay. At various times of the year, weekly rates and special program rates are offered.

Small and quaint, the town of Bad Ragaz is delightful. There is a casino for a little extra fun. Nearby are numerous intriguing castles and villages. The tiny principality of Liechtenstein, with its notable art gallery, is only ten minutes away.

GETTING THERE

Getting to the Quellenhof is not difficult. The hotel will have a car meet you at the Zurich airport if you prearrange it; or there is a train from the airport every hour. Both take about an hour door-to-door. If you choose to rent a car and drive, the hotel is reached by the Munich–San Bernardino tunnel on the Lugano-Milan highway.

RATING

Overall: Lovely, but not lively

⊕ Fine golf course; naturally hot therapeutic waters; elegant ambience; superb medical staff

⊖ Very weak on workout

Main thrust: Mineral water: rejuvenating, revitalizing, relaxing, curative

Cost: Expensive

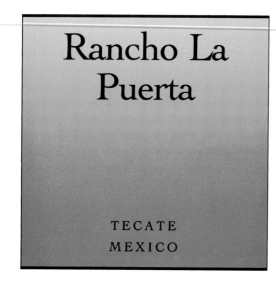

Rancho La Puerta

TECATE
MEXICO

"SOUTH OF THE BORDER" conjures up visions of old men taking a siesta under a lone shade tree with sombreros tilted to keep out the scorching sun . . . of the "Land of Mañana," where you put off for tomorrow what you could be doing today . . . of gringos wolfing down mamacita's sopapillas and chiles rellenos . . . of mariachi bands strumming and strolling. *Forget it!* Why be bothered taking a siesta when there's so much to do and the sun is gently beaming? Why put off anything for another day when today is such an important part of your week's stay? Why eat food designed for heartburn and bellyaches when you can have healthy, home-grown fare? Why shake a maraca when you can shake a leg with the fit people of all ages walking determinedly to their next activity to get even more fit.

Of course, Rancho La Puerta is just barely south of the border. The second you leave the United States you are mere minutes away from your spa vacation. Passing across the border is painless. A short ride through the tiny Mexican town of Tecate begins the transformation from uptight and untoned to loose, limber, and thinner.

One hundred and fifty guests have the use of the 150 acres at the edge of the Sierra Madres and under the spell of mystical Mount Cuchuma. Mexican-Colonial buildings line either side of the meandering paths of Tecate tiles. There are grape arbors and fruit trees, an organic garden, cacti, and flower beds. It is a totally down-to-earth place with holistic overtones, making the visitor aware of the importance of the balance between mind, body, and soul under the harmony of the sun, moon, and stars.

There is no pretension. *Casual* is the key word. People let down their defenses and are kids again. (Incidentally, kids are allowed, but there is a minimum stay of a week for everyone.)

The *only* television is in the combination billiard/Ping-Pong/reading/rec room. The screen is big, but the reception is poor. You don't mind. Neither will you care that there's no telephone in the guest rooms. More than compensating for the lack of a few amenities are the great style of the place, the affordability, the fitness program, and the utter informality.

Accommodations range from stunning "Villa Suites" and "Villa Studios"—with their own gardens, courts, pools and saunas, living room (sometimes a dining room), fireplace, large bathroom, and kitchenette—down

ADDRESS
Tecate, Baja California
Mexico
RESERVATIONS
3085 Reynard Way
San Diego, California
  92103
TELEPHONE
1-800-422-7565
  (California)
1-800-443-7565 (USA)
619-294-8504
CREDIT CARDS
None

to cozy "Haciendas" with everything except the kitchenette, and studio bedroom-plus-bath units called "Rancheros." All have tub and shower, radio, and flashlights (a help in finding your way home after the nightly movie, lecture, zingo bingo, or gab fest). Many units have two bedrooms. Brightly colored native arts and crafts decorate every room. It's quite appealing. If you can't bear to leave it all behind, shop at the spa's Mercado Boutique. Merchandise there is well chosen and well priced.

When you arrive at Rancho La Puerta, you are handed a map of the place and a schedule of activities. If you're like me, you'll have an easier time determining your activity program than deciphering the map. At any rate,

just figure out where you go to sign up for the "extra" services and treatments (massages, facials, herbal wraps, etc.) and do it pronto. Otherwise you may find yourself without a time slot for a bit of pampering by the excellent staff.

As a new guest, you dare not say anything against "RLaP" to one of the return guests (75 percent). They all seem very personally involved and protective. However, by the second day, you will be completely accepted as one of the family (if you put forth even the slightest effort), and then you can partake of the "in group" badinage.

Throughout the day, four or five classes are offered per hour. They include the usual aerobics, stretching, yoga, water exercise, weight training,

Exercise equipment housed in another super-size gym consists of thirty-five CamStar stations, treadmills, Exercycles, free weights, and rowing machine. Here, again, you look out onto the fascinating surroundings.

Brick columns, stone steps, and the ever present Tecate tiles decorate the main pool area. Nearby there's a volleyball court with a basketball hoop. Additional sports opportunities are provided by six lighted tennis courts, five other swimming pools, and a jogging trail around the vineyard. For quieter times, you can wander over to the library and ask the librarian to help you choose appropriate reading material to peruse while cocooned in one of the inviting hammocks.

The idea is to combine treatment, therapies, exercise, and relaxation to bring about beneficial changes in the body and mind. A morning hike in exhilarating air is a good start. With so many lovely mountain trails to follow, what may sound like a chore ends being a pleasure. Less taxing pastimes at Rancho La Puerta include massages, facials, herbal wraps, and scalp treatments at the separate but equal men's and women's health and spa centers. Robes and slippers are provided to wear from one pampering event to the next.

Just walking into the beauty salon is a treat. It is filled with joyous colors and happy faces on each of its three high-ceilinged levels.

Finally, there are private sites where you need not bother with your bathrobe, slippers, or any other apparel while soaking up the sun's rays.

At Rancho La Puerta most of the

and dance, plus the unusual CPR (cardio-pulmonary resuscitation) training, silk-painting, juggling, and "inner journey" (centering your energy and deflecting stress). Go to as many as you desire. Like your room and board, they are included in your package rate.

Each aerobics gym has a unique look—so special that every one deserves a star: Of the six, my favorites are: "The Pine Tree Gym," encased by windows, with deer wandering by; "The Seven Trees Gym," with welcoming mats covering the floor and mirror and windowed walls; and the giant Cuchuma Gym, which features a cathedral ceiling hung with wrought iron chandeliers, stone walls, and a crackling fireplace. Not a bad place to do yoga at dawn.

food is spa-grown and really fresh. One need not worry about getting the *turista* trots—everything is sterilized, pasteurized, sanitized, and probably baptized. Suggested caloric intake is 1000 to 1200 a day. Low fat, low salt, no white flour, and no white sugar ensure that the basically vegetarian menus served in the new Spanish-Colonial restaurant are pure and healthy. Because breakfasts and lunches are buffet style, you must exercise self-discipline and *not* ask for that second helping of pineapple or whatever. Per serving calorie signs are posted at each station. Dinner is served at your table. It's come as you are, sit where you want. (Tables seat from two to ten.) There are always choices on the menu for those who want to maintain their weight or even gain (such as the tri-athletes who come here and use the week to get their minds together as they perfect their bodies).

Coffee is served all day. Smoking is permitted outdoors only. No alcohol anywhere. At 5:00, juice cocktails and hors d'oeuvres are served.

Programs start on Saturdays and are for women only, except for the special couples weeks. Everyone works out her own schedule and then works at her own level. People are friendly and attractive. Because of the moderate price, housewives and working women are able to come and mingle with the sprinkling of celebrities and even heads of state. It's all very convivial.

For early morning walks all year round and brief winter chills, bring a warm jacket, cap, and gloves along with your spa and swimwear, sports clothes, and hiking gear. Proper footwear for all activities is important. Dinner dress is very informal. After nightfall, a light wrap or jacket will come in handy. There is a do-it-yourself laundry room complete with soaps and such.

When I met Alex Szekely, who proudly runs this beautiful, bountiful spa as well as the renowned Golden Door, I commented on how exquisite the air was and how incomparable the climate. "Of course," he said. "That's why my folks chose this particular spot for the Rancho La Puerta. The real world is awash in smog, stress, and strain." Meanwhile, back at the rancho . . . good air, good vibes, good living.

GETTING THERE

The best way to get to Rancho La Puerta is to fly to San Diego and then take a courtesy charter bus for the 1½-hour trip to Tecate. If driving yourself, take I-5 to the Highway 94 turnoff. Drive east on 94 for 40 miles, then take 188 to Tecate's border (open 6:00 A.M. to 12:00 midnight). Cross the border and turn right at second stoplight. After 3 miles you'll see the turnoff for Rancho La Puerta. *Don't forget that you'll need proof of citizenship at the border.*

RATING

Overall: A Mexican stand-out of a spa

⊕ Unique general look; well-done classes; wonderful weather; affordable

⊖ Hard on those without self-discipline

Main thrust: Fitting in fitness between the sun's rays

Cost: Moderate to moderately expensive

Hotel Ritz — Health Club Ritz

PARIS

FRANCE

"WHEN I DREAM OF afterlife in heaven, the action always takes place at the Paris Ritz," Ernest Hemingway once wrote.

As we all know, Hemingway really knew his way around. The Ritz remained on the top of his list of life's pleasures and heads the lists of many other notorious bon vivants. Now the divine action at the Ritz has advanced a further step with the opening of a heavenly and wondrous spa called The Ritz Health Club. If you opt for opulence, this is the place for you.

Situated majestically on one of Paris's loveliest sites, the Place Vendôme, Hotel Ritz sends its rarefied air wafting out to greet you, along with impeccably costumed doormen. Everything reeks of the regal: the awnings, the imposing door, the huge column dedicated to Napoleon Bonaparte, the spread of the elegant building, the chic men and women making their entrances and exits.

Once inside, you see a small reception area, designed to discourage any loitering by mere sightseers. A long wide central passageway (where high tea is served) with oyster white walls, deep-colored, lush carpeting and drapery, elegant furniture, and stately marble columns leads to salons, restaurants, and bars. A small news kiosk sits discreetly at one end.

Two Michelin stars have been bestowed on the Espadon, one of the two beautiful restaurants. The Ritz bars are world-famous gathering spots. For inveterate shoppers, the "Temptation Walk" draws like a magnet. Vitrine after vitrine of French fantasies make the stroll to the far side of the hotel a delight.

Rich fabrics and fine European furniture decorate the 45 guest suites and 143 rooms. Doors are padded against noise; the lighting everywhere flatters everyone; CNN is always on tap for the latest news; *private* telephone lines need only be requested; and beds are dreamy places. Bathrooms continue the Ritz look—marble walls, an amenities package to be cherished, swans-head faucet handles (often in gold) on all fixtures, bathrobes that stay fluffy no matter how many times they've been washed, oversize bathtubs, and endless mirrors.

Directly from your room via elevator, you descend to zillionaire Ritz owner M. Al-Fayed's newest triumph—the spa, used exclusively by guests of the hotel and Ritz Health Club members. There are no separate fees for admission or use of the exercise equipment,

ADDRESS
15 Place Vendôme
75041 Paris
France
TELEPHONE
011-33-14-260-3830
212-838-3110 (Leading
  Hotels of the World,
  in NY)
1-800-223-6800
  (Leading Hotels of
  the World, outside
  NY)
TELEX MESSAGES
RITZ MSG 220 262-
  RITZMSG
TELEX
  RESERVATIONS
RITZRES 670 112
FAX
(001) 33-14-260-2371
CREDIT CARDS
All major

inch exhibits taste and flair. Especially spectacular is the swimming pool. First of all, it is huge. Murals surround the area, with balconies jutting out romantically here and there. At one end is a cupola-ceilinged snack area. Mermaids permanently adorn the bottom of the pool, music plays and lights dance on the water, the trompe l'oeil sky above it is full of sensual clouds, and a double-arc staircase combines with giant pillars for grand entrances. Even if you don't swim, take a peek.

Basic colors of terra cotta (on exquisitely painted walls), beige, and gray keep the atmosphere subdued throughout.

Distinct men's and women's wet areas separate the sexes, but male and female mingle in the large exercise equipment room. (There is also a small room for women who want to work out privately.) Of highest quality and newest design, the Swiss-made machines work like fine watches. All treatment rooms enjoy the luxury of state-of-the-art equipment.

No holds were barred when the squash court was constructed. The King of Morocco loves the game and spends chunks of time there happily bashing the ball.

C'est le spa magnifique!

Smoking is prohibited throughout the spa. Shirts must be worn when exercising. No one wanders about unaccompanied. The action goes on from 7:00 A.M. until 10:00 P.M. daily.

Also underground is the new Ritz Cooking School. It's an elaborate setup, but don't enroll unless your body is immune to sauces and such. Still, you might want to join a session that

pool, Jacuzzis, steam room, sauna, squash court, resting room with ionized air and water beds, or locker areas. Pay as you go for massages, facials, nail and hair care, hydrotherapy, jet spray, ozone (oxygen) therapy, UVA (ultraviolet) treatments (for body, bust, or face), pressure therapy for legs, body peels and wraps. Complete spa plans can be arranged individually.

Decor in the spa appears to be classical Greek with a modern slant. Every

teaches the precise meaning of "cook until done" and other cookbook vagaries. This Ecole de Gastronomie Française Ritz teaches health-minded people a good way to cook cut fresh vegetables.

The Hotel Ritz has been the temporary home of just about every VIP you can think of, though there's nothing homey about it. The staff is superb and service is excellent, but no one will make you feel that you're among old pals. That's the price you pay for the big price you pay. Still, it's great fun to be one of the swells for even a brief moment in one's life.

Paris is the most beautiful city in the world. Treat yourself to a walk along the Seine River, a few hours at the Louvre and the Musée d'Orsay, a shopping spree on the Faubourg Saint Ho-

noré, an excursion to Versailles or Giverney. Then go where kings work out the kinks at that jewel of a spa at the Ritz.

GETTING THERE

Fly to Paris. If you want to be met by a Ritz limousine (and you don't mind the expense), prearrange this with your travel agent or the hotel. Otherwise, take a cab. All drivers know where it is. Remember to pronounce Ritz as though it were spelled "Reetz."

RATING

Overall: A spa for those who want fitness and beauty treatments to include the red carpet treatment

⊕   Extremely elegant; up-to-the-minute spa equipment; great swimming pool; top Paris location

⊖   No spa food program; can be intimidating; so expensive you may find that all your bucks stop here

Main thrust: Ritzy rejuvenation

Cost: Very very expensive

210

The Royal Hotel—Better Living Institute

EVIAN-LES-BAINS
FRANCE

ADDRESS
Rive Sud du Lac de
   Genève
74500 Evian-Les-Bains
France
TELEPHONE
011-33-5075-1400
   (direct dial)
212-838-3110 (Leading
   Hotels of the World,
   in NY)
1-800-223-6800
   (Leading Hotels of
   the World, outside
   NY)
TELEX
385 759 CASIROY
FAX
33-5075-3840
CREDIT CARDS
AE, CB, V, DC,
   Eurocard

THE GOOD NEWS ABOUT THE Royal is that it was built for the King of England by his loving Mom. It seems she spent the summers nearby and wanted her son to frolic close at hand. The bad news is that he never came. Well, that was before 1907. More recently, the Aga Khan made the Royal Hotel his home away from home. What is now the spa area was once his private apartment.

You've heard of Evian, the water; well, this is in Evian, the place. The conglomerate that makes us feel cool and sophisticated drinking Evian water also owns this cool and sophisticated oasis.

The winding road up from the town of Evian and Lake Geneva leads to proud green and white arches. Past them, you enter the hotel garden, lush with phenomenal blue spruce, chestnut, redwood, beech, and magnolia trees.

Elegance is in the air from the moment you arrive, and you know this is not an ordinary spa hotel. The blue and white of the lobby and sitting room reflect the water of the lake below and soothe the soul. There is a large adjoining terrace with a larger-than-life view of both Lake Geneva and the mountains.

Except during the months of December and January, when the hotel is closed, you have your pick of 158 rooms and suites. The normal guest room are . . . well, normal. I was expecting something knock-out. They do all have television (with closed circuit movies), radio, telephone, and a good view. My suggestion is to go for broke—go for a suite. They are sumptuous. Number 321 is an Art Deco delight.

Guests can register for bed and breakfast, half board or full board, and then eat in any of several delightful spots. The main dining room, with its lovely (original) painted ceiling, antique chairs adorned with carved grapes, and flattering lighting, has great style. For the dieters, the beautifully canopied La Rontonde is the watering spot. One unusual treat is that on the one-half or full board you are allowed to take your dinner at the resplendent Casino Royal in Evian, which is part of the same shootin' match called the Royal Club Evian. Wherever and whatever you eat, you're in France, so you'll eat well.

Where the Aga Khan used to play, you can now work out. The elevator takes you to the "Institut Mieux-Vivre"—Better Living Institute (or more simply stated, the superb spa area). There is a boutique and beauty parlor (all the usuals) for the faint at

heart, and numerous facility choices for the heavy of body. Stretching and jazzercize sessions are given in the equipment and exercise rooms. NOTE: You'll need aerobic shoes because the floors are hard.

Most of one entire floor has become a hydrotherapy heaven. Awesome, technologically advanced equipment is used to facilitate relaxation and esthetic improvement in several rooms with exotic names—and it's done with the special waters of Evian. The facilities include a sauna, solarium (tanning machine), beauty care, cabins for massages, facials, wraps, electrolysis, a gigantic Jacuzzi, steam box (without wet heat, but with ozone and oxygen), and, believe it or not, a "laser beam" room where a laser is focused onto

spots of the body for healing. For a respite from all that hard work, go over to the *salon de repose* to rest in a summer house with lovely murals of delicate Art Deco ladies.

Pretty in peach, the spa area invites you to tread softly in your gold-crested white bathrobe. The staff seems quietly frantic. Trying to get all the clients into and out of the right rooms at the right times can be difficult when the spa is busy and the clients are demanding.

For jogging, walking, or watching the deer go by, the par course deviates from the usual facility. You run a little, exercise on the equipment when you come to it, run a little more, and so on. Just be careful where you step—the deer, you know. Other sports from which to choose are paddle tennis,

You've heard of Evian, the water; well, this is Evian, the place.

212

racquet tennis (fine lighted courts), pitch and putt, archery with instruction, hiking with guides. In winter, cross-country and alpine skiing excursions are available.

Swimming at The Royal is a major sport in a major pool alongside colorful umbrellas shading careful sun worshippers. Formal gardens somehow lend a nice touch to the informality.

The Royal owns the golf course nearby and will arrange games.

The "Better Living Institute" (spa) has cooked up a synergy of therapies geared to revitalize the tired, overworked body and unabashedly call the combination "the Biological Cure." I'll tell you what they use, but you'd better have your medical dictionary handy. The list: hyperoxygenation, procaine, phytotherapy, neural therapy, homeopathy, aromatherapy, sophrology, lasers, pulsating short waves, and a soft medicine for wrinkles, falling hair, poorly distributed weight, and phlebology.

Six- or seven-day minimums are required to enter the "Dietetic Program," the "Better Living Program," or the "Super Better Living Program" for ladies and gentlemen. Each of these includes a different assortment of treatments, classes, and exercises (including reaching deep into your pockets). You'll see a doctor or dietitian in the beginning to set your program down in the snazzy red personal agenda (with gold insignia, of course) provided. By the way, the belief here is that slow dieting—you eat up to 1500 calories a day—is the way to go.

"Facial Program" and a "Cellular Treatment Program" are also available.

Not necessarily on the program, but around the hotel are classy, savvy people of all ages, seemingly self-assured and having fun. Clothing requirements are sports and spa attire (don't bother bringing a bathrobe—you'll wear theirs). It's ties and jackets at night for men, and chic resort clothes for women.

The casino is a major draw at night. It is a festive-looking building, all lit up inside and out. Evian's proximity to the lake makes it a fetching place to browse and carouse, especially in May, when the Music Festival is on. Incidentally, everyone in Evian speaks English.

GETTING THERE

Fly to Geneva, connect with bus, taxi, rent-a-car, or helicopter. (There is a helipad right at the hotel.) The drive from Geneva is 28 miles. There is also a train from Paris.

RATING

Overall: The royal treatment for sybaritic spa-goers

⊕ Elegance; archery; hydrotherapy; pampering; tennis and golf; the casino; the food

⊖ An aloof quality, sketchy aerobics program

Main thrust: Revitalization, rejuvenation, and beauty, using Evian waters and unique equipment

Cost: Expensive

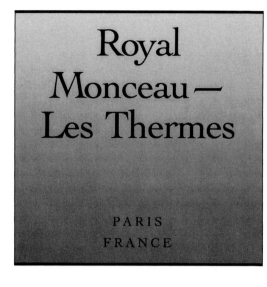

Royal Monceau — Les Thermes

PARIS
FRANCE

ADDRESS
35 Avenue Hoche
75008 Paris
France
TELEPHONE
011-33-14-5619800
  (hotel)
011-33-14-2250666
  (direct to spa)
1-800-221-2340 (Ciga
  hotels)
TELEX
650361 ROYAL
FAX
33-1-45-63-2893
CREDIT CARDS
All major

YOU'RE PROBABLY NOT GO-ing to choose Paris as a weight loss destination, but you might enjoy staying at a truly lovely hotel with a beautiful new spa where you could exercise, be pampered, enjoy restorative treatments, swim, and eat an occasional low-cal (but high-taste) meal. The Royal Monceau provides all that and more to the savvy visitor.

Although the hotel sits serenely on an elegant residential street, it is only a stone's throw from the Arc de Triomphe, the Champs Elysées, and the chic boutiques of Faubourg Saint Honoré. The hubbub of Paris is so near and yet so far.

In the dignified lobby, amid antique French furniture and marble columns, you're likely to see refined travelers and business people from Italy, France, Japan, the United States, and the Arab nations. Conversations are as muted as the carpets are soft. You can count on your appetite being well served in the cheery, trellised Italian restaurant or in the delightful circular French garden restaurant, both of which are off the lobby.

Silk upholstered walls add to the luxury of the 180 stylish guest rooms and forty suites, each with well-equipped baths, amenities packages, air-conditioning, television (including CNN), telephone, mini-bar and twenty-four-hour video films. The rooms are small, but everything you need is there, and the caliber of the service makes up for the modest size of the accommodation.

Now for the spa, Les Thermes. It is enjoyed equally by men and women, who have their respective Roman-inspired wet areas with steam room and sauna but share the body building room (with free weights, the French version of Nautilus, and other machines), the exercise room (exercise bicycles, treadmill, and a couple of smaller body-toning machines), and the classroom for aerobic dancing, stretching, and toning. A garden view enhances the workout experience; so does the dynamic style of the instructors. (I took a class that was more fun than most due to innovative moves done to lively music.)

Treatments and services include water therapy, massages, cellular therapy, lymph drainage, UVA high-pressure tanning (check with your doctor before engaging in this one), every beauty service, and facials using pricey La Prairie products. The Les Thermes personnel count is not high, but then neither is the guest participation.

The heated pool, though not big, keeps lap swimmers satisfied because of the inverted jet stream that pushes against the body. Alongside the free-form pool, lounge area, and garden, the spa restaurant serves delectable food with a distinct French flair. It's hard to believe the calorie count is low when the palate pleasure is so high.

One- to three-day spa plans are available that include room and services but no food. Though guests of the hotel may use the exercise equipment, wet areas, and pool without a fee, treatments and services are extra. When I was there, the spa area was uncrowded and serene. Smoking is allowed, but few, if any, guests light up.

The Royal Monceau is a rather formal hotel. Guests dress stylishly. You'll need seasonal clothes plus an all-weather coat (with layers underneath when it's cold). Comfortable walking shoes are a must. For Les Thermes, pack swimwear and spa gear. Your room comes with a bathrobe and an upscale amenities package.

With Paris at your feet, the Royal Monceau's Les Thermes is a heady choice for a city spa experience.

GETTING THERE

Fly to Paris. Prearrange pickup by the hotel (expensive) or take a cab from the airport. Have the name and address of the hotel written down for the driver.

RATING

Overall: A low-key, high-style city spa

$\oplus$ Luxury surroundings; Paris setting; beauty services and treatments

$\ominus$ No diet program; many of the staff at the spa speak little English

Main thrust: Soothing the highly charged traveler

Cost: Moderately expensive to expensive

The Sans Souci Hotel Club and Spa

OCHO RIOS
JAMAICA

ADDRESS
P.O. Box 103
Ocho Rios
Jamaica
TELEPHONE
809-974-2353 (direct)
1-800-237-3237
   (Elegant Resorts of
   Jamaica)
TELEX
7496
CREDIT CARDS
V, MC, AE, Key Card

"WITHOUT A CARE"—that's the translation of *sans souci*—and that's how you'll be once you're settled into this captivating hillside resort-spa that rises from the Caribbean Sea outside Ocho Rios. How could anyone feel troubled while surrounded by a beautiful, gracious Jamaican staff, lush green landscape, blue sea (and even bluer sky), baby pink buildings, perfect pearly beach, red hot Rastafarian rhythms, and the civilized British atmosphere? You cannot help but fall under this resort's tropical spell.

Much of Charlie's Spa (as it's informally called) at Sans Souci is al fresco—there are open-sided pavilions and gazebos for dining, massages, classes in stretching/toning/yoga, working out with equipment. The soothing sights and sounds of nature, the mystical powers of mineral and sea water, and the variety of outdoor sports are all vital ingredients in the renewal, rejuvenation process.

If you're wondering who "Charlie" is, he's a giant turtle who's made his home in a private mineral bath grotto at Sans Souci. The spa was named after this contented creature.

Outside the gatehouse of the Sans Souci Hotel Club and Charlie's Spa lies the road to town and to the earthy funkiness of down-home Jamaica. Inside, one experiences the safe, cozy relief of privacy, seclusion, and a touch of formality. This is more likely to delight the self-indulgent spa-goer than the young adventurer looking for excitement and a gung-ho fitness program.

The various levels of the resort climb from the sea to the top of a bluff, making it appear larger and grander than it actually is. The grounds are attractive, with terraced gardens, Mediterranean-style architecture, mineral pools, four tennis courts, and the private beach. Indoor-outdoor style buildings serve as the club, boutique, beauty parlor, and the spa. Over seventy rooms and suites with baths and balconies are scattered about, situated to offer ocean views. There are no televisions in the accommodations, but each has a telephone (it takes from two minutes to a half hour to place a call). The plumbing works well, water from the spigots is potable, and the voltage accepts small U.S. electrical appliances without a burnout. As for service, don't expect your wishes to be fulfilled "on the double." The Jamaican way is slow and easy.

The Charlie's Spa program is for one week and is all-inclusive. Other guests of the Sans Souci have the opportunity

to use spa facilities and pay extra for beauty services and special treatments.

A typical spa day begins with an early morning walk followed by breakfast and an exercise class (stretch and tone). Midday there is a water aerobics class, and a gym class is offered at dusk. Throughout the day you can avail yourself of massages, facials, hair care, makeup sessions, and the opportunity to use the exercise equipment (Universal machines, rowing machines, free weights, exercise bicycles). Then, too, you can lounge by the sea, dip into the mineral pools (which are reputed to help skin problems, rheumatism, and arthritis), and play golf, polo (nearby), lawn croquet, volleyball, and a myriad of water sports.

When the weather is heavenly, which it often is, a massage in the open gazebo is absolutely divine.

For calorie-counters, several low-cal choices appear on the menu. Breakfast and lunch buffets are outstanding, with superb tropical fruits. Pasta is always a choice at dinner. Signor Cipriani of Harry's Bar in Venice taught the chefs here how to prepare it *al dente.* Continental in style, the food is surprisingly good.

For a rough-and-ready Rastafarian meal and evening entertainment, you can "fly the gazebo" and go to "The Jungle." It's a ten-minute walk away. Everyone gets a kick out of eating real good Jamaican food in this colorful shanty.

Each night, some activity is on the agenda to keep guests up past 8:30: limbo evenings, beach barbecues, one-man nightclub-type entertainment,

flamenco dancers, and such. If all else fails, try the television room for a cable show or a videotaped movie.

There is a free one-day trip to Ocho Rios for duty-free shopping, plus a chance to climb up to the beautiful waterfall of Dunn's River. Other tours of the island can be arranged for those who want to make the effort.

Guests are of all ages and from all over the world. When I was there, Bloomingdale's had a crew in residence shooting pictures for a catalog. The site is unique, so it's easy to see why they chose it for photographing beautiful resort wear on beautiful bodies.

Charlie's provides a bathrobe and tote bag. You'll have to bring everything else. In season, gentlemen are required to wear a jacket (no tie) to dinner.

Using *self-motivation,* you can get a little fitter and thinner at this Jamaican oasis. Renewal of the psyche will come without strain or pain, and, with a little luck, you'll leave Sans Souci *sans souci!*

GETTING THERE

For your week in the sun, fly to Montego Bay and prearrange a car from the resort to pick you up there. The drive to Sans Souci and Charlie's Spa is about 1½ hours.

RATING

Overall: A swell retreat for the semi-serious, sybaritic spa-goer

⊕ The Caribbean Sea; outdoor classes and services; relaxed, safe, clubby atmosphere; unusual site; mineral spring pools

⊖ Too few fitness classes; self-motivation essential for dieters

Main thrust: Relaxation and rejuvenation using natural elements of the locale

Cost: Moderate to moderately expensive

Grand Hotel Terme Trieste and Victoria

ABANO TERME
ITALY

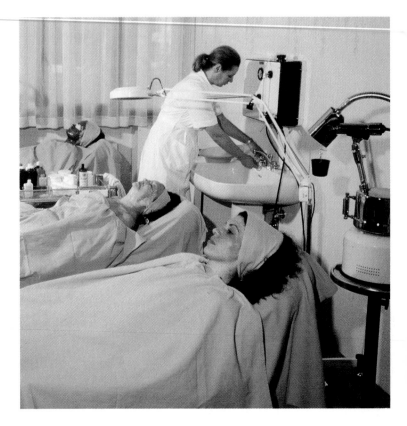

IF YOU ARE ONE OF THE FOLKS whose pockets are not as deep as their need to relax or revitalize those aching joints, the Trieste and Victoria Hotel in Abano Terme, Italy, will take you in, treat you well, and send you home a renewed human being—all for a surprisingly low price tag.

This hotel-spa ages its own curative mud in its backyard vats, using it only when it reaches the miracle mark. Several one-week spa plans are offered; some include beauty services (lymph drainage, facial, bust or stomach toning, etc.), medical exam, inhalations, collagen treatments. Massages and fango or thermal bath therapy plus room and full board (diet or regular) come with each package. (The fango— hot mud and water—treatments, beneficial for many, are taboo for pregnant women and people having some specific medical problems.) Guests can also use the saunas, steam rooms, and exercise equipment. Extremely good rates apply for longer stays and children sharing a room. At any time, this place is a *bargain*, but highest fees are in effect during May and September.

Just minutes away from Padua and only an hour from Venice, the Trieste and Victoria (the bus stops at their door) is a viable solution for the tourist budgeteer. It is not exactly grand, but it is attractive, clean, and has a European flavor. Three thermal (mineral) pools, gardens, a tennis court, lounging areas, dining room, beauty salon, solarium, small fitness room, and spa center are all on the premises. So is a qualified doctor, who prescribes and supervises all treatments. Simple, pleasant accom-

ADDRESS
Via Pietro d'Abano 1
35031 Abano Terme
  (Padova)
Italy
TELEPHONE
011-39-049-669-101
  (direct dial)
212-593-2988 (SRS
  Sales, New York)
1-800-223-5652 (SRS
  Sales, outside New
  York)
TELEX
430250 VITHOT 1
CREDIT CARDS
All major

modations (telephone, air-conditioner, television, mini-bar) keep those perennial guests coming. For those willing to spend a little extra, there are suites with private "cure cabins" where technicians can administer the mud. These contain hydratub, massage table, and a shower of one's own.

GETTING THERE

From the Venice airport, trains run frequently to Abano. The ride takes about an hour. The hourly bus from Venice is comfortable and clean.

RATING

Overall: A good deal for a good rest and some professional old-time rejuvenation

⊕   Fango treatments with source ingredients; swimming pools; family atmosphere; excellent value

⊖   Unexciting clientele; off-the-street, downtown location; no exercise program

Main thrust: Revitalization through fango

Cost: Inexpensive

Verenahof-Staadhof Hotels and Spa

BADEN
SWITZERLAND

THE VERENAHOF AND STAAD-hof hotels are connected physically, share the same management and spa facilities, but are totally different in ambience and architecture.

The Staadhof is newer, starkly modern, and functions very efficiently in every way. It is, in my view, austere. However, all one needs to do for a large helping of charm is to step outside into the delightful courtyard this hotel shares with its sister, the Verenahof, and two other hotels and delight in the flowers, trees, and feeling of intimacy. The Limmat River runs peacefully on the other side.

In the lobby, you can get your first taste of the natural mineral water at very impressive drinking fountains. The surprise is that it is hot and has more than a hint of sulphur—not exactly a taste treat, but it is therapeutic.

If you are going to spring for a suite,

I can suggest #344, with its small living room, bedroom, bath, and wrap-around terrace. The bath is equipped with a second telephone, hairdryer, and tub with handheld shower. All rooms have television and radio.

Now on to the nineteenth-century Verenahof. It has one Swiss star less than the Staadhof's five, and it is more moderately priced. The building (which somehow blends into the gray, starched Staadhof) is gray with many white louvered windows. The greenery on the roof is a nice touch. In the parlor is a skylight, which adds to the charm of the room. One feels immediately comfortable in the reading room, which looks out on the garden, or in the largest of the three dining rooms, which overlooks the water. The director, Mr. Reiber, told me the hotel was meant to give guests space and comfort in a cozy way. It succeeds. Peace permeates the slightly musty air.

Though each room at the Verenahof is different, I'll give you a peek into one. Room #58 is done in pastels and has a homey feeling. It has a small sitting room and a large bedroom. The spacious bathroom has a grand, inviting tub. The eighty-one rooms are well maintained. All have color television, mini-fridge, telephone, and radio. There is a charge for dogs, but no charge for children in the parents' room. Generally, every spa facility and treatment comes with a fee.

The public rooms of the Verenahof are Old World. They are like ladies of a certain age who, bathed in flattering light, can reassume the stunning beauty that once was theirs.

In both hotels, continental food is

ADDRESS
Kurplace 1
CH 5400 Baden
Switzerland
TELEPHONE
011-41-56-22-5251
(direct dial)
CREDIT CARDS
AE, DC, MC,
Eurocard

served. Special diets can be prepared, including those for weight loss. Dining is leisurely, the food tasty and well served. Menus are printed in French, German, and English. Each meal generally offers two first course choices, three choices of main course (accompanied by vegetable and salad), and, for dessert, a tart or ice cream for the indulgent, fruit or cheese for weight watchers.

Beneath the two buildings lies an enormous spa. *That's* what it's really all about. People have been coming to Baden for centuries for the healthful effects of the richest mineral thermal springs in all of Switzerland. I found the thermal swimming pool strangely relaxing.

Although you can stay one day or as long as you want, three weeks is suggested for rheumatic, metabolic, secondary neurological, respiratory, or some cardiovascular disorders. (Water therapy is more often a major focus at European spas than at American ones.)

The massages, facials, foot reflexology, and fango packs are given by old pros. Manicures, pedicures, makeup sessions, body wraps, and body peels are always available; however, there is no hair care.

If a medical checkup is needed, there are three doctors to ensure that it's done properly and to give guests medical advice.

There is every kind of thermal bath one could imagine: open-air, indoor, individual, and one for water gymnastics. Guests can also opt for a carbonic acid or hydro-electric bath. The therapy team is serious and well trained.

All fitness and health services are fairly priced. Unfortunately, they are not included in the room price. However, there are special one-week "Unwind" and "Beauty Programme" packages, which include room, board, transfers to and from the airport, taxes and services, saunas, massages, and other treatments. There are also spa program rates for two- and three-week stays that include the above features plus a medical consultation on arrival to define your personal course of spa treatment.

An important footnote: If you're into aerobics, this is *not* the spa for you. There is a small workout room, but it gets very little use.

As for other pleasures, each week the Verenahof and Staadhof offer a special event or excursion for a small fee. It could be a trip to Lucerne or Basel or a concert.

At the nearby Baregg Sport Center, tennis, squash, and badminton are available to spa guests. Fishing, hiking, and horseback riding can be arranged. I never quite found out what lawn chess is, but if you want it, it's there.

The old city of Baden is truly charming, intriguing, and worth a guided tour. You'll enjoy the shops and casino. For bigger city offerings, take a trip to Zurich, which is only twenty minutes away. The shopping in Zurich is, of course, more exciting than in Baden.

Generally speaking, dress in the hotel and in Baden is casual. You'll need a couple of swimsuits and swim cap, slacks, and shirts. For dinner, men are requested to wear ties and jackets. This is not a place for younger people looking for action. Guests tend to be middle-aged and upper middle class.

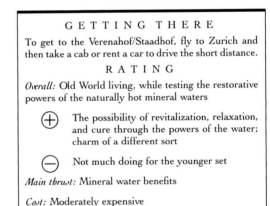

GETTING THERE

To get to the Verenahof/Staadhof, fly to Zurich and then take a cab or rent a car to drive the short distance.

RATING

Overall: Old World living, while testing the restorative powers of the naturally hot mineral waters

⊕ The possibility of revitalization, relaxation, and cure through the powers of the water; charm of a different sort

⊖ Not much doing for the younger set

Main thrust: Mineral water benefits

Cost: Moderately expensive

III
LIVING THE SPA
LIFE AT HOME

The Basic Components for Re-creating the Spa Life at Home

THERE'S NO NEED TO LOSE THAT SPA GLOW AND SENSE OF WELL-being—or to regain those lost pounds—when you leave the spa. It is possible to live the spa life at home. The best part is that it is so easy and inexpensive.

I've culled the best tips from the medical doctors, psychologists, registered dietitians, nurses, nutritionists, estheticians, physical therapists, and exercise specialists of the many fine spas around the world. They have been most generous in sharing their wisdom and experience with me. It is my pleasure to share it with you in turn.

These are the four basic components for re-creating the spa experience at home:

1. Establishing healthy eating habits
2. Exercising
3. Managing stress
4. Looking your best

THE CRITICAL THREE

All the diet, exercise, and beauty treatments in the world won't mean a thing unless you . . .

1. Stop smoking (or better yet, never start)
2. Don't take drugs
3. Keep alcohol consumption to a minimum

Step 1: Establishing Healthy Eating Habits

I F WE ARE WHAT WE EAT, THEN THE LOGICAL FIRST STEP TO ENSURING long-term health and fitness is to establish healthy eating habits. Doing so involves controlling the amount we eat and maintaining a proper balance among the foods we do eat.

EASY AND EFFECTIVE DIET CONTROL

It's simple. Just eat less! Even before you start considering what more nutritious food to eat, you can begin to lose weight. Start by eating 5 to 10 percent less of everything than you normally do. Put a little less food on your plate; that way, a little less will go into your stomach. Soon this will be reflected by a lower number on the scale. No magic formula—it's just logical. And it works! It works even better if you also exercise—anything from walking to total stretching, toning, and/or aerobic fitness routines. But more on that later.

In addition to shaving portions, the bulk of your food consumption should be fresh fruits and vegetables, whole grain products, and some dairy and other protein foods (lean meat, skinless chicken, fish, dried beans/peas/lentils, nuts and seeds). A list of the best of these appears on pages 233–234.

Here are a few easy-to-follow tips to keep in mind to accelerate the *loss of weight* and/or *improve your nutrition:*

- Skip dessert or eat fresh fruit or ice milk, *not* cake, pastries, or ice cream, if you crave that extra course.

228

- Snack on raw vegetables, *not* on candy or chips.
- Broil or bake—*don't* fry or roast.
- Drink a *minimum* of four glasses of water a day (but *not* more than one during any meal).
- Keep sodium (salt), dressings, spreads, gravies, sugar, and caffeine to a minimum.

ADDITIONAL AIDS TO DIETING

- You should always eat three balanced meals a day. That keeps hunger from building up to the point where you're tempted to binge on the next meal you allow yourself. (It's also better for sustaining your overall energy balance.)

- When you eat, put your utensils down between bites. Chew your food well— eat *slowly*. Leave some food on your plate, and don't take seconds.

- Eat only in one or two designated places (not in the car, television room, bedroom, or workplace). Don't eat when involved in any other activity.

- Combat hunger between meals with exercise or other activities. Or else, drink water—and stay away from places where food is kept.

- If you allow yourself an occasional treat, buy one cookie, *not* a whole box, or one ice cream cone, *not* a whole container. Then get back on your diet.

- Drink herbal (no caffeine) tea or hot water with lemon after meals, rather than

---

Fat Facts

- **Excess calories consumed are stored in body fat.**
- **All foods except water and noncaloric drinks have some calories.**
- **Older people need fewer calories than young people.**
- **Women need fewer calories than men.**
- **Desk workers and nonactive folks burn off many fewer calories than physically active people like construction workers, athletes, *and those who exercise*.**
- **Long-term weight loss results from diet *plus* an exercise routine.**

coffee. If abstaining from coffee causes headaches, take one-half cup at breakfast. Decaffeinated coffee is borderline acceptable after meals.

- Whenever possible, eat your protein meal at lunch and the bulk of your complex carbohydrates at dinner.

- Remember that it is more beneficial to eat fruits one-half hour before a meal or two hours after.

Helpful Hints for Food Shopping and Storage

- Work out a calorie budget, then determine menus in advance for the day or week according to that budget. Be sure you also take nutrient content into account in your menu plans.

- Once you've drawn up your plans, make out a shopping list of needed food items and then follow it exactly when you shop—don't throw in last-minute extras. *Never shop for food when you're hungry*—you're just asking for trouble if you do. Also, when shopping avoid the supermarket aisles that tempt you with "trouble" foods. Don't buy snacks for your family and friends that will present a problem to you. Don't buy more than you need.

- Buy nonfat, no-cal foods when possible; low-fat and reduced-calorie foods are your next best choice. *Read the labels* to determine nutritional content and calorie counts. Remember that calories are usually stated on a per serving basis, and one package usually contains several modest servings—sometimes many. Take their stated serving measure into account, not your own. In general, avoid foods high in sugars, saturated fats, sodium, and/or preservatives.

- When making complex carbohydrate choices—breads, pasta, potatoes, and cereals—these are your best choices: whole grain breads, whole wheat pasta, baking potatoes, brown rice, unsalted popcorn, *unsweetened* wheat and bran cereals (avoid granolas, which are highly sweetened), wheat germ, and low-sodium/high-fiber crackers (e.g., Ak-Mak, Wasa, Melba).

- Remember that dairy products and eggs are complete proteins, so include them in your shopping. To avoid the high cholesterol content of eggs, eat only the whites—the cholesterol is concentrated in the egg yolk. To avoid taking in milk fat with milk protein, buy skim milk for adults. Keep in mind that 2 percent milk still has two-thirds as much fat as whole milk, which averages a 3 percent fat ratio *by volume*. The calorie ratio is considerably higher.

- Buy nonfat plain yogurt rather than flavored yogurt, which generally has *more* sugar than ice cream and almost as many calories. If you must buy a spread or dressing, buy low-fat corn oil margarine (soft tub), low-fat mayonnaise, and wine vinegar dressing. You can also make excellent dressings using plain yogurt and seasonings.

230

For nondairy protein, buy dried peas, beans, or lentils, tofu, tuna packed in water, salmon, fresh fish (but note that shrimp, crab, and lobster are higher in cholesterol), and lean chicken or turkey breast. Nuts and seeds, though also protein sources, are high in fat.

Buy *fresh* fruits, but avoid olives and avocados. These have a significant fat content. Similarly, buy *fresh* vegetables. Broccoli, red and green peppers, greens, carrots, and bean sprouts are among the best choices.

Put groceries away as soon as you get home. Put as much food as possible (whether freshly purchased or leftovers) in covered containers; seal any open containers. Take the opportunity to throw out all foods that might cause you a problem.

Finally, to help reduce the temptation that faces you every time you open the refrigerator door, consider unscrewing the light bulb in the refrigerator. What you're not tempted to eat can't find its way to your stomach or thighs.

FOR THE COOK

Broil or bake; *never* fry. Use nonstick utensils or a vegetable cooking spray (e.g., Pam) where you might otherwise cook in oil, butter, or margarine.

Avoid red meat, and cut down on organ meats (liver, kidney, brains). Should you occasionally crave the taste of meat or be pressured into preparing it for family members, be sure to trim off all the fat first. Similarly, skin chicken before cooking. The skin itself is fatty and other fat deposits generally occur in places right under the skin.

Refrigerate stews and soups and then skim off the congealed fat on the surface before reheating and serving.

Raw or lightly cooked vegetables and whole grain products are the best carbohydrate choices for bulk, digestion, and nutrition. They are high in fiber and generally rich in vitamins and minerals—if not overcooked. Use whole grain products whenever possible in your choice of cereal, pasta, bread, or flour.

Avoid preparing meals or snacks that incorporate processed, convenience, or fast foods. White flour and products made from white flour provide mostly "empty" calories in terms of nutrition. These calories absorb very quickly—it's almost as if they know a shortcut to your fat cells. Refined sugar presents the same problem. Processed fats not only make an easy contribution to your fat, they contribute to blood cholesterol levels.

When working with recipes that call for sugar, salt, and fat in some form (butter, oil, margarine), reduce the amount used by half. You'll find your taste buds adjust quickly to the reduced richness. Don't opt for liberal use of sugar substitutes to replace your refined sugar intake. Saccharin contains a substantial amount of sodium, so can subject you to the same risks as overindulging in salt. Aspartame, the newer sugar substitute, has some nutritionists concerned because of alleged bad effects on mood and behavior in some people.

• And then, in line with the admonition we started with—to weigh less, eat less—don't repeatedly taste food dishes as you're preparing them, as so many cooks do. Keep it to a single taste, or if the recipe is one you're confident of, don't taste at all. All those little spoonfuls and sips can add up to a whole serving by the time you've finished creating that culinary masterpiece!

Substitutions for the Calorie- and Cholesterol-Conscious

- Egg whites (or Eggbeaters) for whole eggs
- Herbs for seasoning (add them in the last hour of cooking)
- Low-fat cottage cheese for cream cheese
- Lemon juice and herb seasoning for fish sauce
- Soft-tub margarine containing only polyunsaturated oil for butter
- Nonfat yogurt or skim milk for regular milk, cream, or sour cream
- Nonfat yogurt for mayonnaise
- Nonfat yogurt or lemon for salad dressing
- Nonfat yogurt with fresh fruit for flavored yogurt
- Brown rice for white rice
- Ice milk or nonfat yogurt for ice cream
- Bananas, raisins, shredded carrots, chopped apple for sugar

---

TIPS ON EATING OUT

If you're starved before you go out, cut into your appetite—and thus your temptation to overindulge—by eating raw vegetables at home. To further reduce potentially destructive temptation, let your friends know in advance that pushing food is not a sign of affection in your eyes. You need support, not sabotage. But after that, keep your *thinner* image in your head quietly—don't spend the time talking about dieting. You'll have an easier time sticking to your regimen if the focus of your meal isn't only on the food you are or are not eating. And diet talk can get so boring!

Once at the restaurant, be the first to order and order a la carte. That way you won't be distracted into temptation by the others' choices. Order raw vegetables for nibbling. (Have your waiter remove the bread and butter from the table once the others have helped themselves—or made it clear they don't want any either.) Avoid alcohol—substitute mineral water or low-sodium club soda. Order salads without dressing—substitute a wedge or two of lemon. Remember that broth, consommé, and vegetable soup, though fine from a calorie standpoint, are frequently high in sodium.

Avoid anything that's fried. If you prefer meat to vegetarian main dishes, order skinless chicken, veal, or seafood as your entree, and ask that it be prepared dry and unsalted. Tell the waiter not to bring caloric side dishes, even if they come with the meal. If possible, substitute raw or steamed vegetables prepared without sauce or butter.

Don't even look at the dessert menu. Just ask for ice milk or fresh fruit.

And when you finally leave without having succumbed to temptation, be sure to congratulate yourself. It's an achievement to be proud of.

EAT LESS, EAT SMART

Five groups comprise the food spectrum. They are (1) fruits and vegetables; (2) breads and cereals; (3) milk and cheese; (4) meats, poultry, fish; nuts and seeds; legumes (dried beans, peas, lentils); (5) fats and sweets. You must eat foods from the *first four* each day. (Again, *in order to lose weight, cut down on portions; choose low-calorie products; minimize fats, salt, and sugar.*)

1. **Fruits and vegetables**
   Eat four servings a day. Include one serving of citrus fruit or juice (juice has more calories) for your vitamin C needs; for vitamin A, include deep yellow or dark green vegetables. Unpeeled fruits and vegetables will provide some fiber, minerals, and vitamins. They are low in fat and contain no cholesterol.

2. **Breads, cereals, pastas**
   Eat four servings a day of whole grain or fortified products for fiber plus protein and B vitamins. (One serving = 1 slice of bread, 1 ounce dry cereal, ½ to ¾ cup cooked cereal, ¾ cup whole wheat pasta without sauce.)

3. **Milk and cheese**
   Eat (or drink) two servings a day (more for pregnant women) to supply needed *calcium*, protein, riboflavin, vitamins A, B_6 and B_{12}. (One serving = 1 cup nonfat yogurt, 1 cup skim milk, ½ cup low-fat cottage cheese, 1 ounce low-fat cheese (Neufchatel, Swiss, low-cal American, or mozzarella). While dairy products do have cholesterol, they actually act to reduce the cholesterol in the blood from other foods eaten.

4. **Meat, poultry, fish, eggs, legumes, nuts, and seeds**
   Eat two servings a day for required protein, plus iron, phosphorus, vitamins B_6, B_{12}, and other vitamins and minerals. B_{12} occurs naturally only in animal foods. All meats contain cholesterol. Fish and some shellfish (but *not* shrimp,

crab, or lobster) are lower in cholesterol. Red meats and processed, packaged meats are the worst in this category. Since egg yolks are so high in cholesterol, it is advisable to eat whites only. Iron from whole grains and beans is well absorbed *only* when eaten in conjunction with meats and citrus fruits. Tea and coffee inhibit iron absorption from plant products, but not from meats. Nuts and seeds, as noted previously, provide a lot of fat calories as well as protein.

5. **Fats, sweets, alcohol**
   This is the category that has almost no nutrition and is loaded with calories. The Norwich Inn nutritionist suggested that eating butter or margarine is like eating Vaseline! Saturated fats and sweets are killer foods—devastating to a diet.

EAT LESS—EAT SMART

Step 2:
Exercising

EXERCISE IS ESSENTIAL TO GOOD HEALTH. IT'S ABSOLUTELY NECESSARY to keep your organs in good working order and your muscles from wasting away. (Use it or lose it!) Exercise maintains or improves body tone. It keeps you looking younger, more attractive, more erect. It has a beneficial effect on metabolism and general well-being—combats stress, insomnia, general malaise, and even hunger. A regular program of exercise has been shown to help ward off heart attacks and cardiovascular diseases, lung problems, diabetes, and osteoporosis. You'll find blood pressure and cholesterol more easily controllable.

For these reasons alone it makes good sense to take out time regularly for exercise, no matter what shape you're in right now. If you're sadly out of shape, you'll find the toning effect helps you shed inches—pulls those flabby, sagging muscles back into shape. And it adds a weight-loss dividend to any diet, revving up your metabolism to burn away more (fat) calories than you'd lose by only dieting.

THE THREE COMPONENTS OF A GOOD EXERCISE PROGRAM

The "big three" when it comes to setting up a good exercise program are: (1) stretching, (2) toning, and (3) aerobics. Of these three, aerobics is the most important.

Stretching improves flexibility and helps protect against injury. The movements involved here are floor and standing exercises that allow you to elongate a portion of the body and hold the position (without bouncing) for several seconds while breathing comfortably. It's easy to do and can be done at odd hours. *Stretch daily.*

Toning also improves flexibility but involves exercise that simultaneously builds strength. And it can do wonders for your appearance. Calisthenics, weight training, and aquatic exercises are the exercise forms that make their contribution here, all involving repetitions and work on a muscle group until it is tired. Toning will not result in weight loss, since adding muscle means you're building more body. But toning will reduce inches, since muscle is more compact than fat and toning keeps muscles lean and taut. *Tone three times a week.*

Aerobic exercise keeps your heart and lungs functioning at peak efficiency. It helps control body fat, blood cholesterol, and blood pressure, and it's invaluable for relieving stress. Aerobic exercises include walking, jogging, bicycling, rowing, racquetball, cross-country skiing, and aerobic dancing, among others. The essential qualification is that you engage in the activity nonstop so that you build to and sustain a "target heart rate" (see page 251) for twenty to thirty minutes at a time. Downhill skiing, doubles tennis, and golf, while they are good exercises and do burn calories, are not aerobic—you're not sustaining a constant level of activity for the necessary time to have the desired effect on your heart rate. *Engage in an aerobic activity three to five times a week.*

EXERCISE POINTS TO KEEP IN MIND

First of all, you should *have a complete physical checkup before you start any exercise program.* You risk creating or aggravating a physical problem by simply embarking on a new program of exertion without first taking your general health profile into account. Some exercise movements or levels of activity may not be recommended for you.

Then, for any exercise program to be effective—particularly aerobics and toning—you must *exercise at least three times a week for thirty minutes or more.* Without that kind of regularity, you won't achieve much if anything in the way of change or improvement. Stretching exercises are most beneficial when done daily.

Start slow and easy. Take a couple of weeks to build up to the level of activity and effort you want to establish as routine.

And don't just jump into your exercise routine, especially when toning or doing an aerobic activity. Always take a few minutes *before and after* exercise to *warm up and cool down.* With a proper warm-up, you reduce risk of injury as a result of stressing muscles, tendons, and joints that haven't first been primed for activity. A cool-down after exercise helps your system make a smooth transition from all-out exertion back to routine activity levels.

When exercising, you may find it helpful to inhale through your nose and exhale through your mouth. Breathe normally but deeply.

Take steps to make exercise a stimulating challenge rather than monotonous torture. Exercise with a friend, family member, or group if you need reinforcement to keep you motivated. Vary your program. If you're exercising at a fixed station—

as when riding an exercise bicycle or jogging on a treadmill—watch television at the same time.

If you hate exercising and simply prefer to avoid it as such, find a pastime that keeps you physically active—outdoors is best. Gardening is one possibility. Also, make adjustments in your daily routine to increase your general level of physical activity: Take stairs rather than the elevator when possible. Walk instead of riding. If you drive, park a moderate distance from your destination and walk the rest of the way to where you're going.

AEROBICS GUIDELINES

Choose an aerobic activity that you enjoy and can do easily on a regular basis—for example, swimming, bicycling, or walking. (Walking, in order to be effective, must be briskly done to get your heart rate going sufficiently. Just strolling along won't do it, and will burn only about half as many calories.) Low-impact aerobics—that is, those that do not subject joints to undue strain, as running often does—are far safer than high-impact exercises.

Stay within your target heart range. As you progress, increase duration rather than intensity.

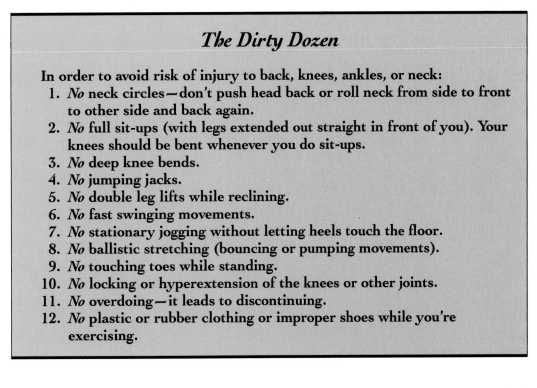

The Dirty Dozen

In order to avoid risk of injury to back, knees, ankles, or neck:
1. *No* neck circles—don't push head back or roll neck from side to front to other side and back again.
2. *No* full sit-ups (with legs extended out straight in front of you). Your knees should be bent whenever you do sit-ups.
3. *No* deep knee bends.
4. *No* jumping jacks.
5. *No* double leg lifts while reclining.
6. *No* fast swinging movements.
7. *No* stationary jogging without letting heels touch the floor.
8. *No* ballistic stretching (bouncing or pumping movements).
9. *No* touching toes while standing.
10. *No* locking or hyperextension of the knees or other joints.
11. *No* overdoing—it leads to discontinuing.
12. *No* plastic or rubber clothing or improper shoes while you're exercising.

TWICE-A-DAY WARM-UP
(5 to 10 minutes)

These warm-ups should be done before every exercise period but can also be done at any time and any place to warm muscles, relax tensions, and invigorate. (The Golden Door suggests doing several of these while on an airplane or in your office.)

1. Stand with knees relaxed. Cross hands in front of your body. Slowly draw them out . . . around . . . and up. Reach for the ceiling as you inhale; exhale as you return to your starting position. Repeat three times.

2. Stand with knees relaxed. Swing both arms in the same direction slowly, then to the opposite direction. Repeat twenty times in succession.

3. Stand with knees relaxed and hands on hips. Lean head first to one side and hold 5 counts. Then slowly move it to other side and hold 5 counts.

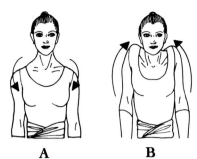

A   **B**

4. Pull shoulders forward and down and hold for 5 counts (A). Then slowly push them up to reach your ears, keeping your head steady (B). Hold for 5 counts. Breathe normally.

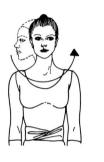

5. With chin down, roll your head slowly from the front around to the side, back to the front (chin down), and to the other side. Repeat this *semicircle* slowly five times. Do not push your head back. Breathe normally.

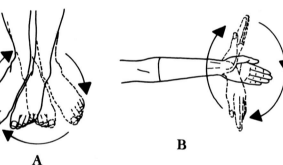

A   **B**

6. Sit on a chair, bed, or bench and rotate your ankles in one direction for ten rotations; then reverse direction and repeat (A). Rotate your wrists for ten rotations first in one direction; then the other (B). Stretch your fingers and then make a fist. Curl your toes and then wiggle them.

A   **B**

7. Stand and march in place, swinging your arms gently, for twelve steps (A). Then step in place lifting only your heels and reaching your arms up for two steps, then down for two steps (B). Repeat this sequence three times.

239

STRETCHING
(Every day)

Home aids: Exercise mat

The following seem to be the favorite stretching exercises of the spas. In any of them, when going from a lying position to sitting, bend your knees, roll over to the side, and gently push yourself up, with hands on the floor.

Consult your doctor first if you have any muscle, joint, or disc problem.

For the Back

(easy)

1. Lie on your back, with hands behind your head (A). Tighten your buttocks and abdomen; flatten your back (B). This combination of moves results in a pelvic tilt. Hold several seconds. Relax. Repeat three times. (Try to keep these muscles taut whenever you sit and stand.)

(You'll have to practice this one.)

2. Lie on your back, with hands behind your neck (A). Slowly raise your head forward using only your arms and shoulders, not your neck (B). Don't force the stretch. Hold for several seconds. Repeat three times.

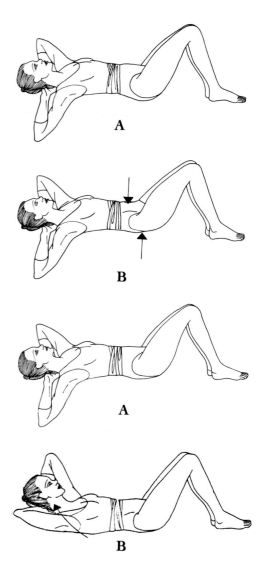

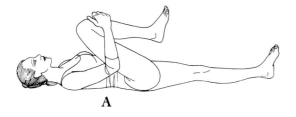

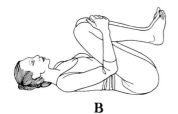

A

B

(easy)

3. Lie on your back, and pull first one leg (A) then the other slowly toward your chest (B), keeping the *back* of your head on the floor. Hold each stretch for a slow count of 20. Then pull both legs toward your chest for a few seconds.

(easy)

4. Sit on the floor, with your right leg straight out in front of you. Cross your left leg over the right leg, setting your left foot flat on the far side of the right thigh. Hold your right arm bent over the left leg (elbow on the outside), and brace yourself with your left arm on the floor. Turn your head over your left shoulder and let your *upper* body turn with it. Your lower body should remain still. Hold this position for 10 seconds. Change sides and repeat.

For the Legs

A   **B**

(You'll have to practice this one.)

1. *For thighs:* Sit. Place the soles of your feet together and grasp your toes, keeping your back and neck aligned (A). Press your knees to either side. Lean your chest to your feet (B). Hold there for 10 seconds. Repeat.

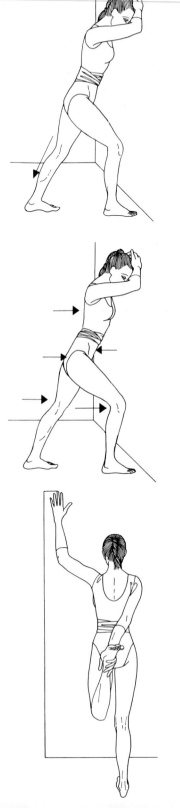

2. *For calves:* Stand next to a wall and lean into it. Rest your head in your hands, bending your right leg with the right foot positioned on the floor near the wall. Extend your left leg straight behind you (toes should point forward). Gently push your hips forward. Hold for a slow count of 20. Reverse leg positions and repeat.

(easy)

3. *For Achilles tendon:* Assume the position for leg exercise #2, but then bend the back knee while keeping your foot flat on the floor. Hold for slow count of 10. Reverse legs and repeat.

(easy)

4. *For knees and quadriceps:* Face the wall, standing. Lean your left hand on the wall, hold the ankle of your left foot behind you with your right hand, and pull the heel into your buttocks. Hold. Reverse positions, making sure you use left hand to right foot. Hold for a few seconds.

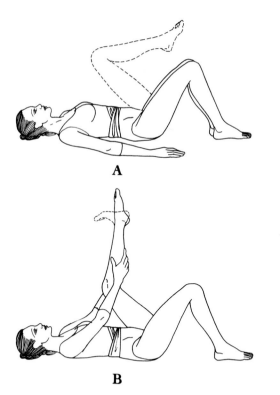

A

B

(You'll have to practice this one.)

5. *For hamstring:* Lie on your back, with knees bent and the back of your head on the floor. Bring one knee to your chest (A); then extend that leg up, straightening it toward your body. Grasp your ankle (or calf) (B). Hold that position for slow count of 10 to 15. Then slowly flex and extend toes ten times. Reverse legs and repeat. (Breathe normally.)

(You'll have to practice this one.)

6. *For hamstrings:* Sit on the floor. Straighten one leg out in front of you; put sole of the other foot against the inside of the straight leg. Lean forward, keeping your back and head straight and aligned, and grasp your toes (or calf). Hold for slow count of 20. (Breathe normally.) Relax. (As you exhale try to lean forward a little farther and hold a few seconds longer.) Reverse legs and repeat.

For the Lower Body

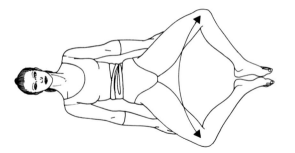

(easy)

1. *For the groin:* Lie on the floor with your knees bent and the soles of your feet touching. Hold for a slow count of 30. (Breathe normally.)

243

2. *For the buttocks:* Lie on your back, bending your knees and keeping your feet flat on floor (A). Contract your buttock muscles, lifting buttocks slightly off the floor as you hold your abdomen muscles tight (B). Hold the position with buttocks slightly raised and muscles tight for a slow count of 10. Release. Repeat. (Breathe normally.)

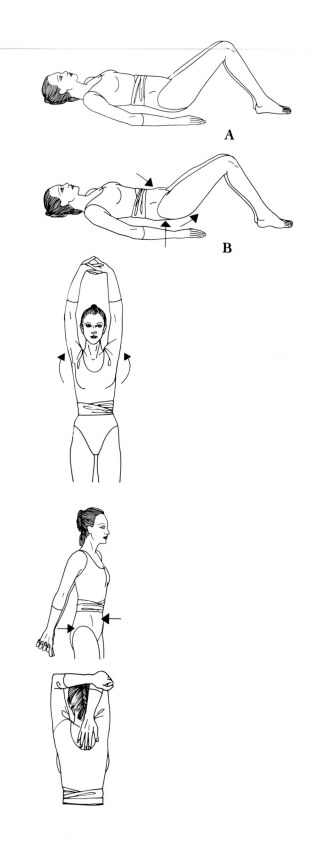

A

B

For the Upper Body

(easy)

1. *For the shoulders:* Stand or sit. Extend your hands up, and interlace your fingers above your head, with palms facing upward. Push your arms back and up *gently.* Hold for slow count of 10. (Breathe normally.)

(easy)

2. *For the shoulders and arms:* Stand or sit. Lower your hands behind you and interlace fingers, then straighten your arms gently. Hold for a slow count of 10. Repeat. Then repeat upper body stretch #1.

(easy)

3. *For the arms and chest:* Stand or sit. Grasp one elbow with the opposite hand from behind your head, then pull gently. Hold several seconds. Reverse hand and elbow and repeat.

For the Whole Body

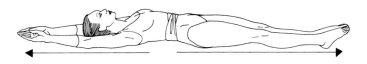

(easy)

Lie flat on your back, extend your toes and fingers in a complete stretch position, and carry the stretch to your limit. Hold it for a slow count of five. Relax. Repeat. (Breathe deeply.) Do this before and after any exercise period. You can also do it standing if you prefer.

TONING
(Every other day)

Home aids: Exercise mat, hand weights, exercise tapes

Randy, the fitness director of the Four Seasons Spa at Las Colinas suggests that if you choose to do only a few exercises (at least every other day) for toning, the "big 4" are lunges, push-ups, abdominal crunches, and crossover crunches. These are starred in the following descriptions.

Remember to warm up for 3 to 5 minutes. Keep knees relaxed while doing all exercises.

For the Legs

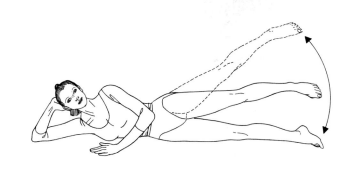

(tiring but helpful)

1. *For the outer thigh:* Lie on your side, with knees together. Lift the top leg up and down (working up to 50 repetitions). Reverse sides and legs and repeat. Keep the motion going smoothly, and exhale as you lift the leg. Afterward, bend the knee of the working leg and pat buttock to relax muscle.

(tiring but helpful)

2. *For the inner thigh:* Lie on your side. Cross the top leg over; exhale and raise the bottom leg off the floor; inhale and lower it. Keep it extended with the foot flexed. Try not to rest it on the floor as you are lowering it. Keep the up-and-down motion going for up to one minute without stopping. Reverse sides and legs. Repeat.

245

★ Lunges

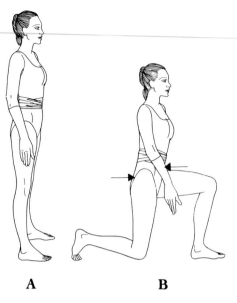

A   B

(tiring but one of the "big 4")

3. *For thighs, hamstrings, and buttocks:* Stand, keeping your abdomen pulled in. Place your feet about shoulder width apart (A). Step forward with one leg (about 24 inches). Then bend the back knee until it touches the floor (B). *Make sure your front knee does not extend out farther than the front foot.* Return to standing position. Repeat fifteen times. Reverse legs. Repeat fifteen times. If you prefer to do lunges as you walk, alternate legs for thirty times. (Start with four to eight lunges and work up.)

For the Abdomen

★ Abdominal crunches

(tiring but crucial)

1. *For the abdomen, back, and torso:* Lie on the floor, with your knees bent, and feet flat on floor (A). *Keep the abdominal muscles taut and the chin tucked in.* You can hold your hands behind your head or crossed on your chest at the base of your throat. Use your abdominal muscles to raise and lower your head and shoulders (B). Your lower back stays in contact with the floor. Raise to the point where your hand could touch your knee and lower until the base of your shoulder blade touches the floor. Repeat fifteen times.

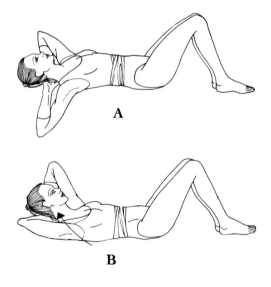

A

B

★ Crossover crunches

2. *Also for the abdomen, back, and torso:* This exercise is the same as the one above except that you reach with the right hand and touch your left knee on the rise for fifteen times. Then reverse and touch the left hand to your right knee on the rise for fifteen times.

246

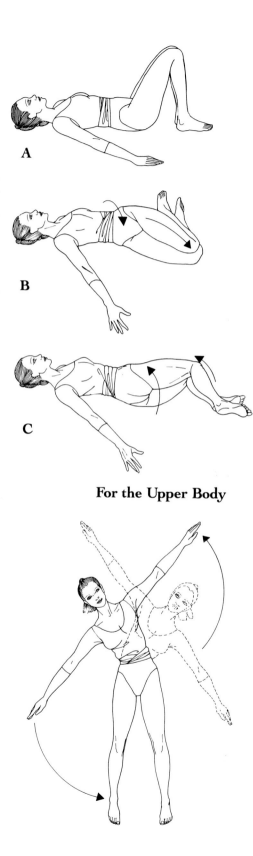

A

B

C

For the Upper Body

(easy)

3. For the abdomen and lower back: Lie on the floor on your back, with knees bent, heels close to buttocks, and arms out to sides (A). Keep your legs together. Slowly drop your knees to touch the floor together on one side (B), then the other (C). Keep the motion going from side to side for ten to thirty times. Breathe normally.

(easy)

1. For the upper body and waist: Stand with your feet apart, knees relaxed. Inhale as you extend your arms at right angles to your body. Bend slowly to one side, then the other. Exhale as you bend. Begin with a few repetitions, increase (to 50) little by little.

247

2. *For the waist:* Stand with your feet apart. Put your right hand on your right hip; hold weight in your left hand. Now bend at waist toward the hand weight; return to erect position (A). Repeat five to twenty times. Now place your right hand behind your head and repeat same bending motion five to twenty times (B). Reverse hands (weight in the right hand) and repeat both sets of motions. You can use a hand weight or improvise with a book or something similar.

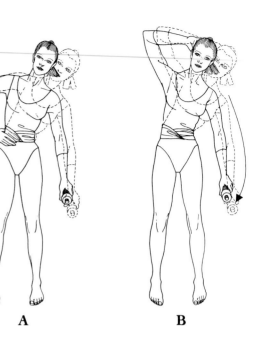

A   **B**

★ Push-ups

(tiring but necessary)

3. *For shoulders, arms, and chest* (using a wall to lean on): Stand facing the wall with feet apart and away from wall, knees relaxed, abdomen taut, back and neck aligned *(do not arch lower back)*, hands shoulder distance apart at shoulder level (A). Lean into wall, keeping elbows up at shoulder and then push out again, keeping your heels on the floor throughout (B). Repeat up to sixty times (start with five).

If you prefer *floor* push-ups, keep your knees on the floor and bent (your ankles can be crossed and up) and your neck and back aligned (don't arch or collapse your back). Keep your elbows out as you lower your body. Raise and lower up to thirty times (start with five).

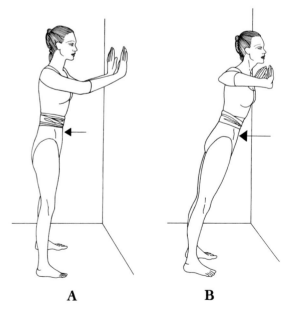

A   **B**

248

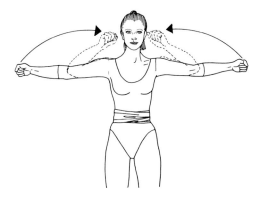

(easy)

4. *For the biceps:* Extend your arms; pull in at the elbows; extend again. Repeat for one minute. (Keep your muscles *taut* or use hand weights of one to three pounds.)

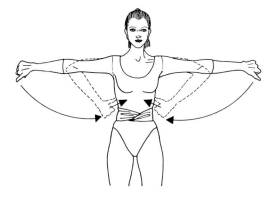

(tiring but necessary)

5. *For the triceps:* Extend your arms to either side, with thumbs pointed down behind your body. Keeping your upper arm in place, rotate your forearm into your body; then push away from your body back to full extension. Continue these rotations for one minute. (Keep your muscles *taut* or use hand weights of one to three pounds.)

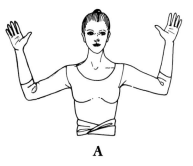

A   **B**

(easy)

6. *For the chest:* Extend your arms, bend your elbows up, and face your palms to each other (A). Then bring your arms together in front of you (elbows still bent) and touch elbows and palms (B). Push your arms back out to either side. Continue this in-and-out exercise for one minute. (Keep your muscles *taut* or use hand weights of one to three pounds.)

249

AEROBICS
(3 to 5 times a week)

Home aids: Exercise bicycle, treadmill, rowing machine, stairs, jump rope, mini-rebounder, cross-country ski machine

Aerobic (cardiovascular) exercise is not only the ace calorie burner, but also works to keep the heart and general circulatory and respiratory systems doing their vital jobs. Stretching and toning are very important exercise forms, but the most important is aerobics.

Set aside thirty-five minutes three to five days a week for aerobics: five minutes for a gentle warm-up, five minutes to reach your target heart rate (see the heart chart that follows), at least twenty minutes *at* your target heart rate, and five minutes to cool down.

Here are the easiest aerobic programs to follow:

* *Walking.* Use a brisk gait and swing your arms, keeping your hands open. Bend your elbows if you prefer. Keep your back and head aligned. *Don't stop moving.* If you are walking in town and come to a stop sign, march in place or keep crossing the available street until the light changes. If you are using a treadmill, increase the incline rather than your speed to achieve your aerobic level.
* *Swimming.* Do continuous laps (no paddling) or jog continuously in the pool (quick walking laps).
* *Jogging.* There is less risk of injury if you jog-walk (alternate jogging and walking).
* *Climbing stairs.* If stairs are not available, use a wooden box about one foot high. Step up on it with one foot, then the other, and back down in rapid succession, putting both heel and toe on step and floor.

In addition, aerobic exercise includes rowing, cross-country skiing, jumping rope, bicycling, racquetball, and aerobic dancing. Exercise equipment manufacturers produce a wide range of machines for aerobic workouts at home. Invaluable to my own home aerobics (and toning) program are my NordicTrack cross-country ski machine and PTS Turbo 1000 exercise bike.

Target Heart Rate (Pulse Beat) for Aerobic Exercise

Age	Target Range per Minute	Target Pulse Beats per 6 Seconds
20	140–170	14–17
25	137–166	14–17
30	133–162	13–16
35	130–157	13–16
40	126–153	12–15
45	123–149	12–15
50	119–146	12–15
55	116–140	12–14
60	112–136	11–14
65	109–132	10–14
70	90–125	9–12
80	85–120	8–12

Take your pulse after a period of exercise. Keep your legs moving slowly while you take your pulse for six seconds. Remember, for the aerobic effect be sure you stay within the target range for at least *twenty minutes* (thirty is best). After forty minutes, there is risk of injury and added benefits are minimal.

If you find it difficult to take your pulse, you can assume you are within your target heart rate range if you are able to talk or hum, but not sing comfortably immediately following your workout. I find it easy to locate my pulse by holding the fingers of one hand rather tightly against my neck just under the chin slightly to one side of the middle.

Step 3: Managing Stress

ALTHOUGH MOST PEOPLE GO TO SPAS TO LOSE WEIGHT, TONE UP, OR get some high-powered pampering, many leave believing that the greatest benefit of all turned out to be their new state of mind. The good news is that by taking only a few minutes each day, you can continue to feel calm, relaxed, and confident long after you've returned to the demands of everyday life.

The Best Stress Busters

- Muscle-relaxing exercise
- Relaxing breathing techniques
- Posture-correction exercise
- Aerobic exercise
- Imagery
- Delegating duties to others
- A healthy lifestyle
- Making out an achievable daily plan
- Massages, facials, baths, showers
- Awareness of the unimportance of certain situations that cause unwarranted tension
- Diverting activity (shopping, movies, etc.)
- Taking advantage of support groups (family, friends, etc.)

The best cure for stress is relaxation. When you relax, stress and tension fade. The relaxation methods and techniques that follow work for many people.

RELAXING THROUGH BREATHING

This is a truly simple technique for alleviating tension, and it doesn't require power—not even willpower!

Begin by relaxing your body and closing your eyes. Push out your abdomen to lower your diaphragm and give the lungs more space to expand. Keep your abdomen out as you start inhaling slowly from the bottom up. Fill your lower chest with air, then your middle chest, then your upper chest (in that order.) Feel the expansion of your upper chest. Now exhale slowly, releasing the air from the upper chest, then the middle chest, then the lower chest. Finally, collapse the abdomen, pushing out that last bit of air and anxiety. Repeat for one or two minutes. Do this several times a day. (I prefer lying flat while I practice this deep breathing.)

RELAXING THROUGH IMAGERY

Imagery is sort of like daydreaming. It involves conjuring up sights, feelings, tastes, sounds, and sensations that are pleasurable. All of your senses (including your sixth one) will come into play. You guide yourself into serenity.

Simple Imagery

Close your eyes. Relax your body, but keep your back straight—propped against the wall or back of a chair or while sitting in the lotus position. Imagine any one of the following that has special appeal to you.

1. You are at the seashore. The air is delightful. Concentrate on the waves, the birds, the sand beneath you and the sun shining gently warming your body.

2. You are in the country, lying in a hammock. A gentle breeze blows. The grass and flowers are beautiful, making the air smell delicately sweet and fresh. Concentrate on the colors and fragrances.

3. You are on top of a mountain. The sky is blue and the air is at once invigorating and calming. Concentrate on your feeling of oneness with nature.

4. Focus on a single peaceful image—a flower, tree, fireplace, brook, etc. Examine it with all your senses.

Use simple imagery to relax each day for a few minutes.

Extended Imagery

1. *The Scarlett O'Hara "I'll worry about that tomorrow" technique:* Relax your body, close your eyes. Visualize a big empty box. One by one, put whatever is troubling you in the box. Put *whoever* is troubling you in the box. (It's okay—people like it in there.) Close the box and shove it to the side. Now relax without thinking of those problems. You can always pull the box over and take the top off when you want to refocus on the problem(s). (I learned this technique at The Kerr House.)

2. *Burying troubles:* This is a technique for getting those anxieties out of sight and out of mind *forever.* (I learned this one at the Centro Benessere at the Hotel des Iles Borromées.)

Seat yourself comfortably and relax all your muscles, especially the shoulders and pelvis. Calmly "feel" your breathing. Close your eyes.

Imagine yourself under a tree in a meadow. The setting is calm and beautiful.

Begin to dig a hole in front of you with a shovel. Slowly make the hole deeper and observe the depth when you finish. Put down the shovel.

Take the troubles that have disturbed you today—physical pains, delusions, or bitterness—and put them in the hole.

Cover this with dirt until the surface is smooth. Observe the clean surface and uninterrupted expanse before you.

Take a deep breath and feel yourself relieved of these worries.

RELAXING BY PLAYING DOWN STUPID STRESSES

The "Stress Bank" idea expounded by a doctor at Canyon Ranch is both amusing and effective. It is used to control unwarranted stress over those rather insignificant everyday situations that tend to make a person nervous and jerky (like getting caught in traffic, double faulting in tennis, hearing your mom tell you how you should have done it, or finding out your plane is delayed).

Think of yourself as having a certain amount of money in the "Stress Bank." Every time you experience stress you use some of that "stress cash," you deplete your life's account. You must manage your money wisely and spend it economically. Don't spend $50 of your stress cash reserve when the situation is worth only 50¢!

The moral is simple—don't get overly stressed about situations that don't deserve it. And most do not!

RELAXING THROUGH STRETCHING

Stand and stretch your body by straightening your back and reaching your arms straight up. Bend your upper body to the right. Hold that position for ten seconds, breathing deeply. Then straighten and bend your upper body to the left. Hold there for ten seconds, breathing deeply. Repeat.

RELAXING THROUGH RELEASING BODY TENSION

To put your mind and body at ease, lie or sit comfortably and tune in to each part of the body as you proceed. Close your eyes and in progression focus on

The weight of your body in the chair
The soles of your feet and toes (relax them)
The joints of your legs (relax them)
Your thighs and pelvic area (relax them)
Your lower body (relax it)
Your waist (relax it)
Your upper body—chest, ribs, vertebrae (relax them)
Your shoulders and arms, hands and fingers (relax them)
Your neck, head, jaw, ears, nose, eyes (relax them)

Now all your body is at rest. Breathe deeply.

This technique is very easy to master, and though it may seem simplistic, it works. Do the progression slowly and really concentrate on your body.

RELAXING BY RETHINKING IDEAS YOU ALREADY KNOW

Because so much stress is caused by feelings of inadequacy, it is helpful to realize that not only your *skills*, but also your *attitude* contributes to the confidence that lessens stress. Confidence is crucial. You can enhance that confidence by preparation (learning, practicing, observing, trying your best, and having a positive attitude). Of course, you must analyze the situation and focus on those parts of the situation over which you have some control (there's nothing you can do about things like weather conditions, an overall competitive environment, or the world economy, so don't concentrate on changing these).

Trying to do more in one day than is humanly possible makes the stress clock tick away. Set reasonable priorities, accomplish those, and fit in whatever else you can. Learn to delegate work to others.

Don't waste your energy and health by obsessing about a mistake made. Forget it. Go on to the next thing. *Everyone* makes mistakes—and lots of them.

Some situations are enormously stressful because they are very serious, even permanent (divorce, the death of a loved one, loss of a job, injury). No amount of stress expenditure will reverse these situations; the only logical route to take is one of accepting the situation and moving ahead mentally to live a different, but still productive and pleasant life. Long-term stress can be extremely detrimental, both emotionally and physically. Take advantage of available support groups—family, friends, coworkers, doctors. They really help.

Being affirmative in one's outlook can lead to positive happenings. Your aims should be in the realm of reality, but occasionally even the most farfetched hopes are fulfilled. Acknowledge that your capabilities are vast, and your possibilities are endless.

Follow the ABCs of a positive mental attitude:

A. Don't think or say *if* (*If* I lose weight . . . ," *If* I find a mate . . . ," *If* I get to take a vacation . . ."). Think and say *when* whenever setting a goal. Don't have the attitude that you *might,* assume that you *will* achieve those things you desire.
B. Keep an attractive, healthy, successful image of yourself in your mind's eye.
C. Deal with others in a kind way, avoiding bitterness and sarcasm. People will react to the way you act. Doors will open, relationships will grow.

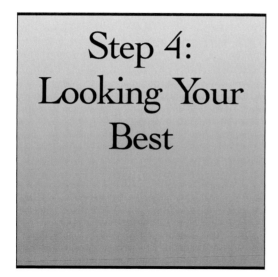

Step 4: Looking Your Best

AS THE ARTIST DAVID HOCKNEY WROTE ON ONE OF HIS PROVOCATIVE paintings, *"Surface is illusion."* The question is, can we make that concept work for us? The answer is yes. An illusion of greater beauty can be created right at home by the magic of makeup, wardrobe, hair, and nail care. Like all good magic, it's done with mirrors—regular, full-length, three-way, and magnifying.

The components of a home beauty program are

- Makeup and care of your face
- Hair care and styling
- Nail care—manicures and pedicures
- Style—choosing clothes that flatter

MAKEUP

As you apply makeup, remember that it is the reflection of light that creates illusion. Light-colored makeup makes an area seem to come forward and widen; it is an emphasizer. On the other hand, darker makeup de-emphasizes and makes the area appear to recede or almost disappear and narrows. Makeup enhances and corrects. Obviously, you must study your face in a good mirror and decide which features and areas you want to maximize and minimize.

Proceed step by step. Not all these steps indicated here need be done. Pick and choose the ones you want to follow. That's what makeup is all about.

257

Necessary Props

Table top (sink)
Mirrors and good lighting
Tissues, cotton balls, swabs
Latex sponges
Sable hair brushes (two big, three small)
Toothbrush or eyebrow brush
Tweezer
Eyelash curler
Makeup pencil sharpener
Makeup remover (cleanser)
Toner
Moisturizer
Foundation
Concealer (two shades lighter than foundation)
Contourer (two shades darker than foundation)
Blush (rouge)
Eye shadows, liners, mascara
Eyebrow pencil
Lip liner, lipstick, gloss

Step 1: Cleanse skin. Most beauticians at spas suggest cleansing cream or lotion on a cotton ball rather than soap to remove makeup and dirt.

Step 2: Apply toner. Use a cotton ball moistened with the correct toner for your skin type. Rub gently all over your face to vitalize, close pores, and pick up any residue of dirt.

Step 3: Apply moisturizer to any dry areas.

Step 4: Apply foundation. Using a latex sponge (most spas use the triangular wedges), dot foundation on your forehead, cheeks, chin, and nose. Blend with the sponge, using outward and upward strokes, then downward. Cover the entire face (including eyes and lips) stopping at the jawline. Be sure you extend foundation all the way to your hairline, and then blend it slightly beyond jawline. This will avoid that mask look. An oil base foundation works well for dry skin; use water base for oily skin. Cream foundation sometimes gives better coverage, but it will make wrinkles show where it gathers in cracks. Liquid foundations get the nod at the spas. Matching your skin tone is preferred unless you wish to add a slightly more pink tone to a very sallow complexion or a touch of yellow to neutralize an extremely ruddy one.

Step 5: Apply contouring makeup. Use a *grayish* brown powder, stick, or foundation two or three shades darker than your regular foundation. Blend all contouring carefully.

- Under the cheekbone (in the hollow)—blend toward top of ear (*emphasizes cheekbones*)

- Along the sides of your nose (*narrows nose*)

- At the tip of your nose (*shortens nose*)

- At the center of your chin (*shortens chin*)

- Under the chin (*minimizes fullness or second chin*)

- Under the jawline (*brings face forward, recedes neck*)

- Along the sides of your face (*narrows face*)

- In the hollow of your temples (*adds interesting dimension*)

To *diminish bags under eyes*, apply a contouring makeup just one shade darker than your regular foundation, blend, apply *concealer* to line under bags.

Step 6: Apply concealer. It should be two shades lighter than your foundation. Choose a concealer that is cream-colored (with a slight *yellow* tinge) rather than off-white. Various uses are

- Under the eyes (*to conceal dark circles*). Blend.

- Above cheekbones, not too low on cheeks (*to highlight*).

- On *blemishes*. Dot then blend slightly.

- On the sides of your face (*to widen face*).

- At the inner corner of each eye next to your nose (*makes eyes appear wider set*).

- Down the center of your nose in a fine line (*for shaping nose*).

- From the outer nostril to the outer edge of your lip (*to minimize fold*). Blend.

- On laugh lines and other lines (*to minimize lines*). Use a concealer pencil or a fine sable-tipped brush for this. Do not go outside the line. Don't blend!

- On any discolored areas (*to conceal discoloration*).

Step 7: Apply blusher (rouge). Use a large sable brush to put dry rouge on the "apple" of the cheek. Blend up and out. Don't get into the undereye area or above or below the ear. Put a little on earlobes to widen the face, across the top of the forehead to lower the forehead, on temples and chin to balance face color, in your cleavage to accentuate the positive.

Step 8: Dust on translucent powder. Dip large sable brush into powder. Shake it. Dust in lightly over your entire face to set your makeup.

A Potpourri of Beauty and Makeup Tips

- Be nice to your face. Don't push or pull the skin. (The eye area is especially delicate.)

- Cleanse your face well each day (no soap unless it is extremely gentle soap). Keep in mind that very cold or very hot water is not good for broken capillaries.

- Night creams (available from most cosmetic companies) are helpful for acid-balancing of skin. Select one that contains vitamins A, E, H (biotin), and/or P (bioflavonoid, which decreases the risk of broken capillaries). Also make sure that all oils are natural.

- Keep in mind that creams, lotions, and cosmetics with an oil base should be used on dry skin. Those with a water base are best for oily skin.

- Avoid a high alcohol content in any product. It dries the skin.

- In a toner, look for one with lemon or citric acid.

- Stay out of the sun or use sun block.

- Change the rubber filler in your eyelash curler frequently.

- Use cotton, sponge, or *middle* finger for blending. Wash sponges after each use.

- Take time to make up properly. (You'll do it faster with practice.)

- If makeup pencils don't sharpen well, freeze them first.

Step 9: Apply eye makeup. If you wear contacts, you should probably insert them before doing your eye makeup. (Just be careful as you apply.)

Eye shadow. Apply dark shadow (can be brown or a dark color) along the crease of your top eyelid. Extend it outward and upward toward the end of either eyebrow. The outer edge of that shadow should be the darkest and triangular in shape. Use a light (beige) color on the eyelid near your nose. Over the iris, you can apply a muted color that will blend with your clothing and enhance your eyes. (Never use a color brighter than your own eyes.) Under the eyebrow, you can opt for a light frosted cream color or a light brown shadow, which can make eyes look larger. Blend each color with a cotton swab. Remember that frosted shadows emphasize wrinkles.

Eyebrow pencil. First brush your eyebrows up with a toothbrush. If necessary,

260

tweeze to get rid of stray hairs (under your brows only). Eyebrows should taper to an end. Never use an eyebrow pencil more than one shade darker than your eyebrow. (One shade lighter is good for brunettes.) Apply with *short*, light strokes. Blend with a cotton swab.

Step 10: Apply lip makeup. Sharpen lip liner and draw a line at the edge of your bottom lip. Then line your top lip. You can actually change the shape of your lips with the liner—experiment. Fill in with lipstick, using a lipstick brush. Take *one layer* of tissue, press against your lips and press over the tissue with powder on a cotton ball. It *will* go through and make your lipstick look yummy. (I learned this trick at The Greenhouse.) Apply a little lip gloss to the middle of your bottom lip for extra sex appeal. Choose lip colors that flatter you. Note that orange lipstick makes teeth look yellow.

HOME FACIAL

There's nothing that brings out the glow of beauty like a good facial. Here's a great facial that you can do very easily at home in less than an hour.

1. Begin by putting your hair in a shower cap or wrapping it up in a towel.
2. Cleanse the skin with lotion.
3. Use corn meal or oatmeal mixed with a little moisturizer or water, or use beauty grains. Massage gently into your face. Avoid rubbing areas with broken capillaries.
4. Rinse well and dry gently.
5. Put cotton pads that have been dipped in cold herbal tea over the eyes. Lie back and leave the pads on for a few minutes.
6. Apply eye cream under the eyes. (Palm-Aire Spa suggests honey.)
7. To the rest of the face, apply a commercial mask for your skin type or use lemon juice mixed with either plain yogurt or egg whites. Recline and leave this on for fifteen minutes (or as package directs).
8. Rinse well.
9. Apply moisturizer to your damp skin.

NOTE: Masks can be used once a week for hydrating and toning skin. Choose one for your skin type. (Lancôme produces one for all skin types.) Some spas suggest masks with only natural ingredients. Read directions on the labels—many warn against applying to the delicate eye area. Most require five to fifteen minutes to "set," during which time you should relax, not talk, keep your face immobile.

PEDICURE

You'll need a foot pan big enough for both feet, water, Epsom salts or bath gel, pumice stone, cuticle remover, toenail scissors or nippers, emery board, orangewood stick, base coat, polish (optional), top coat, lotion, towels.

The procedure:

1. Soak your feet in sudsy warm water (with Epsom salts if you prefer) for several minutes.
2. Pat your feet almost dry and use pumice stone to rub off hard skin.
3. Cut your toenails square across and use emery board to smooth edges.
4. Apply cuticle remover and push the cuticles back with orangewood stick.
5. Apply lotion, massaging your feet. Wipe off your nails.
6. Put cotton between your toes to separate them.
7. Apply a base coat to your toenails; let dry.
8. Apply polish; let that dry.
9. Apply a second coat of polish; let it dry.
10. Apply the top coat; let dry.

Keep your toes separated for fifteen minutes and don't put anything on your feet.

Use an orangewood stick wrapped in a tiny bit of cotton and dipped in polish remover to take off any out-of-bounds polish.

NOTE: Your pedicure should be done before doing your manicure.

MANICURE

For a manicure, you will need an emery board, orangewood stick, creamy cuticle oil, hand lotion, cotton balls, cotton swabs, lotion, polish remover, nail polish (optional), base and top coat (optional), nail dry, cuticle nippers, towel, good light.

The procedure:

1. Remove any old polish with remover on cotton balls. Finish by removing any residue in creases with swabs.
2. File your nails with an emery board to the desired shape. Use the fine side of the emery board to smooth edges.
3. Soak your hands in soapy water and clean under your nails with an orangewood stick wrapped in cotton.
4. Apply cuticle remover and push the cuticles back with an orangewood stick. Then cut dead cuticle skin away with cuticle nippers (optional).
5. Rinse your hands and massage lotion into them. Wipe off your nails.
6. Apply base coat to the nails on both hands; let dry.

7. Apply nail polish on one hand; let dry. Then apply on the other hand and let dry.
8. Apply a second coat of polish just as you did the first.
9. Apply the top coat; let dry.
10. Apply nail dry.

Don't use your hands for fifteen minutes. Use an orangewood stick wrapped in a tiny bit of cotton and dipped in remover to take off any out-of-bounds polish.

HAIR

Take good care of your crowning glory. Wash it with a gentle shampoo, followed by a balancing conditioner for your hair type.

Massaging the scalp with a scalp lotion once a week is also beneficial. Use the lotion on dry hair. Start at the crown of the head and circle out. If you color your own hair, make sure the color is being received evenly. (Most hairdressers will give excellent *free* advice on home correction.)

Here are some spa tips on making your hair work for you:

* Hair styled into your face *narrows your face*.

* Hair styled into the forehead *shortens your face*.

* Bangs *disguise frown lines*.

* Bangs that start from the crown of your head will *disguise a short forehead*.

* Bangs de-emphasize *a large nose*.

* Center parts *accent the nose*.

* Hair styled back from the temples and full at the sides *widens a narrow face* and *shortens a long face*.

* Gray hair, although it can be beautiful, makes you *look older*.

* Hair styled away from the face or cut very short *emphasizes perfect features*.

* "Pony tails" and hair pulled back *emphasize a good profile*.

Doral Saturnia suggests that you put a protein pack (or use mayonnaise) on your hair once a month, leaving it on overnight. Wrap your hair with Saran Wrap, then pin a towel in place over it (turban style).

Our total image is greatly affected by what we wear. Styles and colors can make you appear slimmer or fatter, taller or shorter, more or less confident, powerful, refined, attractive, etc.

At The Golden Door, they have a room full of solid-colored scarves that they hold up to your face to determine which colors are most flattering. What an easy technique this is to use at home to get a general idea of colors to emphasize or avoid when shopping.

Here are some *color* ideas I picked up along the spa road:

- Soft pastel colors are generally flattering and make you appear calm.

- Black and dark colors are "power" colors, making you appear in control, sophisticated, and proper.

- Bright clear colors also show confidence and are "up-beat." Red gets attention and is generally liked.

- Acidy tones and "dirty" mustard to orange shades are rarely flattering.

- Neutral colors such as beige, tan, and gray project confidence and serenity.

- White is always well received. It is *the* color for executive shirts. Women wearing white look either crisp and cool or feminine and delicate, depending on the fabric.

And here are some *style* points I learned at different spas:

- To look *taller*, wear all one color. Don't wear bulky clothes or extra-long jackets. Vertical lines lengthen.

- To look *shorter*, take the opposite approach from above.

- To look *slimmer*, avoid horizontal lines. Wear the brighter colors on your slimmer areas or wear only one color. Dark colors minimize size.

- To make your *bustline* look *smaller*, avoid ruffles and complicated seaming or pockets on top.

- To make your *bustline* look *bigger*, wear an underwire bra, and/or wear tops with added accents (ruffles, pockets, bows, etc.).

- To make your *neck* appear *longer*, wear a V, scooped, cowl, or lower neckline. (High turtlenecks will make your neck look shorter.)

- To make your *hips* and *tummy* appear *smaller*, wear a broader shoulder line, longer tops (*not* full), and pleated pants.

- Long tops that are too big and "gathered" elasticized pull-on pants hide nothing and look awful on everyone.
- Clothes should be altered to fit properly. *Fit can actually change posture* and *posture is important* to the image you project—and, of course, to health.

- To subdue *ripples* and *bulges,* wear a lightweight all-in-one combination bra-girdle.

HERBAL WRAP

The home procedure for an herbal wrap is the same as for aromatherapy, except that you soak a length of linen in hot herbal tea, squeeze it out, and wrap the *hot* linen (blanket-like) around your body tightly. Then you cover that with the plastic wrap (leaving head and arms out). At this point, you lie down on a towel, wrap it around you, and follow the ensuing steps indicated for aromatherapy (cold forehead compress, cold water to sip, slow recovery period). Don't shower or bathe until you re-energize.

Herbal wraps detoxify the body by causing you to sweat out impurities. At some spas, they continue the wrap for an hour, but that is too debilitating for anyone doing it on their own. (Try twenty minutes.)

NOTE: Heat treatments can be harmful to people with high blood pressure and to pregnant women. Consult your doctor if you have any physical problems before indulging in any procedure that heightens your body temperature.

265

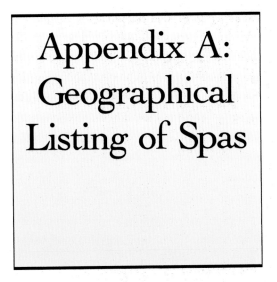

Appendix A: Geographical Listing of Spas

NOTE: Entries are geographical by region, alphabetical within regions.

WEST COAST, HAWAII

The Ashram	Calabasas, California
Cal-a-Vie	Vista, California
Carmel Country Spa	Carmel, California
Dr. Wilkinson's Hot Springs	Calistoga, California
The Golden Door	Escondido, California
La Costa	Carlsbad, California
Marriott's Desert Springs Resort and Spa	Palm Desert, California
The Oaks at Ojai	Ojai, California
The Palms at Palm Springs	Palm Springs, California
The Plantation Spa	Ka'a'awa (Oahu), Hawaii
Rosario Resort and Spa	Eastsound (Orcas Island), Washington
Sonoma Mission Inn and Spa	Sonoma, California
Spa Hotel and Mineral Springs	Palm Springs, California
Two Bunch Palms	Desert Hot Springs, California
Westin Kauai—Kauai Lagoons	Lihue (Kauai), Hawaii

EASTERN UNITED STATES

(The Spa at) Bally's Park Place Casino Hotel	Atlantic City, New Jersey
Bonaventure Resort and Spa	Fort Lauderdale, Florida
Canyon Ranch in the Berkshires	Lenox, Massachusetts
Doral Saturnia International Spa Resort	Miami, Florida
Equinox Hotel, Resort and Spa	Manchester Village, Vermont
Gurney's Inn Resort and Spa, Ltd.	Montauk, New York
Innisbrook	Tarpon Springs, Florida
Le Pli Health Spa	Cambridge, Massachusetts
The New Age Spa	Neversink, New York
New Life Spa	Stratton Mountain, Vermont
The Norwich Inn and Spa	Norwich, Connecticut
Palm-Aire	Pompano Beach, Florida
Regency Health Resort and Spa	Hallandale, Florida
Safety Harbor Spa and Fitness Center	Safety Harbor, Florida
Sonesta Sanibel Harbour Resort and Spa	Fort Myers, Florida
Sun Spa	Hollywood, Florida
Topnotch	Stowe, Vermont
(The Spa at) Turnberry Isle	North Miami Beach, Florida

MIDWESTERN UNITED STATES

Aurora House Spa	Aurora, Ohio
The Heartland	Gilman, Illinois
Interlaken Resort and Country Spa	Lake Geneva, Wisconsin
The Kerr House	Grand Rapids, Ohio
Olympia Village Resort and Spa	Oconomowoc, Wisconsin
The Wooden Door	Lake Geneva, Wisconsin

SOUTHWESTERN UNITED STATES

The Aspen Club	Aspen, Colorado
Canyon Ranch	Tucson, Arizona
The Four Seasons at Las Colinas	Irving, Texas
The Greenhouse	Arlington, Texas
Maine Chance	Phoenix, Arizona
The Phoenix Fitness Resort	Houston, Texas
Tucson National Resort and Spa	Tucson, Arizona

Southern United States

The Greenbrier	White Sulphur Springs, West Virginia
Hilton Head Health Institute	Hilton Head Island, South Carolina
Southwind Health Resort	Cartersville, Georgia

The Americas Outside of the United States

CANADA

King Ranch Health Spa and Fitness Resort	King City, Ontario

MEXICO

Rancho La Puerta	Tecate, Baja California

JAMAICA

The Sans Souci Hotel Club and Spa	Ocho Rios

Europe

ENGLAND

Champney's Health Farm	Tring, Hertfordshire
Grayshott Hall Health and Leisure Center	Grayshott, Surrey

FRANCE

(Hotel) Ritz — Health Club Ritz	Paris
The Royal Hotel — Better Living Institute	Evian-les-Bains
Royal Monceau — Les Thermes	Paris

GERMANY

Brenner's Park-Hotel and Spa	Baden-Baden
Hotel Nassauer Hof	Wiesbaden

ITALY

(Hotel) Des Iles Borromées — Centro Benessere	Stresa
(Grand Hotel &) La Pace	Montecatini Terme
(Grand Hotel) Orologio	Abano Terme
(Grand Hotel Terme) Trieste and Victoria	Abano Terme

SWITZERLAND

Badrutt's Palace Hotel — The Acapulco Spa	St. Moritz
(Clinic) La Prairie	Clarens-Montreux
(Grand Hotel) Beau Rivage — Belmilon Beauty and Fitness Spa	Interlaken
Hotel Limmathof and Spa	Baden
Le Mirador Hotel — Revitalization Center	Vevey
Quellenhof Spa and Golf Hotel	Bad Ragaz
Verenahof-Staadhof Hotels and Spa	Baden

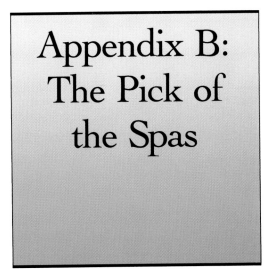

Appendix B: The Pick of the Spas

THE TOP SPAS
(in alphabetical order)

UNITED STATES — THE TOP TEN
Bonaventure Resort and Spa
Cal-a-Vie
Canyon Ranch
Doral Saturnia International Spa Resort
The Golden Door
The Greenhouse
La Costa Hotel and Spa
Palm-Aire
The Phoenix Fitness Resort
Safety Harbor Spa and Fitness Center

OUTSIDE THE UNITED STATES
Brenner's Park-Hotel and Spa
Champney's Health Farm
Grayshott Hall Health and Leisure Center
(Hotel) Des Iles Borromées
Rancho La Puerta
The Royal Hotel — Better Living Institute

THE MOST LUXURIOUS SPAS
(in alphabetical order)

UNITED STATES
Cal-a-Vie
Canyon Ranch (if you stay in a casita)
Doral Saturnia International Spa Resort
The Greenbrier
La Costa Hotel and Spa
The Golden Door
The Greenhouse
(The Spa at) Turnberry Island

OUTSIDE THE UNITED STATES
Badrutt's Palace Hotel—The Acapulco Spa
Brenner's Park-Hotel and Spa
(Hotel) Des Iles Borromées—Centro Benessere
(Hotel) Ritz
The Royal Hotel—Better Living Institute

THE FINEST FITNESS SPAS
(in alphabetical order)

UNITED STATES
The Ashram
The Aspen Club
Canyon Ranch
The Four Seasons at Las Colinas
The Greenhouse (indoor program)
The Golden Door
La Costa Hotel and Spa
The Phoenix Fitness Resort
Safety Harbor Spa and Fitness Center
Sonesta Sanibel Harbour Resort and Spa

OUTSIDE THE UNITED STATES
Champney's Health Farm
Grayshott Hall Health and Leisure Center
(Hotel) Des Iles Borromées
Rancho La Puerta

THE BEST BEAUTY AND PAMPERING SPAS
(in alphabetical order)

UNITED STATES
Aurora House Spa
Bonaventure Resort and Spa
Cal-a-Vie
Doral Saturnia International Spa Resort
La Costa Hotel and Spa
The Four Seasons at Las Colinas
The Golden Door
The Greenhouse
Maine Chance

OUTSIDE THE UNITED STATES
Brenner's Park-Hotel and Spa
The Royal Hotel—Better Living Institute
Hotel Ritz—Health Club Ritz

THE BEST SPAS ON A BUDGET
(in alphabetical order)

UNITED STATES
(The Spa at) Bally's Park Place Casino Hotel
The Four Seasons at Las Colinas
The Oaks at Ojai
Olympia Village Resort and Spa
The Palms at Palm Springs
Safety Harbor Spa and Fitness Center
Southwind Health Resort

OUTSIDE THE UNITED STATES
(Grand Hotel &) La Pace
(Grand Hotel) Orologio
Rancho La Puerta

THE BEST LONG-RANGE WEIGHT CONTROL AND LIFESTYLE SPA PROGRAMS

(in alphabetical order)

UNITED STATES
Canyon Ranch (special program)
Doral Saturnia International Spa Resort (special counseling)
The Heartland
Hilton Head Institute
La Costa Hotel and Spa (special program)
Palm-Aire (special program)
The Phoenix Fitness Resort

OUTSIDE THE UNITED STATES
Le Mirador Hotel—Christian Cambuzat Revitalization Center (special program)

THE BEST "QUICK-FIX" WEIGHT LOSS AND DE-TOX SPAS

(in alphabetical order)

UNITED STATES
The Ashram
Bonaventure Resort and Spa
Cal-a-Vie
Canyon Ranch
Doral Saturnia International Spa Resort
The Golden Door
The Greenhouse
La Costa Hotel and Spa
The Oaks at Ojai
Palm-Aire
The Palms at Palm Springs
The Norwich Inn and Spa
Safety Harbor Spa and Fitness Center

OUTSIDE THE UNITED STATES
Champney's Health Farm
Grayshott Hall Health and Leisure Center
(Hotel) Des Iles Borromées—Centro Benessere
Rancho La Puerta

THE BEST PSYCHOLOGICALLY FOCUSED SPA PROGRAMS
(in alphabetical order)

UNITED STATES
Canyon Ranch (special counseling)
The Golden Door (special program)
The Kerr House

OUTSIDE THE UNITED STATES
Grayshott Hall Health and Leisure Center (special counseling)

THE BEST ATHLETIC SPAS
(in alphabetical order)

UNITED STATES
The Aspen Club (skiing, tennis, hiking, racquet sports)
Bonaventure Resort and Spa (golf, tennis)
Canyon Ranch (tennis, hiking, racquet sports)
La Costa Hotel and Spa (golf, tennis)
Doral Saturnia International Spa Resort (using The Doral Hotel and Club)
   (golf, tennis)
The Four Seasons at Las Colinas (golf, tennis, racquet sports)
The Greenbrier (golf, tennis)
Marriott's Desert Springs Resort and Spa (golf, tennis)
Palm-Aire (golf, tennis)
Sonesta Sanibel Harbour Resort and Spa (tennis, racquet sports, water sports)

OUTSIDE THE UNITED STATES
Badrutt's Palace Hotel and Spa (skiing, ice-skating, tennis)
The Quellenhof Spa and Golf Hotel (older clientele) (golf)
Rancho La Puerta (hiking)
The Royal Hotel—Institut Mieux-Vivre/Better Living Institute (tennis, golf)

THE BEST "MAGIC WATERS" SPAS
(in alphabetical order)

UNITED STATES
The Greenbrier
Safety Harbor Spa and Fitness Center
Spa Hotel and Mineral Springs

OUTSIDE THE UNITED STATES
Brenner's Park-Hotel and Spa
(Grand Hotel &) La Pace
(Grand Hotel) Orologio
The Quellenhof Spa and Golf Hotel
Verenahof-Staadhof Hotels and Spa

The Most Delicious "Spa Food"

(in alphabetical order)

UNITED STATES
The Aurora House
Cal-a-Vie
Doral Saturnia International Spa Resort
The Golden Door
La Costa Hotel and Spa
The Kerr House
The Phoenix Fitness Resort
Safety Harbor Spa and Fitness Center
Sonoma Mission Inn and Spa
Southwind Health Resort

OUTSIDE THE UNITED STATES
Brenner's Park-Hotel and Spa
(Hotel) Des Iles Borromées — Centro Benessere
(Grand Hotel &) La Pace
Le Mirador Hotel — Christian Cambuzat Revitalization Center

New and Promising

Canyon Ranch in the Berkshires
King Ranch Health Spa and Fitness Resort
Topnotch

276